Queering Families

REPRODUCTIVE JUSTICE: A NEW VISION FOR
THE TWENTY-FIRST CENTURY

*Edited by Rickie Solinger (senior editor),
Khiara M. Bridges, Laura Briggs, Krystale
E. Littlejohn, Ruby Tapia, and
Carly Thomsen*

Queering Families

Reproductive Justice in Precarious Times

Tamara Lea Spira

UNIVERSITY OF CALIFORNIA PRESS

University of California Press
Oakland, California

© 2025 by Tamara Lea Spira

All rights reserved.

Library of Congress Cataloging-in-Publication Data

Names: Spira, Tamara Lea, author.
Title: Queering families : reproductive justice in
    precarious times / Tamara Lea Spira.
Other titles: Reproductive justice ; 12.
Description: Oakland : University of California Press,
    [2025] | Series: Reproductive justice : a new vision for
    the twenty-first century ; 12 | Includes bibliographical
    references and index.
Identifiers: LCCN 2024032828 | ISBN 9780520386198
    (hardback) | ISBN 9780520386204 (paperback) |
    ISBN 9780520386211 (ebook)
Subjects: LCSH: Gay-parent families—United States—
    21st century. | Reproductive rights—United States—
    21st century.
Classification: LCC HQ75.28.U6 S65 2025 |
    DDC 306.85096/60973—dc23/eng/20241122
LC record available at https://lccn.loc.gov/2024032828

34 33 32 31 30 29 28 27 26 25
10 9 8 7 6 5 4 3 2 1

For Isa and Adela,
which is to say for all children,
especially the martyred children of Palestine.

May we—*may all of us*—
enact our sacred obligations
toward the dead
with the same reverence
tenderness
and grace
with which we tend to our newborn babies
cradled vulnerably in our arms.

May we mourn
the shattered parts of the whole
the futures never allowed to unfold
the brutal blunting of life
the violence of our own complicity
cutting off
the life of one
the lives of all
massacred at the source.

Cradles ratcheted:
our collective life source
obliterated
by the worlds we sow
we unleash
we unravel
as we worship ourselves in
Power's warped mirrors.

May we mourn.

May we act
with an atonement so fierce
a determination so strong

a dedication so uncompromising
so resolute
so as to put everything on the line
which it is.

May our atonement
be so fierce
so as to bring us all
to a time and place
where we all bask together
in the silver moonlight
justice pursuing justice
freedom pursuing freedom
truth pursuing truth.

Heaven transmuting stars into flesh
sunshine into skin
memory into presence
and there
somewhere
beyond our wildest dreams
the babies dance again.

CONTENTS

ACKNOWLEDGMENTS

I dedicated my dissertation and first manuscript—a project about the politics of memory—to my father, a soulmate and best friend whom I lost when I was nineteen. In the dedication, I likened him to a comet—one whose life blazed out prematurely, burnt short because of the intensity of his light. Nineteen years later, my first child, Adela, was born, with their sister Isa following two years later. This project, a continuation of the last, is dedicated to the intergenerational light that continues to emanate, reverberating forward, back, and in all directions to illuminate pathways to the multiple and more beautiful worlds that we must create with and for our children and predecessors.

As I was finishing this book in October of 2023, the slow-drip genocide of colonialism in Palestine ratcheted up to full-scale genocidal bombardment and all-out attack. We watched aghast, gutted by unconscionable violence, as entire genealogies of Palestinians—and the possibility of a future itself—were wiped out. I came to more deeply understand the stakes of abolishing the world built by colonialism and slavery, and replacing this death-world with the dreams, memories, and lived realities of communities that live beyond the private nuclear settler family and its regimes of extraction and ecocide at all costs.

This book is for my children, which is to say all children; for our babies need a world in which their entire generation is free to dream, create, live, and make manifest the futures our ancestors whisper in their ears before they are forgotten once more. I am grateful to the Palestinian, Black, Indigenous, queer, migrant, trans, liminal, marginalized, criminalized, and otherwise institutionally devalued communities who refuse the category of surplus and insist upon their inherent rights to etch the world in their names. Without these movements, and their poetry, I would not exist. Nor would the questions I humbly offer here exist.

For my teachers: Anna M. Agathangelou, you prefigure life in the pursuit of struggle as revolutionary love lived through poetry and deep care. You expand the edges of my mind, my heart—and potentiality itself—with a brilliance that infuses and transforms everything. Thank you for radically remaking worlds in our midst every day. Angela Y. Davis, you model an unflinching political clarity, a searing intellect in the service of revolution, and radical love. Your lessons always bring me back to center, deepening my commitment to radically open futures. Neferti Tadiar, your razor-sharp acumen and uncompromising brilliance form a template for the scholarship to which I aspire. Ana Maria Enríquez-Enríquez, you always trusted me to follow my instincts and do the work; because of this, I do. Lisa Rofel, thank you for your generosity and for your willingness to open institutional doors for me. I am especially grateful for your mentorship as an anti-Zionist Jewish queer feminist. Michael Lazzara, thank you for meeting me and for listening to and reading my words a million times, and then again. Your warmth, care, and, above all, kindness make all the difference. I also thank Steven Volk, Paola Bacchetta, Rabab Abdulhadi, Gina Dent, Veronica Carrizales, Joyce Cunha, Annie Hilar, Charisse Domingo, Claude Marks, Nina Serrano, and the other teachers and mentors who have fostered my growth throughout the years.

I am indebted to those who raised me, teaching me what *family* means as verb and praxis of profound love: Andrea and Philip M. Spira, you created the world for me, giving your all to raise the next generation with a lighter and brighter flame—and thus a future. Your collective belief in my intellect and creativity from the time I was very young has shaped me more than anything. Mom, you are the embodiment of perseverance and care; each time I love, fully, you are here. Dad, your exuberance colors the very essence of my being. There was no greater gift than to learn from you, through example, to run enthusiastically toward love, with no holds barred. I hope this project echoes somewhere that you can hear and receive it as testimony to the inextinguishable forces of intergenerational love. Freddie Tilford-Allen, my second mom, you have always shown up for me through thick and thin and threadbare and abundance yet again. Sweet memories of childhood beaches and weekly brunches sustain me. For my other mothers: Noel Silverman, Laurie Peck. I miss you. I thank my grandmother, Leona Spira, whom I often see in the round flurry of the leaves, her art shaping my sensibilities and worlds four decades after her passing. I thank Louis Gecenok, Tara Bozorgi, Charlie Tilford-Allen, Luther Brock, Susan and Mike Klonsky, Maria Coward, and Jon and Susan Gross, who have all served as important parental figures for me and as grandparents for my babies. I thank Sue and Bob Merz, who have taken me in as your own. This book is also for my auntie Carol Ziff, a quiet genius who transitioned to the other world at the start of the pandemic. Carol, your unparalleled wit, your unforgettable laugh, and the art that you are ring through my bones. May you and Phil continue to soar like the birds you used to "fish" for outside your apartment window in Chicago as children, among other creative games that foretold lifetimes of creative brilliance.

I am grateful for my brother Josh, whose fierce passion, intensity, and humor inspire me to always aspire toward profound friendship and love as that which matters most in life. Josh, you are both my sweetest memory of our shared past and a dream of futures for our children to come; Dad would be so proud. I thank my "sisters" Talya and Daniella Mizrahi, for whom I learned how to care when I was, myself, a child. Our entangled experiences of survival formed me, strengthening my commitment to you even, and especially, through our differences. I thank yet another "sister," the brilliant Samira Bozorgi. Thank you, Sammy, for loving the Spiras so much and for giving your heart and soul to our entwined and growing families. I would also like to thank my cousins: Ariela Meyers and Larry Ziff. Last but not least, I thank the entire Merz extended sibling crew, Jenna, Marissa, Scott, Scott, Josh, and Jessica: I love you.

I am inspired by the many children who grace my world and who motivate me daily. I love you, Miles Spira; Seychem, Sequoia, and Seyge Turcotte; Ishan and Nayimah Raza; Ezra and Xavier Smith-Deylami; Amaya Hava Alexander Mongia; Zayd Yusuf Ryder Olwan; Izzy Klonsky; Remy, Noa, and Mila Meyerson; Cessa and Joey Petenuzzo; Violet and Oliver Merz; Joey and Nico Hodgson; Addy Creech-Huynh; Deluvina Zamora Valdez Quade; Nico and Mikah Koomas-Asrani; and the "big kids" Flora Machado Doremos and Leithian Shore and Aman Porcello. I also want to acknowledge all the babies we have lost. I write for the children with whom ours needed to grow up but cannot.

To my friends, old and new, who tether me to this earth, while acting for a better world—Anjali Asrani and Joey Koomas, Cindy Bello, Kineret Alexander, Feng Kung, Magalí Rabasa, Emily Davidson, Lupe Arenillas, Tristan Josephson, Mónica Enríquez-Enríquez, Shirin and Holly Smith-Deylami, Pete and Briana Hodgson, Becca and Bao Creech-Huynh, Michelle and Lauren Taylor, Keith Feldman, Laura Okin, Em Thuma, Sophie and Carwill Bjork-James, and countless others—I thank you.

To my coconspirators, my soulmates, born of the same stardust: your hands and hearts alter the substance of this book at its core. Amanda Klonsky, you are family and a foundation: your love sustains us all. Diane Machado, Ítalo Acevedo, DAR, Lana Porcello, and Morgan Bassichis: thank you for meeting me in the place where our multiple lives cross, never turning away from what we have been and what we can be. Claire Chase, I loved you before and beyond your first note—and always will. Nadia K. Raza, the glint in your eye reminds me of the taste of freedom, inviting me into wonderful trouble and, above all, beautiful struggle. Heather Turcotte, you ground me in multiple worlds. Thank you for never asking me to suppress my wild fire—but instead challenging me to grow larger and bolder. Dana Olwan, your quiet strength brings me to a new place on the edge of joy, sorrow, and hope that magnifies my resolve to never give up. I will always fight for a world in which our babies do not have to do the same. Megan Shaughnessy-Mogill, thank you for accepting me exactly as I am and for entering the fire of transformation so that we may finally heed Cassandra, in outrageous laughter, fugue state and all.

I write for and with those who continually make queer home with us here up in Washington State and who have infused the rainy Pacific Northwest winters with warmth. Vero Vélez, your luminous spirit encircles me, teaching me that in nurturing, loving, and forgiving ourselves we enact revolution. Thank you for beckoning me into our other shared lifetimes, while lovingly nurturing Adela, Isa—and the babies yet to come—into this one. Mariangela Mihai, we found each other at the end of this project this time around, and it all made sense. I am forever changed by our journey back to the profound places where linden meets cypress and our poetry entwines. Thank you for holding me with grace in my mess, for sharing bottles of seltzer, for howling in laughter and tears, and for honoring the revolutions that we lost, the ones we will win, and the struggles that continue *hasta la victoria, întotdeauna. Te iubesc.*

I am lucky to have true friends within the academy who believe in my work with generosity and shared commitment. I thank Kalindi Vora, friend and the former director of the University of California, Davis Feminist Research Institute, where I drafted the first chapter of this book. I thank my writing partner, Jennifer Denbow, for reading every word of this manuscript and for making it so much stronger. I thank Keith Feldman for reading nearly every word of everything I have written leading up to this book. The brilliant Alexandra Kimball spent countless hours listening to my ideas and sharing her meticulous research. Alex, your commitment to combating lies—regardless of the consequences—so that our children do not live in shame emboldens me. Anita Starosta was the most incredible editor who both pushed my writing to a further place of clarity and deepened my ideas. This book would not be what it is without Anita's labor, intelligence, and care. Michael Needham was an editor, champion, and interlocutor since this project's inception. I am thankful for his editorial support and constant encouragement. I also thank my colleague-comrades at Fairhaven College and Western Washington University, and especially Dolores Calderón, Clayton Pierce, Kristen French, Elaine Mehary, Shirin Deylami, Vicki Hsueh, Cathy Wineiger, Jenny Forsynthe, Tuti Baker, Ceci Lopez, John Bower, Lourdes Gutiérrez Nájera, and Nada Elia. I am grateful to Western Washington University for supporting me with a sabbatical to write.

My students have astounded me with their activism, keeping me on my toes. I thank students in my Queering Families courses since 2020, as well as alumni including Andrea Tomkins, Aleyda Cervantes, Belina Seare, Dayjha McMillon, Kyles Gemmel, Alia Taqieddin, Madi Stapleton, Tahlia Natachu, and Mollie West. I am grateful for the research assistance of Madi Stapleton and Dayjha McMillon, with whom I conceptualized this project in its nascence, as well as Abby Baker for her meticulous editorial support. I thank WWU's Students Against Apartheid, the Arab Students Association, Jewish Voice for Peace, Students for Justice in Palestine, and No New Whatcom Jails, as well as students across the country fighting for a free Palestine and the abolition of all systems of carceral control. Thank you for prefiguring—and enacting—a world in which we can insist upon a future for generations to come.

As abolitionist feminists argue, we must account for the ways that past organizing efforts shift worlds by enabling revolutionary imaginations to come. This insight is especially germane now as we watch the world erupt in intersecting movements for abolition, decolonization, and an end to all forms of oppression. I am grateful to my decades-long comrades within Critical Resistance, Justice Now, the International Jewish Anti-Zionist Network, Jewish Voice for Peace, Friends and Family Members of the Disappeared, and the various mutual aid networks that have held me over the years. Thank you for showing me what it means to demand loving futures in a world that does not want us to live. Dean Spade, Morgan Bassichis, Mariangela Mihai, and Vero Vélez stand out as exemplars of this work to whom I turn for inspiration as activist-scholars. I also thank my sisters Fatima Khan, Kate Matthias, and Sophie Rosenblum, fearless cofounders of Protect Their Future, for teaching me what it means to fight with ferocity for a world in which *no* child suffers needless illness or death. My comrades within Whatcom Families for Justice in Palestine—and especially Erum Mohiuddin, Teizeen Mohamedali, Natalie Baloy, Nasreen Mughal-Barrows, Alison Merz, Jessi Radovich, Neah and Andy Monteiro, Asch Kapowi, Elaina Ellis, Phoebe Wall, Hisham Khayyat, Iliana Bradley, Anna Ebreo, Cathy Wineiger, Yoav Litvin, and others—came together quickly in heartbreak. Thank you for reminding me, through example, that the only way we can love our babies is by fighting for all children in times of genocide through collective struggle.

I thank the entire team at the University of California Press for the smooth, supportive process of publishing this book. Aline Dolinh and Summer Farah were so attentive and supportive. Thank you to Elisabeth Magnus for the meticulous copy edits and communication. Naomi Schneider shepherded me through the process with such kindness and care. I am grateful for her collegiality and feminist commitments. Rickie Solinger was a champion from day one, always ready to help me work out an idea or navigate the process. This solidarity meant the world to me, especially as I sat at my computer, my mind spinning—my infant on one knee, my toddler on the other—as I worked to make sense of what it mean to usher in queer abundant futures for all children amid the pandemic, wildfires, Fascist resurgence, heightened racial violence, active genocide, and so much more.

Finally, this book is for the core of my extended queer family—a family that knows no limits but begins right here in my heart. Adela Sky, my world was forever altered when heaven spilled open, bringing you to us and awakening in me a joy, awe, and wonder that I never imagined possible. Isa Dawn, you turn the world over with the sheer magnitude of your strength, your unbridled sweetness lighting up a new corner in my heart. And my Alison, my start and my beginning, my hummingbird and wildflower and soft grass prairie and blue heron and sun and moon and stars: you are a paragon of generous love that knows no ends and enacts the queer politics to which I aspire. Thank you for listening to the constant hum of my whacky ideas, for altering your world so that it might meld with mine, for throwing up the house so we can further strengthen the foundation. Thank you for welcoming in love, new and old, for supporting me to write in lockdown, societal abandonment, and beyond with an infant and toddler, and for holding everything down, always. Thank you for traveling from stars to the depths of the ocean so that we might continue to grow and expand what it means to make family infused with love and multiplied by love. The dreamy family we have built seeds hope in perilous times, expanding and growing more gorgeous each day.

ABBREVIATIONS

ACLU   American Civil Liberties Union
ARTs   advanced reproductive technologies
BPP   Black Panther Party
CBC   Center for Bioethics and Culture
DC   donor conceived
DCP   donor-conceived people
DHHS   Department of Health and Human Services
DSR   Donor Sibling Registry
ICWA   Indian Child Welfare Act
IVF   in vitro fertilization
OFWHC   Oakland Feminist Women's Health Center
OOC   Out of Control Lesbian Committee to Support
          Political Prisoners
SVCC   St. Vincent Catholic Charities
TWGR   Third World Gay Revolution

The Beginning and the End of the World

Queering Families in Precarious Times

> Our generation must walk the spiritual path that is available to us only in this time, with its own unique combination of wisdom and creation.
>
> —adrienne maree brown[1]

July 2019: I wake up raw from a nightmare that cuts through me, a dystopic dream of separation from loved ones that floods me with feelings of alienation and communal disconnection that are so indicative of our political times. In the dream, a friend yells at me. We are both unable to surmount the wall of pain stemming from our different histories of trauma and oppression. I have gone to bed amid grotesque news clips of Trump, and groundwater being poisoned, and Brexit, and the story of the migrant child who remained in detention the longest. Like many around me, I am unnerved.

December 2019: Adela, our two-year-old who has been murmuring sweetly in their sleep, sighs from their bed across the room and rolls over to hug their stuffed bunny. Conceived on the day of the 2016 presidential elections, Adela has brought unbridled bliss, sweetness, and joy in a time of much despair. Adela sighs in bed peacefully as I lie in the same room, gripped by fear, with the cries of migrant children separated at the border from their loved ones ringing in my ears. I am reminded that my child does not flinch before reaching to touch my eyelash or kiss my cheek. Adela's love has not yet been tempered by fear of vulnerability or the possibility of intentional harm. Adela often brings my long-deceased father into the room when I need him the most.

November 2020: Seven months into COVID-19 and on the eve of the 2020 presidential election, I sit long into the night holding our five-month-old, Isa, who came to us in the early months of the pandemic. Isa is a gift from the ancestors, a love letter, and a serene soul who steadies my nerves. Isa's radiant smile requires me to recommit to a future on days that might otherwise feel intolerable. During the recent wildfires that left a furious trail of smoky skies along the Pacific Coast, a friend told me that we would need a new form of humanity to withstand these times. So, too, adrienne maree brown tells us that each generation possesses the combination of wisdom and creation required to withstand their times. As I hold Isa in my arms, it occurs to me that her generation embodies this new humanity; this new humanity is here.

I begin with these moments to foreground my own stakes in this book, which is about the promises and perils of queering reproductive justice in precarious times. I write on a precipice of fear and hope, with a terror that we have brought our babies into an uninhabitable world and a profound belief in the unique wisdom of this generation, culled from our ancestors' survivals.

It is my obligation to create conditions so that the fear and hope may meet.

June Jordan once wrote that children begin the world again and again because they have no choice but to live: their existence is predicated upon the existence of a future.[2] What does this mean in times marked by migrant babies locked away in detention camps and the mass slaughter of a largely child population in Gaza? What do these words mean amid a more general war on youth[3]—or during an ecological catastrophe that leads youth climate activists to declare that their futures have already been stolen?[4]

In *Queering Families: Reproductive Justice in Precarious Times,* queering reproductive justice—that is, demanding the conditions for collective life against considerable odds—reflects a commitment to radical interdependency that continues in this genealogy. Here I use *queering* as a verb to align myself with movements that dare to rip at the edges of respectability to unapologetically demand a world in which we all belong. To queer reproductive justice is to theorize the political project of cultivating future generations—and thus of lovingly kindling futures—in increasingly perilous times.

Queering reproductive justice is the antithesis of reproductive genocide. "Reproductive genocide," writes the Palestinian Feminist Collective, "refers to the policies, discourses, and practices that delimit, restrict, target, or diminish the life-giving capacities, choices, access, short-term health, long-term health, and life chances of communities made vulnerable by systemic military violence and occupation, besiegement, settler colonialism, and/or imperial warfare."[5] This statement speaks directly to the assault in Gaza and could also refer to the situation of babies ripped from caregivers at the US-Mexico border.

Additionally, as reproductive justice movements have long argued, an assault on the right to reproduce family according to one's wishes, and thus to nurture future generations, has been a central feature of racial capitalism, colonization, and US empire. This assault is emblemized in residential boarding schools for Native American peoples and in the theft of Black children through the slavery/prison nexus, among other histories, that bring us to our current juncture. Moreover, reproductive justice movements have laid bare the eugenic dynamics of stratified reproduction and "institutionalized kin-lessness"[6] that have informed experiences of pregnancy, childbirth, and child-rearing, and have impeded the reproduction of marginalized communities across multiple generations.[7]

Anchored in this ongoing racial, colonial, and imperial history, *Queering Families* traces the shifting meaning of queer family in the late twentieth and early twenty-first centuries. From the 1960s to the 1980s, many queers—and particularly queer mothers—faced protracted custody battles, having their children removed by courts that deemed it was in "the best interest" of children to be shielded from "homosexual lifestyles."[8] Long-standing tropes of the queer as a dangerous child molester loomed large, as sexuality, morality, and the capacity to parent were closely entwined in legal discourse and public opinion.[9] Three decades later, queer couples increasingly vie for the legal right to partake in the private nuclear family under racial capitalism and its oppressive state institutions, raising significant tensions between a liberal mainstream LGBTQ+ rights movement and radical struggles for decolonization and racial and economic justice. In 2019, for example, LGBTQ+ people won a legal settlement against Bethany Christian Services, one of the major agencies implicated in the separation of migrant children from their caregivers, for refusing to work with prospective LGBTQ+ foster parents.[10] Instead of challenging the harmful work of the private Christian agency, they participated in it.[11]

Taking such tensions as a point of departure, *Queering Families* asks how those who often lack the biological capabilities for coital reproduction have become drawn into a vortex of ethical conundrums and political challenges in the late twentieth and early twenty-first centuries.[12] The book asks how many privileged queers, once deemed unfit to participate in social reproduction through parenting, could become active, albeit contradictory, agents within the US state's necropolitical policies, with attention to their related instabilities, contradictions, internal hierarchies, and stratifications. It examines the fraught politics of adoption, as well as debates surrounding advanced reproductive technologies (ARTs). *Queering Families* maps the arc of increased queer investments in the nuclear biogenetic family, the US settler imperial state, and racial capitalism over the last forty years. Simultaneously, it engages the contradictions of a reproductive justice agenda that still often takes heterosexual conception as the unmarked norm.

Throughout, *Queering Families* excavates an alternative history of queering reproductive justice and of family abolition that was born in Black and queer-of-color feminist movements of the 1970s, and traces that history through to the present. By *family abolition*, I refer to the generative process of proliferating networks of care, love, and support to crowd out the rigid, hierarchical, nuclear heteropatriarchal white settler family.[13] Revitalized in contemporary queer movements for mutual aid, prison abolition, disability justice, and decolonization, these movements kindle sacred intergenerational life amid a war in which the most vulnerable of children are positioned at the front lines. *Queering Families* revisits these genealogies to uncover modes of family making that have been buried, ignored, or forgotten in dominant queer scholarship and praxis, and that can lay the groundwork for nurturing future generations.

WAITING IN THE WINGS: QUEER CROSSINGS IN A WORLD ON FIRE

In her 1997 memoir of queer motherhood, *Waiting in the Wings*, Cherríe Moraga tells the story of her son, Rafael Angel, who was born prematurely at twenty-eight weeks. Rafael spent three months in the NICU. The memoir compiles Moraga's journal entries as she watches her infant straddle the razor-thin line between life and death. Ultimately, Moraga realizes that even her "tightest hold against death cannot keep Rafaelito here" and that he "needs to be free to decide: to stay or to leave."[14] He stays.

In addition to documenting Rafael's fragile early days, *Waiting in the Wings* is a story of loss—of a time when the state ratcheted up its abandonment of, and attack upon, entire communities. It voices a refusal to forget the revolutionary dreams, possibilities, and lives of comrades who were rapidly being subsumed into the apparatus of neoliberal amnesia.[15] Throughout, Moraga shows how Rafael's life is entwined with the deaths of the many "HIV-positive sisters and brothers" and "sister poets gone and surviving with cancer."[16] This is especially significant in a time when, to quote contemporary scholar Myisha Priest, "death [was] ... becoming an occupational hazard of Black female intellectual life."[17] Moraga chronicles this loss in real time, bearing witness to a great backlash, characterized by dramatic state disinvestment from communities and by aggravated state assault against those deemed surplus to the new world order.

Moraga's text thus refuses a progressive history of success. Rafael's survival is not a metaphor for queer assimilation and triumph. Rather, Moraga casts a more complicated narrative, framing Rafael's story to be the "story of one small human being's ... struggle for survival/for life in the age of death/the age of AIDS."[18] She mourns and memorializes the departures of many loved ones who were dying en masse—be it through overt state assault, abandonment, or insidious structural violence. Rafael thus emerges into the world in a time when other worlds are shutting down. Inviting the emergence of new worlds, *Waiting in the Wings* reverberates into our present. Written from a moment when radical feminists of color diagnosed the world to be "on fire," it echoes forward to contemporary times when we too are called upon to "create out of the raw smithy of [the] fire a shape different than ... [our] inheritance."[19]

In a poignant passage, Moraga finds an unpublished poem of Tede Matthews, the beloved AIDS and solidarity activist who died at the age of forty-two in 1993. Entitled "Angel Wings," the poem depicts an angel who visits Matthews in his last days of life.[20] The angel's "tears [wash] ... away [Matthews'] lesions" in preparation for Matthews's journey to "heal the earth" by taking flight himself. Matthews, a dear friend and comrade, was diagnosed right after Moraga became pregnant, his death also coinciding with Rafael finally being healthy enough to leave the NICU. Moraga is stunned to find this poem after Matthews's death, tucked away in his belongings: Angel is the middle name she has already given her son.

Here Moraga holds life and death in simultaneity, sensing the liminal space where her loved ones have met before. She writes:

"Rafael is a poem. *El milagro* of what has passed and what will go forward. He is history and future as Tede now knows, as Audre was given the daily glimpse of for fifteen years, battling cancer. Through Rafael I have been given the gift of bearing witness to a soul's decision to take hold of an earthly life."[21]

Moraga forges a queer temporality that allows Rafael to cohabitate with Matthews and Lorde in the present.[22] To celebrate Rafael's life, Moraga theorizes, is to dwell in "a kind of queer balance to this birthing and dying," informed by a commitment to honoring our dead, at the same time as it is to stay anchored in a belief in and fight for the future.[23] In this sense, Moraga enacts what Ruha Benjamin calls a "kinship with the dead,"[24] which, "as a creative process of care and reciprocity," is indispensable to our movements for reproductive justice.[25] As Benjamin argues, the severe deprivation of life and kin from Black people, in particular, requires a "practice of making kin ... *with* the materially dead/spiritually alive ancestors in our midst," compelling a "stubborn refusal to forget and to *be forgotten.*"[26] Moraga thus embraces the continuity between what Benjamin calls the "materially alive" and the "spiritually alive."[27] In an act of remembrance that honors continuity, Moraga's words speak to a copresence and kinship with the dead. It is within this kinship with the dead that new life takes form.

This motif of coexisting life and death recurs in Moraga's 2001 foreword to *This Bridge Called My Back*, where she recalls, in the wake of the 9/11 attacks, sitting with a ten-year-old Rafael and watching a storm as thunder claps across the sky. Frightened, Rafael asks if "a new world is emerging and [he] ... will lose [her]" in the transition from old to new.[28] As Moraga reflects upon the question, she wonders: "Is this in fact what we are bearing witness to, the end of one epoch and the painful birthing of another?"[29] Once again, the child inhabits the queer precipice of life and death, acting as a harbinger for shifting worlds.

Moraga's words offer important insights into how our dedication toward the future of our children is also a dedication to our ancestors and movements past. Such concerns animate *Queering Families*. In her beautiful theorization of "decolonial love," queer Native scholar Christine Finley deepens understandings of this convergence by issuing "a call … a desperate scream to ancestors and ghosts to help, love, and guide us beings to a future of care and responsibilities to one another."[30] Finley frames "decolonial love" as something that "extends beyond temporal and terrestrial realms" and as something that must draw "from and among ancestors, ghosts, and those who live in the ghastly thresholds of social life—the criminalized, the marginalized, and the disappeared."[31] Finley expresses a powerful respect for the dead as teachers who can guide the next generation. In her refusal to disavow the dead, Moraga also invites this intergenerational connection. This contradicts the mandates of neoliberal multiculturalism and homonormativity that require a disassociation from community members who cannot assimilate into the dominant order. Instead, Moraga welcomes intergenerational continuity across the borders of death and life. This continuity is paramount to a politics of queering reproductive justice.

Queering Families rejects these colonial binaries of life and death, shaped by the call to listen deeply to those residing beyond and between worlds to bring about a new form of collective healing and justice. To make our children's lives possible is to refuse a biopolitical order that makes millions surplus. Simultaneously, it is to honor the queer crossings of the worlds that have passed and those that have yet to arrive. It is to stand firm against a politics of abandonment, disposability, and betrayal.

"How many more must die," M. Jacqui Alexander asks while reflecting upon Gloria Anzaldúa's death, "before we internalize the existential message of our fundamental interdependence—any disease of one of us is a disease of the collectivity, any alienation from the self is an alienation from the collectivity?"[32] Like Moraga, Alexander turns to the ancestors, urging that we remember them and acknowledge an interconnectedness that flies in the face of assimilationist progress narratives. Queering reproductive justice requires a commitment to this "existential message of our fundamental interdependence," all the while tending to the *milagros* (miracles), like Rafael, that are always waiting in the wings.[33]

REFUSING DISPOSABILITY: FORGING RADICAL INTERDEPENDENCIES IN A WORLD ON FIRE

Part of a larger genealogy that informs *Queering Families*, Moraga's text allows me to articulate several key political principles that ground this book, especially from my vantage point as a queer parent and daughter and student of the queer-of-color and anti-imperialist lesbian movement histories that Moraga and others central to this book helped to shape. Refusing a series of binaries—between self and other, between arrival and departure, between earthly form and spirit, between living and dying—Moraga's work opens up a queer space in which to counteract the harsh losses of the past and their mandated amnesias that have been part and parcel of the neoliberal imperative.[34] The complex passage between the revolutionary period of the mid- to late twentieth century and the counter-revolutions that followed required, in part, a forgetting of revolutionary dreams, possibili-

ties, and lives. This forgetting, as I argue elsewhere, with Anna
M. Agathangelou and Morgan Bassichis, has been central to the
rise of homonormativity and neoliberal multiculturalism.[35] The
inclusion of particular sexual and racial minorities in racial capitalism and US empire became a central feature of a more flexible
geopolitical order, creating, to quote Jodi Melamed, "new privileged subjects, [by] racializing the beneficiaries of neoliberal multiculturalism as worthy neoliberal citizens and racializing the los-
ers as unworthy and excludable."[36] Moraga refuses this schema.
Instead of trading historical memory for the lure of inclusion, she
honors and remembers those who have been lost. She understands
her son's life to be predicated upon those who came before him—
whose dreams and struggles will help seed his own.

Waiting in the Wings stands as one queer narrative of family
that commits to a collective politics of solidarity that neither
forsakes our dead nor accepts the subjugation of others. This
principle becomes paramount, I argue, in thorny issues of queer
family building practices through ARTs and through the adoption and foster care systems in a political landscape that has
increasingly pitted multiply marginalized communities against
one another. Often framed in binary ways, debates over whether
it is a right for nonsexually procreative LGBTQ+ people to
partake in dominant family-building processes fall into two
camps. Either they end up celebrating queer family building at
any cost, or they valorize the bionormative heteropatriarchal
nuclear family as the only option.

Rather than accept this binary, *Queering Families* draws from
the dreams opened up by Moraga and her contemporaries. It
asks, instead, why choices are framed as such—and what alternatives for queering family and reproductive justice lie just
beyond the frame. By rooting a queer politics of reproductive

justice back within these radical genealogies, this book refuses the narrow parameters that constrain the choices we have been offered. It proposes queering reproductive justice as a political project that cherishes the lives and safety of the most vulnerable as a litmus test for the survival of all.

This leads me to the second principle that takes us back to the archive of Black queer and feminist-of-color radicalisms: radical interdependency as the key to collective survival. As Audre Lorde wrote in the 1980s, "If there is any lesson we must teach our children, it is that difference is a creative force for change [and] that survival and struggle for the future ... [are] the very texture of our lives."[37] Lorde's words underscore the political task of raising youth as integral to the larger revolutions we wage—revolutions upon which our children's futures hinge. Lorde remained true to this principle of mutual interdependency as she lay in her deathbed, more than a decade later, envisioning her cancer cells to be white racists in apartheid South Africa, both of which needed to be eradicated.[38] Throughout her writing, she firmly reminded her readers that to care for the other was an act not of "altruism" but rather of "self-preservation," because the individual could not be healthy and whole until the collective was.[39] She believed so deeply in our shared fate that she linked her battle for survival with the struggles of Black and other oppressed people in South Africa and globally; at the same time, she entrusted her dreams to the children who were yet to come.

This radical interdependency inspires the present book as part of a longer lineage. "We have come to realize," echoed Gloria Anzaldúa, "we are not alone in our struggles, nor separate, nor autonomous.... We ... are connected and interdependent."[40] In this vein, *Queering Families* theorizes the project of queering reproductive justice grounded in the principle of the indivisibility of justice and the profound interconnectedness of our fates. With the term *indivisibility of justice*, I draw from June Jordan, who argued persuasively that "freedom [was] indivisible or ... nothing at all."[41] Positing that no part of her could be free until all parts were free, Jordan understood the ways that until the individual and collective body was empowered and free from harm, the struggle continued.

Informed by this genealogy, *Queering Families* proposes a praxis of queering family and reproductive justice that extends the radical politics of transformation articulated by these ancestral luminaries into an open future. To queer reproductive justice is to bring together the mandates of the reproductive justice movement—the right to have children, the right to not have children, and the right to raise our kin in healthy and life-affirming environments so that they might flourish[42]—with the project of queering, which entails a refusal, failure, or resistance to adhere to normativity's stranglehold. To queer reproductive justice is also to create networks of love, support, and care among and for the most vulnerable, and especially for our children in their "refus[al] to grow up toward normative ways of being an adult," with equal attention to our dead.[43] Queering reproductive justice, as praxis, thus expands the aforementioned political mandates of solidarity, mutual survival, and recognition of the how our pasts, presents, and futures are intertwined.

AGAINST ALL ODDS: QUEERING UTOPIAN FUTURITIES

Queering Families is inspired by the invitation to kindle intergenerational reciprocity in precarious times, when protecting the lives of the most vulnerable is supposed to be impossible. This entails fighting for a world in which we create communities of care to encircle, cherish, and uphold the lives of those who defy normativity's violent stranglehold and who are continually deemed to be unworthy of life. This brings me to a final principle that animates a queer reproductive justice praxis: the creation of kin is also an act of wagering a future against all odds.

Here I turn to Alexis Pauline Gumbs, who reads Black feminist writers from the 1970s to the 1990s as a model of what it means to answer "death with utopian futurity" as a fundamentally "queer thing to do."[44] Gumbs traces the arc of Black queer mother artists who "appropriated motherhood as a challenge and refusal," resisting eugenic systems that "allowed and endorsed violence against the bodies of Black women and early death for Black children."[45] Black feminists "audaciously centered an entire literary movement" that asserted Black women's "reproductive autonomy"—both literally and in their more general capacity to create new worlds, writ large.[46]

Mining the archive for an insistence upon life—and even utopia—in the face of genocide, Gumbs extends José Esteban Muñoz's precept that "queerness exists for us as an ideality that can be distilled from the past and used to imagine the future."[47] Returning to Muñoz's frequently cited words, Gumbs argues for a queer politics of Black mothering as a direct "rejection of a here and now and an insistence on potentiality or concrete possibility for another world."[48] Utopia is not a naive form of hope for Gumbs. Nor is hope an ahistorical formulation that is disconnected from daily practice. Rather, to insist upon utopia through a practice of hope is to fight for nothing less than the worlds that future generations deserve. It is to live into better futures in the present in order to orient ourselves toward the better worlds that are always possible.

This corresponds to what Tina Campt calls a grammar of Black feminist futurity, which is

> a performance of a future that hasn't yet happened but must. It is an attachment to a belief in what should be true, which impels us to realize that aspiration. It is the power to imagine beyond current fact and to envision that which is not, but must be. It's a politics of prefiguration that involves living the future now—as imperative rather than subjunctive—as a striving for the future you want to see, right now, in the present.[49]

Campt describes the labor of "living in the future *now*—not because the future is ever guaranteed, but because there is no other alternative."[50] A politics of prefiguration compels one to step into the lives and worlds one deserves in the face of claims that this is impossible in material ways. It is the antithesis of ignoring social conditions. Rather, it is the steadfast insistence upon cherishing life in a world hellbent upon one's destruction and the destruction of one's children: a core principle for a queer politics of reproductive justice.

Queering Families takes courage from these traditions that have long insisted fiercely upon the realization of a future that "is not, but [that] must [be]," and that inspire a political praxis for our times.[51] Queering reproductive justice, I argue, must explode an LGBTQ+ family politics that is beholden to dominant disciplinary understandings of the possible, and well beyond "pragmatic" calls toward assimilation into racial capitalism, dominant nationalisms, the imperial settler state, and the already violent private nuclear family form.[52] Here I appreciate Dean Spade's critique of a pragmatist politics that discourages radical political demands before they even take form. Spade challenges the ways that our movements cede to the myth that it is neither "reasonable" nor "winnable" to fight for "a radically different world."[53] Instead of focusing upon "wins" in the service of a world we don't even want, Spade argues, queer and trans movements ought to, instead, demand the conditions that we need in order to survive, and more.[54]

This framework of demanding utopia in troubled times resists the hegemonic normalization of mass death and large-scale ecological destruction from which no one is immune. As movement philosopher Grace Lee Boggs has argued, there has never been another historical period in which the "challenges have been so basic, so interconnected, and so demanding, not just to specific groups but to everyone living."[55] Writing presciently before her death in 2015, Boggs compelled her readers to wrestle with a fundamental decision to either transform radically or accept "the devastation and the extinction of all life on earth."[56]

Boggs set forth the stakes in no uncertain terms, arguing that "our lives, the lives of our children and future generations, and even the survival of the planet depend on our willingness to transform ourselves."[57] She called for common cause among all communities for the purpose of planetary survival. Importantly, the experience of extinction is not a new phenomenon, especially for Black and Indigenous communities. "Imperialism and ongoing colonialism," writes Robyn Maynard plainly, "have been ending worlds for as long as they have been in existence."[58] What has shifted, however, is the reach of these conditions, especially as more communities are drawn into what Kim Tall-Bear calls the "ever widening circle" of threat.[59] For TallBear, this expansion of threat creates a possibility for new solidarities among unconventional allies who must see themselves as inhabitants of a shared planet—and whose futures are thus entwined.[60] This context frames Boggs's analysis, which names the deep transformative work that will require widescale participation if we are to facilitate collective survival.

THE CHILD-AS-PROXY AT THE ENDS
OF THE WORLD

Queering Families locates the question of queering reproductive justice—of demanding the conditions for collective life against all odds—as a commitment to radical interdependency. The book thus belongs within a genealogy of radical Black feminist, Indigenous, and queer-of-color work. As a queer mother and abolitionist, I write, in particular, from a specific historical conjuncture of ever-widening precarities in which competing claims upon the future across the political spectrum hinge upon the question of children and their futures.

Competing claims over children's futures often find expression in moral panics. Gayle Rubin has famously argued that debates over sexuality, reproduction, and children function as a screen for larger geopolitical contestations in times of national instability, carrying an "immense symbolic weight" that stands in for other national fears.[61] The trope of the innocent child in peril has, historically, been effective in galvanizing nationalist fervor because, as Erica Meiners elaborates, "invoking real or imagined children produces an irreproachable purity."[62] For to oppose the protection of the child "is almost unthinkable— tactically impossible, an intimate violation."[63]

A heightened moral panic also forms the historical backdrop for *Queering Families*, which I write in a moment when, to draw from Rebekah Sheldon, the figure of the child carries an emotional charge that is heightened by widespread societal insecurities. As Sheldon argues, contemporary "conditions of planetary threat" lead to an atmosphere in which "the child, the fetus, and the reproductive woman [*sic*] become subjects of intense discursive investment."[64] These dynamics feature prominently in contemporary political debates, amid intersecting crises of ecological, political, and economic precarity. As planetary threats amplify, actors on all sides of the political spectrum invoke the figure of the imperiled child to justify a wide range of political agendas and issues—from guns in schools, to health care access for transgender youth, to pandemic-era masking in schools, to children's book bans, and more.

Within this context, the Right mobilizes the bogeyman of a secular "wokeness" that threatens to encroach upon conservative worldviews. Parents crowd school boards and influence state legislatures to police everything from the teaching of history to the provision of gender-affirming care. Here the image of the imperiled child mobilizes publics, as political leaders call upon Christian "mamas" to "lay down [their lives] ... for [their] children ... to advocate for their children's innocence," to quote *Daily Citizen* author Nicole Hunt.[65] Meanwhile, the GOP's 2023 "Parents Bill of Rights" demands the teaching of content that is "rooted in the history and culture of Western civilization" and invokes a so-called parental "right to know" if a school employee or contractor acts to "change a minor child's gender markers, pronouns, or preferred name" or grants transgender or gender-nonconforming children the right to appropriate bathrooms, locker rooms, and sports programming, thus effectively waging war upon LGBTQ+ children, employees, and families.[66] The trope of childhood innocence is constructed in opposition to the specter of a racial, sexual, and national Other, who threatens the purity and sanctity of a white life. This stems from a history of "childhood innocence" as a concept that, as Robin Bernstein has demonstrated, emerged only in the mid-nineteenth century and gained purchase in direct opposition to dominant constructs of Black culpability.[67]

This rhetoric exemplifies the ways that the trope of childhood innocence acts to preserve the ideals of whiteness, heterosexuality, and reproductive normativity. It also further encodes which children are imagined to be worthy of protection—and which are not—as well as who is even imagined to be a child in the first place.[68] For the Right, the figure of the imperiled child is a dog whistle, despite the material, environmental, economic, and health harms caused to actual children by the policies being promoted.[69] This leads historian Michael Bronski to conclude that what "is ... foremost a plea for an imagined innocence of the past ... has nothing to do with actual children."[70]

However, it is not just the Right that mobilizes the figure of the imperiled child in the face of perceived existential threats. Discourses of children's rights and well-being have also been highly effective at organizing liberals and progressives in contradictory ways. This has been especially the case in the era of COVID-19. Take, for example, Urgency of Normal, a campaign that coalesced in Blue states, bringing together "for the child" rhetoric with a quest to resuscitate racial capitalism at all costs. Initially started up in 2020 as an informal coalition of physicians based in San Francisco and New York, Urgency of Normal opposed school closures, expanding to argue for the *unmitigated* opening of schools as vaccines became available to adults. They argued that pandemic mitigations in schools and classrooms amounted to a "kids-last" policy—even in a time when vaccines were not yet available to most youth. Challenging mask requirements and opposing teachers' unions, the group issued its own form of for-the-child rhetoric that strung together cherry-picked data to promulgate the false narrative that COVID-19 did not medically affect kids.[71] This was especially dangerous to disabled and immunocompromised children, as well as children in intergenerational households or living with vulnerable family members. Moreover, this narrative capitalized upon the real suffering of parents, papering over important questions like sick pay, a spike in homelessness and hunger among children, and necessary financial supports for struggling parents.

Urgency of Normal reframed the discussion in ways that explicitly excluded critical discussions of supports like universal healthcare or safe affordable childcare, also foreclosing key questions about why children could not access a hot meal or vital services outside of schools, and refusing to join with a simultaneous national struggle to shift state expenditures from prisons and war into community supports. It thus abetted the concerted attack that has taken place upon the already-inadequate social safety net. It was here that the neoliberal and neoconservative agendas converged. What had once been a stance associated with neoconservative groups (such as Moms for Liberty, funded by the Koch brothers) was repurposed for Blue states. This move shifted the discourse by mainstreaming the antimask, antimitigation message under the pretext of doing it "for the children."

In both its neoconservative and neoliberal instantiations, child-as-proxy logic silences key questions about the real harms and dangers facing children under racial capitalism, as neither the Right nor the Left commits to actions that come anywhere close to addressing the ecological, economic, and political catastrophes that our children are inheriting. Instead, they advance moralizing calls to save children that actively deflect us away from the deeper conditions that actually pose threats to children. These contradictions grow all the more unbearable amidst an active genocide. *Queering Families* shifts the discussion to ask how both positions eclipse the real work that we must do to combat the systems, such as settler colonialism, prisons, and racial capitalism, that plunge current and future generations even deeper into ecological and economic catastrophe. The book thus seeks to push past the child-as-proxy to raise questions about what kinds of solidarities a queer politics of reproductive justice requires.

This context frames *Queering Families*, which locates debates surrounding reproduction in a political landscape where crises of ecological and economic precarity come to a head. A politics of queering reproductive justice, I argue, must resist the affective draw into child savior discourses grounded in moral panics. Rather, we must abolish the harmful systems that imperil current youth and future generations of all living creatures.

QUEERING REPRODUCTIVE JUSTICE: TENSIONS, GENEALOGIES, CONVERSATIONS

A queer politics of reproductive justice rejects the ways in which contemporary LGBTQ+ family discourses align with both neoliberal and neoconservative ideologies and frameworks. It also probes the deeper processes of slavery, racial capitalism, and colonialism that have made those frameworks and ideologies possible—processes that have long ended worlds and that, if allowed to continue, will drive all living creatures to extinction. Challenging a dominant politics of the possible that hinders radical imaginations before they can take form, this book demands no less than utopic futures, even—and especially—in a world plagued by ecocide, intensified racial stratification, public health emergencies, rising Fascism, and other threats. *Queering Families* thus politicizes discussions over queer family in times when the figures of the child, the family, and the parent come to acquire heightened cultural and political resonance.

The book addresses core debates surrounding reproduction among people for whom procreative intercourse is not currently the primary mode of creating family. It engages debates surrounding adoption, foster care, ARTs, gamete donation, and the place of DNA in queer family. Since such family building has also included adopting children from poor families of color, including migrant, Black, and Native families, it echoes historian Laura Briggs's question about how what was once "a fierce fight [of queers] to keep their own children in the seventies and eighties" somehow warped into the articulation of a "'right' ... to take other people's children."[72] Simultaneously, *Queering Families* nuances overly simplistic critiques of adoption, foster care, and ARTs, which often resort to the biogenetic family as the default and the most authentic and just kinship formation. Ultimately, I argue for a queer politics of family abolition that moves us beyond the private nuclear family unit, be it hetero- or homonormative. I ask how these debates about family making, especially when framed in binary ways, can also become a site for the displacement of larger structural questions about all living beings' futures in a world under peril.

Here it is helpful to take a step back to lay out some of the core tensions between reproductive justice and queering family, the two broad areas of scholarship and praxis that *Queering Families* brings together. Within the first area, trailblazing Black feminist legal theorist Dorothy Roberts warned of a landscape in which proliferating reproductive technologies accessible only to an elite few would exacerbate a racial caste system that penalized and criminalized women of color, particularly Black women.[73] In *Killing the Black Body* (1997), Roberts juxtaposed the increased reproductive surveillance experienced by Black women with the largely unfettered expanding commercial market of reproductive technologies that these same Black women could not access. What did it mean, Roberts asked, that—in a time when reproductive technologies were being celebrated as harbingers of reproductive freedom—ever more Black women could barely access basic health and economic supports and were under increasing state scrutiny and criminalization?

Roberts was drawing on Angela Davis's 1993 essay "Surrogates and Outcast Mothers," in which Davis analyzed the politics of the then-new reproductive technologies for communities that had long experienced reproductive exploitation. Davis was particularly attuned to racial, gender, and labor politics; she raised piercing questions about the specter of an alarming future in which "poor women—especially poor women of color—[might be] transformed into a special caste of hired pregnancy carriers."[74] While reproductive technologies were ultimately neither inherently emancipatory nor oppressive for Davis, she argued that their implications could not be abstracted from slavery's racial and sexual economies. Nor could those implications be assessed without considering racialized labor arrangements that had continually exploited the reproductive labors of immigrants in particular.[75]

Debates about the ethics of ARTs were recast on a transnational stage when, at the turn of the twenty-first century, biocapitalist economies of sex, care, body parts, and reproductive labor burgeoned.[76] These discussions voice a structural tension of a commercially driven ART industry embedded within racial capitalism and the US settler state: that reproductive technologies would only further exploit the reproductive capacities and labors of the most marginalized in order to furnish the families of the most elite. *Queering Families* contributes to these theorizations, attending to the ways that queered desiring parents figure into these arrangements.

Despite the paramount importance of these debates, however, the vast majority of them envision the default mode of reproduction to be heterosexual conception. They often construe all forms of conception outside heterosexual intercourse as problematic—particularly given the histories through which, to quote the editors of *Queer Kinship*, "queerness denotes an excess or perceived deficiency in relation to the normative family."[77] At times they go so far as to take issue with *all* non-normative pathways to creating families, promoting an unnuanced rejection of ARTs that exacerbates obstacles for queer reproduction. This creates erasures so glaring that Laura Mamo and Eli Alston-Stepnitz must make the explicit assertion that "LGBTQ reproduction is part of reproductive justice."[78]

Problematizing the binary of ARTs as intrinsically oppressive or liberatory, *Queering Families* complicates notions of queer family as inherently flawed or lacking by politicizing blanket notions of biological ownership and inherent genetic connection. I challenge the narrative that the consumer of ARTs is always white, heterosexual, and upper class—a story that does not reflect the empirical demographics of LGBTQ+ families, who are, by and large, more economically disenfranchised and racially diverse than their heterosexual counterparts.[79] I also draw from feminist science and technology studies scholarship that complicates a "pure" or "old-fashioned" notion of heterosexual reproduction as inherently unproblematic.[80] By offering a more nuanced account of queer reproduction, *Queering Families* proposes an antiracist queer-of-color feminist analysis that neither pathologizes LGBTQ+ reproduction nor perpetuates the celebratory and largely uncritical thrust of much of the scholarship on LGBTQ+ conception.

Ultimately, the book contributes to an emergent discussion of queering reproductive justice that works against the dichotomy of queer reproduction and reproductive justice. I join chorus with sociologists Marcin Smietana, Charis Thompson, and France Winddance Twine, who call for a politics that might challenge "the binary mode of seeing ART as increasing the reproductive choice of LGBTQ+ intended parents while compromising the health of reproductive labourers and those unable to access the technologies for reasons of economic, national, racial and other kinds of stratification."[81] I am inspired by Natalie Fixmer-Oraiz and Shui-yin Sharon Yam, who point to the capaciousness and flexibility of reproductive justice frameworks to argue for a politics that stretches the "reproductive justice movement" to "a critical edge in its consideration of LGBTQ+ lives."[82] Fixmer-Oraiz and Yam highlight coalitional efforts of differentially oppressed communities who face vastly different but entwined obstacles to reproductive autonomy. They name the ways in which queer and reproductive justice movements crosscut with broader struggles for environmental justice, disability justice, immigration, trans rights, prison reform, and more. By bringing together those struggling at the margins of reproduction in different spaces of precariousness, Fixmer-Oraiz and Yam call for a nimble politics that refuses the ways that multiply marginalized communities come to be pitted against one another.

Inspired by this conversation, *Queering Families* theorizes queering reproductive justice as a transgressive political act that extends beyond the institution of the family as a bounded unit. I argue for a politics of family abolition that is rooted in a commitment to abolish all institutions under white supremacy, racial capitalism, colonialism, and heteropatriarchy. I locate family abolition in the project of decolonization and abolition in ways that have yet to be imagined. This requires us to move beyond a discussion about the ethics of queer reproduction as simply being one of individual choice. Rather, following Laura Mamo, I raise questions about how our choices are "situated and, therefore, made legible within conditions of inequalities and normative ideals of what and who make a family."[83] Ultimately, *Queering Families* works toward the creation of kinship forms that foster, sustain, and cherish radical life—especially among those who have continually been subject to reproductive genocide—in a time when conditions for life are becoming dramatically foreclosed.

CHAPTER OVERVIEW

Queering Families traces the figure of the queer parent through the late twentieth and early twenty-first centuries. It locates debates around queer family in a time when, to quote Melinda Cooper, the legitimacy of one's family came to rest upon its capacity to adhere to norms of "private family responsibility" more than to norms of gender or sexuality per se.[84] Chapter 1, "The Long Story: The Nuclear Family and Its Other(s)," begins with radical political critiques of the US state, racial capitalism, and US empire that emerged from New Left queer family formations. It grounds the project in a time prior to the consolidation of the neoliberal privatized family form—and prior to its eventual embrace throughout the homonormative turn. I offer a genealogy of the lesbian custody movement of the 1960s to the 1980s, with particular focus on the radical critiques of the private nuclear family as an instrument of white supremacy, settler colonialism, and racial capitalism. My archive is composed of the narrative writings and poetry of lesbian moms of this era. Reading the work of Beth Brant, Pat Parker, Deborah Miranda, and Minnie Bruce Pratt, I tease out a radical critique of the nuclear family as an institution used to separate loved ones from kin on the basis of race, class, sexuality and gender. This provides a historical yardstick with which to gauge significant shifts in more contemporary queer family discourse that I trace in subsequent chapters.

Chapter 2, "Opposing Figures: Good Families, Religious Liberties, and the Queering of Reproductive Justice," examines queer adoption and foster care politics. I analyze two key legal cases through which lesbian couples have sought to sue the state and the private Christian foster care and adoption agencies subcontracted by the state to manage social services. The first case, *Dumont v. Gordon* (2019), involves a couple wishing to adopt through Bethany Christian Services in Michigan, the largest Christian adoption agency in the country, implicated in the kidnapping of migrant children and babies stolen from their caretakers at the US-Mexico border. The second case, *Marouf v. Becerra* (2018), involves a lesbian couple who sued the US Department of Health and Human Services and the US Conference of Catholic Bishops for denying them their application to apply to foster unaccompanied minors. Bringing these cases together, this chapter theorizes the historical movement from a time when queers were deemed unfit to participate in social reproduction through parenting, to another—a time when mainstream LGBTQ+ political strategy is to make legal claims upon children whose capacity to remain with their families of origin has been severely undermined by racial capitalism and US imperial and colonial control. This analysis opens up a broader history through which the most privileged of LGBTQ+ subjects were able to gain purchase upon respectability vis-à-vis legal adoption just as they were folded into the neoliberal project of antisocialist privatization, militarism, and US empire building.

In examining the complexities and pitfalls of queer participation in the "family regulation system," chapter 2 warns of the consequences of an uncritical engagement with those systems.[85] However, chapter 3, "Your Children Are Not Your Children: Queer Investments in the Biogenetic Turn," argues that a queer politics of reproductive justice must be just as critical of bionormative understandings of family that have gained purchase within LGBTQ+ parenting circles of the past quarter century. Centering DNA politics, the chapter details the rise of the Donor Sibling Registry (DSR), a network that has, since 2000, worked to connect children with others born of the same gametes in "the conviction that it is healthiest for donor-conceived children to connect with those who share genetic material through a sperm donor."[86] First, I complicate the privileging of definitions of family that are structured through biology, biogenetics, and patriarchal bloodlines. I examine the implicit racial, colonial, and gendered projects embedded in the renorming of family as biological, asking what it means when DNA is used to arbitrate the authenticity of family. Finally, I demonstrate that far from being neutral, claims to a unitary model of biological heredity rest upon notions of queerness as pathology and lack, which also carry with them racial and colonial histories and epistemologies with which we must contend.

Interspersed throughout chapters 2 and 3, I include counternarratives of queer radicalism that disrupt hegemonic projects of LGBTQ+ family. Chapter 4, "Queering Family Abolition: Intergenerational Archives of Care," maps a less considered genealogy of queering family: family abolition. I turn to the archives of care produced by radical queer feminists of color from the 1970s to the present. I first read the intergenerational writings between Audre Lorde, Cherríe Moraga, and their children, Rafael Angel Moraga and Elizabeth Lorde-Rollins, for the ways they challenge hierarchical notions of the private family to embody transformative care. I next trace this ethos in queer collective activism of the 1990s and 2000s. The histories that chapter 4 unearths voice an insistence upon abiding care for the most marginalized in times of abandonment, thus embodying a core principle of abolition feminism: the rejection of a hierarchical, rigid, and punitive colonial and carceral institution—in this case the private nuclear family—and its replacement with more humane and sustainable structures of collective care.

The Epilogue, "Dreams and Nightmares: Reproductive Dystopias, Reproductive Utopias" situates major arguments of the book amid developments in the world of ARTs and federal adoption policy. I turn to fertility capitalism and the 2023 Supreme Court case *Haaland v. Brackeen* to highlight the stakes of all that gets lost when LGBTQ+ family discourses become disarticulated from a fundamental commitment to reproductive justice. Against these nightmares, I offer counternarratives of queer reproductive justice that bring the struggle for queer family squarely into a broader movement for reproductive justice, decolonization, abolition, and planetary survival that *Queering Families* has highlighted.

CHAPTER ONE

The Long Story

The Nuclear Family and Its Other(s)

Nuclear Family, a recent docuseries by Ry Russo-Young, tells the harrowing story of the 1991 legal battle between the filmmaker's moms, Robin and Russo, and Robin's sperm donor, Tom Steel, who sued Ry's mothers for custody when she was nine years old. While Steel initially agreed to the family structure that Russo-Young's mothers proposed, this changed over time, escalating to a custody battle for Ry. What ensues is a painful process in which Steel, a progressive gay lawyer, resorts to arguing that all children need fathers and that lesbians are bad for children's identities.

The story of *Nuclear Family* grows all the more tense as the viewer learns that Steel is dying of AIDS, which adds another layer of tragedy to a narrative about queers vying for access to the limited forms of kinship allowed to them under the law. As Steel faces impending death, his claim upon Ry hinges on the delegitimization of Russo, Ry's nonbiological mother, and Ry's sister, Cade, thus reifying heteropatriarchal biogenetic definitions of family as exclusively based on DNA. In response, Robin and Russo double down on the legitimacy of the private nuclear family, claiming strict boundaries between Steel as "friend" and their private nuclear unit as "family."

In this conflict, both arguments perpetuate hegemonic ideas of the nuclear family as an exclusive domain. In her work on the illegibility of queer belonging, Elizabeth Freeman argues that our capacity to imagine intergenerational queer kinship is haunted by a linguistic inconceivability. Because "we lack names that would individuate the participants within larger forma-tions," Freeman argues, "we tend to use the language of com-munity or even nation, which does not distinguish the individ-ual relationships within it."[1] Russo-Young's story functions as a case in point of these limitations. As the adults wincingly fall back into conservative notions of family that contravene their stated political ideals, no party wins.

Glimpses of a counternarrative and alternative political imag-inary, however, appear a few minutes into *Nuclear Family*. Archival footage from the 1979 March on Washington for Gay and Lesbian Rights flickers on the screen. A blurry protest sign reads, "Down with Nuclear Family: Root of All Sexual Oppression," bobbing up and down in an ephemeral flash. "Down with Nuclear Family: Root of All Sexual Oppression" contrasts starkly with the traps that ensnare all three adults in the film. It serves as a fleeting vis-ual reference to a different sensibility and political ethos.

This chapter expands upon this counternarrative to elaborate a different vision, one kindled as movements of the late twentieth century declared the nuclear family to be an instrument of oppression and articulated family otherwise. Throughout the 1960s and 1970s, as Michael Bronski argues, queers sought to be free from the nuclear family's structures, violences, and limita-tions. Feminist, gay liberation, and other New Left organizations coalesced to envision "a utopia that would finally liberate women from the burdens of reproduction, while also creating a social structure in which children could safely function as independent beings who [were] not frightened or shamed out of exploring their sexuality."[2] Activists sought to collectivize the responsibility for childcare, as queers called for "both an end to the nuclear family and the involvement of gays and lesbians in the raising of children."[3]

In the decades that followed, however, these expansive notions of family were largely contained within the site of the nuclear monogamous family again: they gave way, ultimately, to marriage equality movements of the early twenty-first century that prioritized the nuclear family for the reproduction of kin and the provision of care. Those earlier energies were captured by a backlash that worked to contain "the liberation movements of the 1960s," as Melinda Cooper argues, and to redirect "the antinormative and redistributive promise of these movements" through a powerful call to "family responsibility" that co-opted queer, feminist, and anticolonial movements of prior decades.[4] This process materialized in the lesbian custody movement, where, according to Daniel Rivers, custody battles once rooted within "larger resistance ... [against] heterosexist, racist, and misogynistic attitudes about the proper structure of the American family" were eventually channeled into the more conservative, whittled-down goals of legitimacy and inclusion.[5] Thus the radical intersectional reach of early lesbian moms' activism "would survive only in muted ways as lesbian and gay parental and domestic rights emerged by the late 1990s as a central focus of the mainstream LGBT freedom struggle."[6]

This chapter offers a genealogy of a time prior to the consolidation of this limited family form. I first outline prominent critiques of the nuclear family that animated diverse sectors of the Left from the mid-1960s to the 1970s. I next focus on some of the less chronicled protagonists who highlight the broader—colonial, capitalist, and white supremacist—context informing the struggle for lesbian custody. Writings by Beth Brant (Bay of Quinte Mohawk) and Black lesbian poet Pat Parker, in particular, set our histories of queer custody movements within the context of a settler colonial state that, founded on genocide and slavery, has continually stolen children. Reading Brant's and Parker's texts as political and theoretical writings situates the struggle against state-sanctioned kidnapping and family regulation within deeper, communal histories of resistance. In closing, I speak to the ensuing backlash that sought to reprivatize the family amid a broader reassertion of imperialism, white supremacy, and militarization, both domestically and abroad.

This context allows us to understand the eventual hegemonization of the private nuclear family within LGBTQ+ family politics. Over and against this context, I articulate an alternative queer politics of family that brings the tragedy of *Nuclear Family* into stark relief. These histories remind us of a time and place when queers and feminists worked to reveal how the nuclear family was itself a tool of oppression. They also center the racial, colonial, and capitalist violence that activists unearthed to be a key function of both the heteropatriarchal and the homonormative nuclear family.

This chapter thus provides another vision of family, one rooted in notions of collective care and a commitment to the liberation of all. Taking the reprivatization of the family in the post-1970s period to be a form of backlash against these dreams, I pose an alternative to the political dead ends that entrap the protagonists of *Nuclear Family.*

THE NUCLEAR FAMILY AS THE ROOT
OF OPPRESSION: SOME HISTORIES

In a 1979 speech at the National Conference of Third World Lesbians and Gay Men, Audre Lorde called upon her audience to vow to collectively care for all children within the community. Speaking to around five hundred people at this historic event, Lorde delivered a key message:[7] "Our future lies in our young people," she stated.[8] This includes, she clarified, "not only about those children we may have mothered or fathered ourselves, but about all our children together ... [who] ... are our joint responsibility and our joint hope."[9] Lorde's words articulated a commitment to what Alexis Pauline Gumbs calls "an avowedly socialist" approach to parenting that characterized Black and Third World queer feminisms of the era.[10] This commitment would surface the next day, when activists holding a sign calling for the abolition of the private nuclear family participated in the 1979 March on Washington for Gay and Lesbian Rights.

Lorde's call was in dialogue within feminist and gay and lesbian liberation movements of the times. "Liberationists," writes legal scholar Michael Boucai, identified marriage and the nuclear family as "the centerpiece of an intricate system of unwarranted sexual regulation."[11] Their critique, Boucai explains, coalesced in feminist and "gay [and lesbian] liberation's attacks on the 'patriarchal capitalist family' ... [where] specific grievances against the nuclear family," ranging from its gendered division of labor to its constraints on desire, "were multiple and crosscutting."[12] Highlighting largely occluded histories of "gay liberation's dream of structures beyond the procreative nuclear family,"[13] Boucai reminds his readers of the archive of early gay liberation's "feisty manifestos imagining the demise or even the 'abolition of ... the bourgeois nuclear family'" that were so common in this era, and notes the influence of prominent feminist texts.[14] Kate Millett's watershed *Sexual Politics* (1969), for instance, declared in no uncertain terms that a sexual revolution must strike directly at the patriarchal monogamous family, which she called "a patriarchal unit within a patriarchal whole."[15] Lesbians, too, levied arguments against what Adrienne Rich called "compulsory heterosexuality," revealing the political underpinnings of marriage, the nuclear family, and heterosexuality itself.[16]

Importantly, this critique was not exclusive to feminists and queers. Rather, it took place amid broader activist cultures of the era. By the 1970s, diverse sectors of the Left also took on the private nuclear family as part of their work of liberating adults and children alike. As historian Andrew Lester argues, this dynamic could be seen within the Black Panther Party (BPP), for example, and in New Left formations where activists "experimented with utopian alternatives to the nuclear family norm," and "organizations and movements ... [sought] alternative ways to experience belonging while refusing to conform to the white normative nuclear family ideal."[17] BPP cofounder Huey Newton was influential among feminist and gay liberationist subcultures within the San Francisco Bay Area, and his critique of "the bourgeois nuclear family as the basic unit of capitalism" reverberated widely. It surfaced, for example, in the extensively circulated "Gay Manifesto" (1969), in which the Committee for Homosexual Freedom called marriage "a rotten, oppressive institution" and argued that the liberation of gay people relied upon an outright rejection of the nuclear family and of "straight values," which could not dictate queer social relations.[18] The group Third World Gay Revolution (TWGR) also drew on the BPP. Using the Panthers' direct language, TWGR's 1970 sixteen-point platform argued that "all oppressions originate[d] within the nuclear family structure" and made the abolition of the nuclear family one of its key political demands.[19]

A series of efforts to practice collective care for children accompanied these ideological critiques. The BPP started breakfast and community education programs,[20] the Young Lords organized breakfast and childcare programs, and gay and lesbian liberationist, feminist, and anti-imperialist organizations incorporated childcare collectives into their work.[21] The Boston Gay Men's Liberation Front identified child-rearing as "the common responsibility of the whole community."[22] The Prairie Fire Organizing Committee likewise argued that "collective child care was a practical expression of our feminist politics and a political responsibility."[23] The committee thus introduced childcare teams and children's political education in order to free women to participate in broader political work.

These projects represented a radical break from the nuclear family as diverse but interconnected communities committed to creating a new society that would take the nurturing of children beyond the private monogamous nuclear family. They situated the institution of the family in relation to other oppressive institutions of the settler state under white supremacy, capitalism, and imperialism, and they also forged the ideological space for the envisioning and practice of diverse forms of kinship that—in overtly political acts—broke with the nuclear family. These projects thus gave rise to new articulations of family less beholden to the powers that be.

QUEER AND LESBIAN MOTHERS'
MOVEMENTS AND THE WEAPONIZATION
OF CUSTODY

These efforts formed a backdrop against which collective efforts coalesced to support queer moms threatened with the loss of their children. From the mid-1960s to the 1980s, thousands of queer parents, largely mothers, previously in heterosexual marriages, routinely faced the threat of custody loss after coming out.[24] Thousands more either settled out of court or stayed within their marriages because of economic, physical, social, and legal coercion.[25] In response, a movement emerged to critique the "legal kidnapping," abetted by the state, that was waged to punish queers for coming out.[26]

As Daniel Rivers argues, lesbian moms' activism of the 1960s–1980s had an especially radical bent, given many of its leaders' prior experiences within civil rights, Black freedom, and antiwar struggles of the era.[27] "What were the reasons?" wrote Minnie Bruce Pratt about the loss of her children to her ex-husband after she left him for a woman. "Power of a man over / a woman, his children: his hand on power he lacked ... / Terror of a man left alone / the terror at a gesture: my hand sliding from her / soft pulse neck, to jawbone, chin, mouth met."[28] The movement thus framed the denial of custody as one expression of a backlash that sought to reassert hegemony over the nuclear family through legal and extralegal patriarchal violence.

The denial of custody is, for Pratt, a political act—and a form of direct punishment for acting on her desire for her woman lover. Framed this way, each threatened loss of children was not an individual occurrence. Rather, it was emblematic of a larger system of control that entrapped mothers and children.

Custody cases thus raised "very large questions about the institutionalization of human relationships, and about the entity called the family—that battleground, open wound, haven, and theater of the absurd," to quote Adrienne Rich.[29]

Queers also centered the importance of bodily autonomy and of control over one's sexuality in the struggle for the custody rights of lesbians, single mothers, and anyone who happened to "bust open the egg" of the nuclear family, as Lois Thetford, cofounder of the Lesbian Mothers National Defense Fund, put it.[30] Leaders emphasized the racialized and economic forces that limited sexual autonomy by keeping queers trapped in heterosexual marriages and nuclear families against their will. The groups Black Women for Wages for Housework and Wages Due Lesbians, for example, highlighted the coercive nature of marriage and the private family under racial capitalism. As they argued, Black, lesbian, and poor women would never be able to seize control over their own reproduction under the current racial and political economic systems. Until mothers were remunerated for their domestic labor, they would be burdened by "the threat of seeing [their] ... children taken away ... always hanging over ... [their] heads," as a 1976 flyer warned.[31]

Utilizing this analysis, Wages for Housework understood the attack upon welfare from the 1970s onward to be a backlash and a "well-orchestrated campaign ... that relentlessly targeted ... women as parasites consuming state budgets."[32] This especially affected lesbians, a high number of whom were on welfare because they lacked access to a husband's income. The dismantlement of welfare, they argued, attempted to roll back the gains of feminism through a targeted attack upon lesbians, and especially poor and Black women, who either broke with or had never been part of the nuclear family.[33]

Informed by these conversations, the custody movement located the removal of children from lesbians at the crossroads of multiple intersecting systems of oppression, working to forge a "broad antiracist, reproductive rights political coalition [as] ... an important way to organize against what they perceived in the late 1970s as a rising conservative backlash."[34] The New York group Dykes and Tykes (which included Audre Lorde) joined in solidarity with racial justice and anti-imperialist organizations of single Black mothers and campaigns challenging the forced sterilization of women of color.[35] The Lesbian Mothers National Defense Fund took it upon itself to "support all single mothers facing poverty and the hardships of raising children in a patriarchal society."[36] They joined a variety of anti-imperialist and anticolonial movements, from campaigns against US intervention in Latin America to campaigns supporting the self-defense of domestic violence survivors, such as Yvonne Wanrow, a Native woman who was accused of killing her abusive husband.[37] These coalitions voiced deep understandings of the entwined systems of oppression.

This critical ethos shaped and was shaped to a notable extent by feminist poets of the era who shared Audre Lorde's edict that "poetry is not a luxury."[38] It is important to consider the material role of writers, print culture, and writing in movement organizing—supported by a robust network of feminist bookstores and culture of poetry readings as protest—that blurred the boundaries between poetic sensibilities and political consciousness. Many worked to "write / what happened," as Pratt put it, even when it meant "a return / to the cold place where I am being punished."[39] More broadly speaking, feminist poets of the era were important in the creation and circulation of a political consciousness that "traversed scales of the intimate and the geopolitical," as I argue elsewhere, thus allowing for a critique of imperialism, colonialism, and heteropatriarchy on both the intimate and the structural levels.[40]

The poetic sphere emerged as a crucial space for the generation of political visions and thus for the birthing of alternative histories and the forging of solidarities that could help guide movement organizing. Literary works were simultaneously theoretical and political texts. They constitute a critical archive for us to read in order to nuance our analyses of oppression and resistance.

In what follows, I turn to the writings of Beth Brant and Pat Parker in conversation with several of their interlocutors. Coming out in the 1970s in her thirties as the mother of three children, Brant left her husband. Notably, Brant did not become a formal writer until she was forty, when she was encouraged by Michelle Cliff and Adrienne Rich to publish her writings and edit the works of other Native feminist writers; this makes her gift of language all the more stunning.

A staunch believer in the interconnectedness of radical movements for self-determination and collective freedom, Parker used her poetry to link struggles across the scales of the intimate to the international. This was an outgrowth of her work in multiple movements—from her early days in the Panthers, to her work against intimate partner violence, to her health activism as the director of the Oakland Feminist Women's Health Center, to her influential role in the early days of lesbian grassroots publishing networks.

Taken collectively, the writings of Brant and Parker articulate the ways that histories of slavery, white supremacy, settler colonialism, and racial capitalism undergird the nuclear family. Their work thus helps to frame the problematics of the private nuclear family within a broader racial and colonial history. As I argue, these writers—and their larger movements—challenge the contemporary, often uncritical uptake of the private nuclear family within LGBTQ+ circles that is naturalized in *Nuclear Family* and beyond. These writings therefore nourish a political consciousness that troubles whitewashed, depoliticized ideologies of the nuclear family that large portions of the LGBTQ+ family movement have since uncritically embraced.

FRAMING THE LONGEST STORY: CUSTODY LOSS WITHIN THE SETTLER STATE

> I had no name for the terror I felt, no explanation for
> my inability to eat or keep food down, the swift loss
> of 40 pounds, a sudden thyroid problem that made
> my hair fall out, my heart palpitate, my skin grow
> grey and dry…. All I knew was that my children
> were being held hostage, and only my "good
> behavior" could save them. I had to be a "good
> mother." Bad mothers lost their babies.
> —Deborah Miranda[41]

In a beautiful 2015 obituary for Beth Brant, Deborah Miranda reflects on the importance of Brant's writing in her own life.[42] A queer Two-Spirit Ohlone-Costanoan Esselen writer, Miranda found a lifeline in Brant's work when she herself was threatened with the loss of her children. Miranda captures the utter terror that this threat sent through her, reducing her to "a tiny, tiny soul inside a body more like a robot than a human being."[43] Brant's writing helped Miranda come to grips with her own intergenerational terrors to face a core truth: "In my family, mothers *did* lose their children. Children *did* lose their mothers."[44] Locating this experience within a collective history loosened the strong hold of fear.

Miranda references Brant's "A Long Story" (1983), a fictional account that moves between the stories of two mothers, across the span of a century, whose children were stolen from them.[45] "A Long Story" intersperses the first-person narration, set in 1890, of "Annie," a Mohawk mother whose kids are taken to a boarding school in Philadelphia, with the 1978 story of Mary, her descendent, a Native lesbian mom whose daughter has been taken from her by her vindictive ex-husband.[46] By entwining these stories, Brant articulates the long durée of reproductive violence that links her protagonists across generations. She also attests to the power of intimacy, forging a path for the reclamation of lost selves forged in the connections between lovers, kin, and ancestors. This analysis, in turn, opens into a decolonial and intersectional queer praxis that must be implemented in our grassroots movements if contemporary LGBTQ+ movements for reproductive justice are to abolish structures of colonialism, white supremacy, and violence, and replace them with more humane systems of care.

"A Long Story" is best understood within the context of Brant's larger oeuvre, which weaves together stories of different Native women dislocated from themselves and their communities, crisscrossing between entwined systems of the settler colonial state—boarding schools, foster homes, the courts, and the nuclear settler family itself—only to find themselves in companionship with one another. One place where "A Long Story" appeared was in Brant's 1985 anthology of poetry, *Mohawk Trail*, in a larger section called "Long Stories" that assembles different accounts of mothers and daughters who are separated from one another by different state institutions. Notably, the section includes "The Fifth Floor, 1967," a story—dedicated to the poet Mary Moran, who endured forced psychiatric hospitalization—

about a Native woman who was locked away from her children in a psychiatric ward for refusing to have sex with her husband. Brant's sensitivity to these issues is no doubt informed by her own experience of forced psychiatric hospitalization.[47] By layering these entwined histories, Brant locates the state's violent seizure of Native children at the crosscurrents of multiple intersecting systems of oppression. She highlights the power of connection across bars, cages, and history to form intimacies that can transform unfathomable despair.

Brant challenges dominant institutions that violently wrench children from their families, from the boarding school, to the hospital, to the child welfare system, to the private settler nuclear family. She demands an abolition of them all. These threads all coalesce in "A Long Story," in which a series of repeating motifs connects Mary, a Native lesbian mom in the late twentieth century, and "Annie," whose children are kidnapped and placed in a boarding school a century prior. Both women's lives are bound together by institutions that seek to steal their power and their capacity to practice family on their own terms. Simultaneously, the story also highlights distinctions between the two, particularly as Mary is able to receive life-giving intimacy with her lover, Ellen, and thus to receive support that is wholly unattainable for "Annie."

The first theme that coheres the two women's stories is that of the living dead. Both mothers remark that they must be dead when faced with the staggering loss of their children. At the story's opening, Annie sits by the fire, quivering with cold and terror two days after her children have been stolen.[48] "I hold myself tight in the fear of flying apart in the air. Can they feed a dead woman? I have stopped talking. When my mouth opens, only air escapes. I have used up my sound screaming their names."[49]

Unable to accept food or warmth, "Annie's" body does not respond to fire and blankets. She declares herself "a dead woman," articulating the impossibility of any imaginable future without her children.[50] This dynamic is paralleled in a vignette in which Mary awakes from a nightmare, convinced that her daughter, Patricia, is dead. As Mary wanders the house and enters Patricia's empty bedroom. She marvels at the paradox that her heart still beats as she feels such pain, asking, "How is it possible to feel such pain and live?"[51]

Mary's and "Annie's" children have been stolen from them by a state that justifies its actions in papers, documents, and grammars that are not available to either woman. This leads to a second theme that binds the stories: the power of the hegemonic word. Neither mother has legal recourse to get her kids back. Across the generations, the hegemonic word is delivered by patriarchal colonial state authorities, as the power to shape the dominant historical narrative—and to occlude all other historical realities—emerges as a key function of the law.

Brant highlights the crushing power of legal documents in the form of treaties and custody papers. We "signed the papers ... [and that] gave them the rights to take our babies," states "Annie," underscoring the ludicrous power of a piece of paper.[52] Mary, too, battles legal papers, her broken treaties dressed up in fancy garb but brutal nonetheless. "My lawyer says there is nothing more we can do," she says, resigning herself. "I must wait ... as if there has been something other than waiting."[53] Mary refers not only to the time she has already spent separated from her daughter but also to the accumulated wait for all of the children who have been stolen before hers.

This continuity also emerges in the letters penned by the children to their mothers, as children are coerced to write words to punish their grieving moms. "The agent was here to deliver a letter," states "Annie." "I screamed at him and threw curses his way [, throwing] … dirt in his face as he mounted his horse."[54] The letter "Annie" receives burns her hands; it is written by "two strangers with the names of Martha and Daniel" who claim to be "living the civilized ways."[55] In response, she refuses the names, "Daniel" and "Martha,"[56] given to her children, and she recoils, rejecting the premise of these letters and their foreign signatories.[57] "Annie" decries how the colonizers "steal our food, our sacred rattle, the stories, our names."[58] Like "Annie," Mary knows it is not the true voice of her daughter who speaks in the letter as she arrives home from work to a letter from her daughter Patricia. Mary anxiously paces her house, disturbed by the idea of Patricia's "father standing over her, coaxing her, coaching her[, turning the] letter … ugly."[59] Mary is devastated to see no mention of Ellen in the letter.

This discursive power that the state wields through a control of language is not simply symbolic. It manifests materially in the bodies of Brant's characters, who come physically undone. In one example, "Annie" looks mournfully at her son's shorn braids. As her husband wraps the braids in cloth, "Annie" remarks that he is "tak[ing] pieces of [their] son away."[60] This vignette cuts into a nightmare from which Mary has just awakened. In it, her daughter is dead. Like "Annie's" son, she has also been taken apart; her body is being returned to Mary in pieces.[61] Corporeal dislocation abounds across time and place.

Brant's words bring urgency to the imperative for an intersectional and anticolonial analysis of the origins and consequences of the private nuclear family, confronting the reader with a visual metaphor for the devastation that colonialism wreaks upon the individual and collective body. This violence turns inward as

"Annie" takes a knife to her hair, clothes, and body and throws everything into the fire to express her rage.[62] She tosses her shorn hair into the fire, replicating the violence done to her son's locks.[63] Mary too takes to tearing all that is around her: sheets, curtains, all the things that used to adorn Patricia's room. "Like a wolf, caught in a trap, gnawing at her own leg to set herself free," states Mary, "I begin to beat my own breasts to deaden the pain inside."[64] This corporealizes the devastation that internalized violence brings when vulnerable members within communities are left to shoulder the burden of oppression alone.

As Kim TallBear argues, the settler state depended upon the destruction of Native families—and the imposition of the nuclear reproductive monogamous settler family—as a key facet of the colonizing process. The boarding school was one part of the crusade to assimilate Indian children and turn them from their own ways.[65] The image of children in pieces in "A Long Story" represents this process, as Brant greets the reader with the broken bones, psyches, and corpses produced by colonialism. An ethical reading of such images demands a reckoning with the breaking of native kinships and families that colonialism requires, opening into a critique of the nuclear family as the cornerstone of a queer reproductive justice. By rejecting the atomization represented in these stories across multiple generations, Brant also advances understandings of the modes of discipline—namely, the brute stealing of babies from their kin—required to silence many forms of life lived beyond the private family. This bespeaks the ways that the nuclear family's consolidation and naturalization were possible only through entwined systems of settler colonialism and heteropatriarchal terror.

Brant's writing, however, does not simply offer critique. It also practices a "gathering of spirit" that mends what has been broken and enlivens spirits. In the face of devastation, Brant, the writer, does what her protagonists cannot often do: she reappropriates the word. "We write," Brant states in an essay on queer Native literature, "not only for ourselves but also for our communities, for our People, for the young ones who are looking for the gay and lesbian path, for our Elders who were shamed or mythologized, for the rocks and trees, for the wingeds and four-leggeds and the animals who swim, for the warriors and resisters ... for our mothers, fathers, grandmothers."[66] Brant partakes in a "gathering of spirit" in order to "retell" the "story that hasn't changed for hundreds, maybe thousands of years," as she describes her writing process.[67] In so doing, she taps into something larger, evincing the collective historical experience of a long story that coheres community across space and time.

Likewise, Mary enacts this healing work, especially with Ellen, activating the power of queer intimacies that are fundamentally rooted in profound care. Mary and Ellen share in a desire that can, at least momentarily, "[cut] through the heartbreak [that the two] ... share."[68] Brant thus not only "reconstitutes how Indigenous lesbian bodies have been marked by settler colonialist discourses," as critic Ari Burford argues, but also "sheds the diagnosis, resisting the legal system and embodying an erotics of power."[69]

As a nurse, Ellen helps to heal, knitting broken places back together. Brant works with the reappearing image of knots, ties, braids, and plaits that might tie things together again, just as Ellen has lovingly stitched a patch on her daughter's overalls: "chain stitch, French knot, split stitch."[70] This comes through powerfully as Mary's despair is met with Ellen's loving touch, the two women's hairs braiding together. As Brant writes:

> She comes to me in full flesh. My hands are taken with the curves and soft roundness of her. She covers me with the beating of her heart. The rhythm steadies me. Heat is centering me. I am grounded by the peace between us. I smile at her face above me, round like a moon, her long hair loose and touching my breasts. I take her breast in my hand, bring it to my mouth .... Our bodies join. Our hair braids together on the pillow. Brown, black, silver, catching the last light of the sun. We kiss, touch, move to the place of our power.[71]

Broken bodies are made whole once again. As the prose slows down, it steadies the reader through the cadence of a beating heart. The reader is stilled in an inextinguishable drive toward intimacy and life itself. Mary and Ellen's hairs braid together as the two bodies entwine, Brant plaiting together stories of survival that are strengthened as parts of an interconnected whole. The roundness of Ellen's body and her moon-shaped face encircle and draw the reader in as Mary returns to a profoundly collective place of power and joy.

The connection between Mary and Ellen is a beautiful example of what contemporary scholars Qwo-Li Driskill and Lisa Tatonetti call a "sovereign erotics," which they define to be "a return to our bodies as whole human beings [who] can disrupt colonial gender regimes that have attempted to disavow and colonize native genders and sexualities."[72] They name Brant as a foremother of a contemporary Two Spirit revival whose work has been critical for the nurturing of future generations. This "sovereign erotics" is embodied in Brant's characters who reclaim the possibility for radical transformation—one that is attained only through a rejection of colonial divisions of kin and self, and a reclamation of the body. As a form of "medicine,"

Ellen's mouth kisses Mary's entire body, healing as it "[stops] at swells of skin, kissing, removing pain."[73] Brant infuses a life-giving intimacy into Ellen and Mary's relationship.

This corporeal return is repeated when, at the end of the story, Mary has a vision in which all of the vengeful fathers and judges are ground to dust, disappearing into the wind. Amid the flurry, Mary stands firm, her heart slowing down and "blood pumping" back into her "veins, carrying nourishment and life."[74] Proclaiming her identity as a lesbian—which she will "not cease to be"—Mary rejects what Brant elsewhere calls a "self-hatred ... so coiled within itself [that serves to] deny our part in creation."[75] Mary comes home to her full self in a radical reclamation, memory, and creation. The reader is left with the image of a revitalized woman, committed to a fight that will—like the blood pumping in her veins—continue until she dies, reverberating forward into generations to come.

Thus for Brant the struggle for queer family and reproductive justice is inextricable from the project of decolonization and the abolition of cages, walls, and state-enforced borders. This, in turn, nuances the critique of the nuclear family as a tool of sexual oppression that animated radical feminist and queer movements of the mid- to late twentieth century. In particular, Brant's work adds vital historical and political context to the conversation on lesbian custody, rooting the state-sanctioned kidnapping of children from mothers deemed to be "unfit" within a legacy of settler colonial state violence. Furthermore, as Krista L. Benson argues, Brant's writings offer a much-needed decolonial approach to prison abolition by illuminating Native women's understandings of how carceral regimes, such as imprisonment and psychiatric lockdown, have been thoroughly shaped by colonialism.[76] Brant's writing therefore urges a commitment to dismantling colonialism if one is truly serious about ending the excruciating practice of the state-sanctioned kidnapping of children as a mode of political discipline and the enforcement of the heteropatriarchal settler state.

Brant's work makes decolonization an urgent priority to any movement interested in dismantling the nuclear family. This challenges the contemporary, often uncritical uptake of the private nuclear family within LGBTQ+ circles that is naturalized in *Nuclear Family* and beyond. Brant calls forth modes of collective intimacy that, as future chapters argue, are indispensable to a queer reproductive justice praxis. Additionally, Brant's work taps into a wellspring of resiliency and power, inspiring imaginations of struggle that are fundamentally collective. This intervention is extended by Pat Parker, who builds intergenerational legacies to muster the strength to resist assaults upon herself and her children.

PAT PARKER'S LEGACY

An activist who read her poetry at countless political events, Parker supported the Lesbian Mothers Defense Fund as well as the case of Jeanne Jullion.[77] Parker also struggled to retain custody of her own (adopted) daughter, Anastasia, after the birth mother's family learned of Parker's sexuality.[78] Her beautiful poem "Legacy" addressed this custody battle in the context of her broader work to support queer mothers facing the loss of their children. It invites Anastasia into intergenerational histories that can guide her in difficult times.

Parker wrote "Legacy" when Anastasia was two years old, just a few years before her tragically untimely death to cancer in

1989, at the age of forty-five. Addressed to Anastasia, it is the final poem in Parker's brilliant 1985 anthology *Jonestown and Other Madness* and a dignified rebuttal to all those "who think ... that children and lesbians together / can't make a family" and are therefore "perverse."[79] In response to accusations of "perversity," Parker writes a love letter in which she turns to three generations of family to communicate to Anastasia the legacies "in blood" and "in spirit" that will anchor her throughout her lifetime.[80] In so doing, Parker identifies for Anastasia a source of power within their shared lineage of formerly enslaved peoples, whose fight and resilience she offers to her as a gift.

Parker opens the poem sarcastically, speaking back those who accuse queers of corrupting children by rising nightly only to feed their babies "Lavender Similac," thus drawing on tired tropes of a posited gay agenda that, quite literally, never rests.

> There are those who think
> or perhaps don't think
> ....
> that we have different relationships
> with our children
> that instead of getting up
> in the middle of the night
> for a 2am and 6am feeding
> we rise and chant
> *you're gonna be a dyke*
> *you're gonna be a dyke*[81]

Parker's language creates a flippant tone as she mocks the fears and fantasies of those who dare rip her away from her child.

This shifts quickly, however, as Parker responds with dignity and grace, addressing Anastasia directly.

Child
that would be mine,
I bring you my world
and bid it be yours.

The conditional tense that would cast any doubt on whether
Anastasia is Parker's child is met with a promise: "I bring you
my world."[82] For Parker, this means sharing the stories of three
generations of family, each of whom faced their own battles and
"took risks ... to chisel the crack ... [of racism and social strife]
... wider" so that their descendants might one day be free.[83] It
means sharing a beautifully capacious vision of family, vast and
deep enough to embrace Anastasia through life's most difficult
moments—a lesson that rings all the more poignant in retrospect, given Parker's death to come.

And thus begins Parker's exegesis of the strength and love
encircling Anastasia. The genealogy commences with her grandparents, Addie and George, both the children of slaves who toiled
to create a future that would outlive them. This commitment to a
future was funneled into the twenty-two children that Addie
birthed, many of whom did not survive their first year of life.[84]
Parker describes her grandparents' lives spent in pursuit of building homes, family, and community with their own hands. Short
and direct sentences convey a clear sense of purpose, while their
actions—"building," "preaching," "cleaning"—express lives lived
in pursuit of goals.[85] What results is an inner peace, revealed not
only in the lives of Addie and George—and next, Ernest and
Marie—but also in their deaths. All of "Legacy's" protagonists
die in peace. Having performed the work that they needed to do
on this earth, they all "lay down / and die."[86] To lie down peacefully is to surrender; it is a rite of passage and, when the time is
ripe, an act of agency to which all living beings are entitled.

Parker neither idealizes the past nor takes for granted the lessons that follow. Rather, she culls them, recognizing their immense value. This reflectiveness is testimony to a rich inner world that nourishes Parker's more public and visionary persona. This comes to a crescendo toward the end of the poem, as Parker narrows her gaze inward on her daughter and speaks directly from the heart. "Each generation improves the world for the next," she writes.[87]

> My grandparents willed me strength.
> My parents willed me pride.
> I will to you rage.
> I give you a world incomplete.[88]

By naming the world to be incomplete, Parker acknowledges the long durée of a struggle in a perpetual revolutionary process. To create a world worthy of one's children is to commit to a multigenerational task. It is to insist on hope in the face of daunting conditions; there is no other choice. And it is to insist on being a part of a collective, even when the system wishes to isolate you. As strength grows into pride, which grows into rage, Anastasia inherits these lessons. She becomes the bearer of the sacred mandate to pass along this responsibility to the next generation.

Parker articulates a form of inheritance that exceeds bloodline and heteropatriarchal notions of kin with an expansive notion of family alive in her community. As Cheryl Clarke puts it, for Black poets of the 1980s, Parker served as a key "fore-sister ... [who] made it possible for ... a sisterhood of lesbian poets ... [to interpret] the love that ... [had] finally begun to shout its name."[89] A generation later, Black feminist poet and critic Mecca Jamillah Sullivan notes just how much Parker's work kindled possibilities for future "black girls, queer kids, trans folks, womanists, lesbians, feminists and radicals in-becoming," many of whom did not learn of Parker's work until after her death.[90] Here family is expansive and communal, as one generation opens up possibilities for the next.

Parker's inclusive family departs drastically from a bionormativity that would later overtake mainstream notions of queer family, in line with the broader leftist queer and feminist cultures described earlier in this chapter. As historian Angela Hume documents, Parker co-raised children with her comrades at the Oakland Feminist Women's Health Clinic (OFWHC).[91] Offering the first community-led sperm bank and insemination clinic, OFWHC also made expansive queer family possible. Parker thus exemplified a queer reproductive justice practice for all.

Parker further theorizes expansive queer family in the lesbian mothers' anthology *Politics of the Heart*, in which she elaborates directly on her experience of family as extended, non-nuclear, and beyond biology. "The family structure we utilized is not new. Extended families have always existed in Black culture. We simply modified it slightly."[92] With characteristic humor, Parker places her queer Black family squarely within a genealogy of Black kinship structures. Anastasia and Cassidy, Parker's child from a previous relationship, enjoy relationships with each other and with adults in their extended family, forming part of a larger network of cousins, aunties, uncles, godparents, and grandparents. These values are passed down to Anastasia, who "has no idea what sexual preference is but ... knows that her godfather Joe loves Julie ... her godfather Charles loves Pablo ... [and] ... her mama Pat loves her mama Marty and they both love her."[93]

Parker's capacious vision of family accompanies her ideological critique of the heteropatriarchal nuclear family. "The left must give up its undying loyalty to the nuclear family.... The nuclear family is the most basic unit of capitalism and in order for us to move to revolution, it has to be destroyed. And I mean destroyed.... As long as women are bound by the nuclear family structure we cannot move toward revolution."[94] This passage comes at the end of Parker's fiery speech—delivered at BASTA! Women's Conference on Imperialism and Third World War and later published in *This Bridge Called My Back*—in which Parker issues a clear charge for revolution. After critiquing the complicity of elite feminists willing to sell out their working-class and poor comrades of color, Parker speaks to the necessity of a broad, multiracial feminist movement in support of larger anti-imperialist, Third World, antiracist feminist revolutions across the globe.

While Parker thinks on a grand scale to envision worldwide revolution, she centers the importance of the intimate sphere, and especially the family, in her discussion of institutions that need to be transformed. Here we hear echoes of Brant's call to intimacy as a political act that creates life amid the death-making conditions of imperialism and settler colonialism. For Parker too, the nuclear family is a structure that binds, holding women back from their revolutionary potentiality as political agents.

In "Legacy," Parker offers an alternative to the oppressive nuclear family, providing Anastasia with a larger context that she can use in the construction of family otherwise. She offers a vision of what it means to supplant the nuclear family, thus engendering what Ruha Benjamin has compellingly called a mode of "black kinfulness" that challenges the "assault on black kinship [that] is ever-present and pernicious."[95] By teaching Anastasia about all the ancestors, Parker does precisely this. This resistance to biogenetic notions of the family is paramount to the visionary and revolutionary queer reproductive justice praxis.

Parker's rejection of the exclusive family is distilled in the last stanza of the poem as Parker instructs Anastasia to live her cherished life to the fullest in accordance with the lessons she has inherited. What this rich legacy offers Anastasia far exceeds any power that bigots may hold over her. Like Brant, Parker draws directly upon the strength of ancestors to teach her child about a collective strength that knows no bounds.

> These be the things that I pass
> to you my daughter
> if this is the result of perversion
> let the world stand screaming.
> You will mute their voices
> with your life.[96]

Parker ends "Legacy," the last poem in her book, with the image of her daughter's brilliant life, a force that far eclipses the muted voices of all who oppose her. Here the passing down of wisdom cannot be contained by bloodline or genes. Rather, by insisting upon life as the final word of an anthology filled with so much death, Parker implores Anastasia to claim what is rightfully hers. In a world unbefitting of her sacred life, Anastasia is given the charge to always live as brightly as possible.

BACKLASH AND THE QUEERED FAMILY

The docuseries *Nuclear Family*, with which I began this chapter, points to some of the traps—especially the reification of the family as private and exclusive—that have imperiled movements for queer family. However, an antidote to this draconian vision of the private nuclear family is found, precisely, in the work of Brant, Parker, and the movements surrounding them as archives of the bold efforts of queer mothers' movements of the late twentieth century. At great cost, they worked to create family otherwise and, in their writings, militated against privatized, enclosed formations.

Thus, while Brant's "Long Story" draws attention to the deeper colonial violences underwriting the nuclear heterosexual family, Parker's work underscores the ways that Black subjects have always been set in opposition to this specific and exclusionary family structure. It is important to revisit these visions in a time when dominant queer imaginaries of family have been overwhelmingly co-opted and enclosed by bionormative and atomized ideas about family.

Offering lived alternatives, these writings typify what Saidiya Hartman theorizes as the "wayward lives" and "beautiful experiments" that unfold in scenes of Black intimate life to forge modes of kinship that cannot be circumscribed by the dominant power of culture or the law.[97] Drawing their power from historical forms of living and making kin that have always fallen outside the nuclear family, Brant and Parker also exemplify what theorist Neferti Tadiar calls the forms of life that "fall away" from the grasp of dominance.[98] Read in the context of movement history, finally, their writings underscore the power of collectivity—with lovers, kin, and community across the generations—to demand expansive notions of family outside the strictures of biology or state recognition.

Unfortunately, as we now know, history followed other pathways. At the turn of the century, these capacious understandings of family overwhelmingly came to be boxed back in. Here the archive of Black and Third World feminists foretelling the backlash to come is vast.[99] Writing in 1988, a British collective of Third World and Black feminists concurred that a big shift was underway. While "once there [had been] ... a plethora of local Black women's groups ... in solidarity with ... the Irish and Palestinians, Eritreans and Namibians, Chileans and the people of El Salvador," they wrote, a vast geopolitical transformation had taken hold; feminists now "collude[ed] in the ... redirect[ion]" of their struggles.[100] The authors diagnosed the splintering of a radical politics of solidarity among different oppressed communities waging revolution and the dawning of a politics of collusion and competition.

This backlash played out everywhere: from the NGOization of social movements, to the recruitment and incorporation of select minoritized groups and individuals into the upper echelons of state and corporate power.[101] It also reverberated in the academy, with the co-optation of hard-won knowledges that had emerged from feminist, antiracist, and queer radicalisms.[102] By the early 1990s, queer Menominee poet Chrystos declared that feminism had been "gutted by academia ... our freedom to speak to each other co-opted ... by those who do not share .... [our] oppression."[103] This backlash was internalized within intimate networks of family and kin, as queer, antiracist, Indigenous, and women-of-color feminists keenly understood. Gloria Anzaldúa wrote of the consequences of these restructurings on an intimate level, theorizing them as indicative of a new phase of colonialism that she labeled "intimate terrorism."[104] While in "the 'dominant' phase of colonialism," she wrote, "European colonizers [had] exercise[d] direct control over the colonized," movements had internalized "the white colonizer's systems of values, attitudes, morality, and modes of production."[105]

It was a core interest of the US state, moreover, to break solidarity among Black people—as Audre Lorde argued in reflect-

ing on the US military invasion of Grenada in 1983. She understood that, for a state intent on waging a successful political
backlash, it would be necessary to erode intimate intracommu-
nal bonds of trust. Alarmed to watch the state test out "the concern long expressed by the Pentagon as to whether or not Black
soldiers could be gotten to fire upon other Black people," Lorde
cautioned readers to remain vigilant.[106] "How does a system bent
upon our ultimate destruction," she asked, "make the unaccept-
able gradually tolerable?"[107] With this question, Lorde worked to
denormalize the pitting of comrade against comrade.

Just like Parker and Lorde, June Jordan brought this back to
the level of sexuality and the family to write powerfully about
the attempted strangulation of creative life force in the neoliberal quest to commodify every essence of human being.[108] In her
poem "From Sea to Shining Sea," Jordan named the dawning of
a toxic "natural order" that required the suppression of erotic
connections to ensure subjects' complicity with domination.
Jordan saw the numbing of self to be a vital component of state
projects to enjoin US citizens to support military crusades at
home and abroad.[109] In "From Sea to Shining Sea," she counter-
poses this with the metaphor of a pomegranate split wide open,
juicy and succulent, and bursting with sensuality and vitality.
Issuing a collective enlivening of the senses, Jordan called for
the revitalization of a revolutionary movement driven "by
desire."[110]

Parker predicted this internalization of backlash, warning
her readers of the political dangers of a queer and feminist
embrace of the family as an exclusive, private, and hierarchical
institution. In the foreword to *Jonestown and Other Madness*, the
anthology in which "Legacy" appeared, Parker senses imminent
backlash, positioning her poems as a political intervention. The

"madness" in the namesake poem references the Jonestown Massacre, the catastrophic 1978 cult murder of over nine hundred primarily Black people at the Jonestown encampment. However, Parker is equally interested in other, more mundane spaces where madness is unfolding—in particular, the family. As she writes:

> This book came about because we have become too quiet. We go about our jobs and raise our families and turn our minds away from the madness that surrounds us.... It is frightening to me that we live with the madness, that we continue to move through our lives as if these ... were normal occurrences. We are a nation in great trouble. It is time for those with vision to speak madly before the madness consumes us.[111]

This is a call to readers to engage backlash's multiple fronts—from the intensification of police and vigilante violence to the revitalization of homophobic legislation across the country—and a warning about a dangerous complicity setting in. Parker thus deliberately places "Legacy" at the end of a collection that includes poems on more overt political struggles surrounding racism, sexual violence, US imperialism, lynching, and homophobia. And she names the domestication, privatization, and depoliticization of the family as a key political concern.

Parker's warnings were prescient. In the decades that followed, older generations would bear witness to a mainstreaming of queer movements and LGBTQ+ families in previously unimaginable ways. Scholars and movements critiqued the mainstreaming of once-radical movements, pointing out that "racial, gendered, and sexual dissidence would be folded into the machinations of multi-cultural pluralism, homonormativity, and imperial feminism," as neoliberalism moved to funnel revolutionary aspirations into pleas for inclusion, prioritizing issues such as marriage, hate crimes legislation, and military inclusion over a robust social justice platform centered on redistribution.[112]

Julie Enszer speaks to this loss tenderly in her obituary to Beth Brant in 2012. She begins with the observation that, prior to her passing, Brant felt lost in the world because, like so many of her contemporaries, she "had lost her context."[113] Enszer writes that "[Brant] died surrounded by her family—daughters, sons-in-law, grandchildren—but she lost contact with the writers, artists, and activists who were an important part of her world."[114] This becomes all the more poignant when we consider the premature loss of Parker, Lorde, and so many of the movement's Black, Native, and queer luminaries, prophets, and poets of color who built the movements that this chapter has engaged.[115]

This loss of collectivity was structural, and a key dimension of this transformation would be the privatization of the public sphere. Gay marriage, for instance, was critical to state efforts to shed responsibility for the collective care of queer subjects dying of AIDS, as Melinda Cooper argues in tracing the interventions of neoliberal economists into the AIDS crisis. Neoliberals hypothesized that, by promoting gay marriage, they could most effectively remove state responsibility for the care of its citizens. Gay marriage thus served two functions: to discipline nonrespectable queers unable to adhere to these new norms and to became a "substitute for social insurance and [thus] the most efficient means of minimizing the social costs of healthcare."[116]

This policing of sexuality, race, and class was linked to the privatization of welfare, which was another key arena for targeting dissident sexualities as a means of reducing social spending. As Laura Briggs demonstrates, politicians' mobilization of racist tropes about reproduction was critical to the successful gutting of the welfare system. Briggs traces the fallacious mythologies of the Black "welfare queen" and the Latinx "breeding machine," which she argues were weaponized to push through the divestment of state expenditures from the family.[117] Thus, as Dorothy Roberts famously argued, welfare reform became central to the neo-eugenic reinvigoration of a key means for "schemes to restrict Black fertility," shifting any sense of public responsibility for the care of children and families to a program geared to curtail Black families' capacity to reproduce.[118] The state thus transformed dominant understandings of welfare from a program to support the state's citizens to "a means of modifying poor people's behavior," especially pathologizing primarily Black mothers whose fertility, pundits spun, needed to be restricted.[119]

These pressures to privatize the family infused the domain of the LGBTQ+ family proper, as revolutionary movements were supplanted by nonprofit organizations and NGOs whose main agenda was to access mainstream institutions. This "formalization of lesbian and gay family activism," as cultural historian Liz Montegary puts it, moved largely away from "coalitional work in the name of redistributive justice and toward identity-based and increasingly professionalized calls for rights and recognition."[120] An extensive body of scholarship on homonormativity and homonationalism would trace this shift, decrying the ways that "same-sex marriage advocacy .... [had] introduced a new celebration of the traditional trappings of the institution of marriage, complete with blood diamonds, white gowns and destination weddings in colonized locales," as Dean Spade and Craig Willse colorfully put it.[121] However, returning to luminaries like Brant and Parker, as well as their broader movements, is critical to highlight the stakes and consequences of these historical transformations. Put simply, we must re-anchor a queer politics of reproductive justice within abolitionist, anti-imperialist, and anticolonial movements for justice and life.

CONCLUSION: TWO HANDS OF HOPE
AND SACRIFICE

As in the opening scenes of *Nuclear Family*—in which the protest sign demanding other family forms vanishes into a sea of protesters—many of the commitments to a radical politics traced in this chapter were overtaken. As they were drawn into neoliberalism's seductive fold, the most privileged elements of LGBTQ+ communities helped to remap the boundary between those worthy of rights and liberties and those who were to be defined as expendable; the nuclear family often mapped the boundaries between legitimacy and aberration.[122] However, by animating the heterogeneous critiques of the nuclear family that developed in the Left, feminist, and queer political cultures of the 1960s–1980s, this chapter has probed beneath the surface, asking what histories had to be erased in order for the naturalization of the nuclear family to congeal. Turning to the new worlds opened up by radical movements and writers of the late twentieth century who risked all to change the family and the world, I have presented a history of family conceived otherwise.

The sacrifice to build a different future is expressed powerfully in Minnie Bruce Pratt's poem "Shame," published in *Crime against Nature*, which was written as she was losing her two sons. Pratt recounts this experience fifteen years later, when her children are no longer minors and she can therefore be with them again. Pratt reflects upon the untenable "choice" she was given: to retain custody of her sons by remaining in the closet, or to live an honest life.

Speaking to the simultaneous horrors and possibilities that came out of the struggle, Pratt uses the image of two hands:

> In one hand the memory of pain.
> I re-read these poems and begin
> again (again, it's been fifteen years)
> to cry at the fragmented naked faces,
> at the noise of the crying, somewhere
> inside us, and even now, like an old wind.
> In one hand, the memory of pain.
> In the other hand, change. When
> did it begin?[123]

Pratt grapples with the impossible crossroads she faced when confronted with a nightmare choice: either succumb to her ex-husband's threat to take away her children if she left him or live an out life without them. Electing to be true to herself, Pratt suffered, alongside her children, the brunt of retaliation. Yet she also taught them, through example, what it means to demand the space to resist conformity with violent structures. "Shame" articulates a contradiction of this history: while countless children and parents suffered, the result was a transformed world.

The powerful image of two hands leaves us with hope and possibility, in an alternative to the dominant pathways to queer parenthood that I will explore in chapters 3 and 4. Pratt understands her sacrifices to have ultimately resulted in victory, even as she voices the immeasurable cost. Of course, at the time, risking all, she did not know that she and her children would come through hell intact, "grown up, survived, no suicides."[124] It is only in retrospect that Pratt can look back and marvel at how she and her children made it through, emerging victorious and bittersweet.

Pratt's words humble the contemporary reader, reminding us of the costs dearly paid. This grows all the sharper in the face of

Pratt's unexpected death in July of 2023. After a sudden bout of illness, Pratt crossed over to the other side, joining Beth Brant and Pat Parker, as well as her long-term partner Leslie Feinberg, Michelle Cliff, Audre Lorde, Adrienne Rich, and many others in this chapter. Here I am chilled by Minnie Bruce Pratt's response when I asked her about details of Beth Brant's writing just prior to her diagnosis in 2022. "Mournfully, [Brant] is gone now," she wrote, "and [she is] not here to tell us."[125] In these correspondences, Pratt promised to tell me about details of her case that had not been publicly shared.[126] Her illness and death cut our conversation short.

With Pratt now among the ancestors, it behooves us to remember the histories that these luminaries bring to the surface as a frame of reference against which to gauge the present. This chapter has paid homage to the sacrifices of a generation who fought hard to imagine and live out the family otherwise, and upon whose shoulders rest current movements for queer family, however contradictory they may be. This history also serves as a political and ethical yardstick against which we can measure future trends and debates, engaged in the upcoming chapters, in the struggle for queer family.

CHAPTER TWO

Opposing Figures

*Good Families, Religious Liberties, and the
Queering of Reproductive Justice*

In 2017—approximately four decades after the lesbian custody cases discussed in the previous chapter—the ACLU filed a lawsuit in Michigan against Bethany Christian Services. Contracted to facilitate child services in their county, the agency denied Dana and Kristy Dumont, a married lesbian couple, their application to foster children in their area. This case coincided with several similar cases across the country. In *Marouf v. Becerra* in Texas, for instance, the litigants were barred from submitting an application through Catholic Charities to serve as foster parents because they did not "mirror the holy family."[1] As in the Dumont case, the only agencies contracted in Marouf's area to manage foster care were conservative religious organizations. Consequently, the doors were shut on these prospective parents who wished to foster or adopt children as a way of building their families.

This chapter traces dominant legal discourses surrounding contemporary LGBTQ+ family that foreclose the more visionary and radical enactments of family that the previous chapters engaged. I am interested in how contemporary LGBTQ+

family advocacy efforts continue in the vein of custody struggles of the 1960s–1980s to challenge the legislating of the heteropatriarchal family. Simultaneously, I examine how these efforts often reproduce hegemonic notions of family that depart quite drastically from critiques of the nuclear family that animated diverse sectors of the Left through the 1980s. In turning away from queer articulations of family explored in prior chapters to official legal discourse, this chapter proceeds on a different register to offer a critique of LGBTQ+ movements' uncritical uptake of dominant ideologies of family. I conclude with counternarratives that join with earlier histories of queer and feminist radicalism foregrounded in earlier chapters.

The Dumont and Marouf cases above raise several germane issues that frame the broader discussion of LGBTQ+ adoption in the twenty-first century in ways that depart from earlier debates. These issues are especially pertinent now as claims to "religious liberty" are tested out as a legal strategy by a conservative movement aiming to roll back legal protections for LGBTQ+ people. The strategy was brought to the public light with the now-infamous Masterpiece Cake Shop case, in which a baker refused to sell a wedding cake to a gay customer, and has most recently led to the 2023 Supreme Court's decision in favor of an Evangelical Christian wedding website designer in Colorado who refused to provide her services to LGBTQ+ couples.[2] However, while these cases involved private businesses, the "religious liberty" defense is taken to a new level by state-contracted organizations that claim the right to deny social services to communities whose beliefs don't align with theirs.[3] Funded by taxpayer dollars, organizations like Bethany Christian Services and Catholic Charities test the legal waters to see just how far the "religious liberty" argument can be stretched.

In the contemporary cases above, the question of religious liberty, opposed to claims to equal protection under the law, frames a plethora of cases, thus requiring close scrutiny and analysis. It serves as a pretext for everything from current attacks upon trans youth,[4] to the denial of care to LGBTQ+ elders in state-contracted nursing homes and care facilities.[5] Indeed, as Columbia Law School's "Law, Rights, and Religion Project" argues, state-contracted private Christian organizations are currently implicated in "a wide range of discriminatory acts against unmarried pregnant and parenting persons, including denial of employment, housing, public benefits, and access to social services."[6] This context also informs *Fulton v. City of Philadelphia*, a 2021 foster care case, in which the Supreme Court determined that Catholic Social Services could refuse to certify same-sex couples as foster parents.[7]

The denial of LGBTQ+ parents' right to foster must be situated amid a broader neoconservative strategy of reasserting the heteropatriarchal family under the guise of "religious liberty." At the same time, despite the importance of this context, this chapter argues for moving beyond the dichotomous framework of competing individual rights that current iterations of LGBTQ+ movements have come to embrace. In its place, it proposes a queer reproductive justice paradigm that is rooted in a fundamental commitment to abolition, decolonization, and anti-imperialist feminist politics and movements. Queer reproductive justice is committed to cherishing the lives of the most vulnerable as a litmus test for our interconnected collective survival across generations. This calls upon us to build robust networks of communal care rooted in a fundamental respect for the planet and all living beings, those who came before us, and those who have yet to come.

Queering reproductive justice must also be anchored in a politics of decolonization and abolition that refuses to silence the state's ongoing work to break native families and Black kinfulness. This chapter challenges LGBTQ+ rights movements to do just this. I call for a consideration of the ways that multiple vectors of power—including race, class, ethnicity, citizenship, coloniality, disability, and more—inform which families are split apart and which are venerated across genders and sexualities. This paradigm thus makes it important to ask which children become guardians of the state to begin with and what it means for the mainstream LGBTQ+ movement to seek claims to these children as a matter of justice.

My argument proceeds in two stages. First, I interrogate the discourse of the stable, respectable, and deserving couple that litigants present in their appeal to be considered as viable parents by state-contracted adoption agencies.[8] I draw from Dean Spade, who argues that rights-based frameworks do very little to improve the life chances and conditions of transgender and queer people for whom respectability is neither possible nor desirable, particularly of those for whom the structural conditions of racism, poverty, anti-Blackness, colonialism, ableism, and more are inseparable from the injustices, reproductive and otherwise, that they face. I examine the underside of two loaded tropes—the "good queer family" and "the best interest of the children"—and argue that both feed the further marginalization of all who cannot fit the mold.[9] Emblematizing a larger neoliberal politics of respectability, these figures shore up the very justifications mobilized by the state to forcibly remove so many children—particularly children of color, poor children, and the children of queers—from their families and communities. The "good queer family" and "the best interest of the children" thus reinforce the boundaries between legitimate and illegitimate families, and they inaugurate further tropes—ones that are racialized, queer-phobic, and transphobic—regarding child welfare.

Second, I question the ways in which this framing obscures the collusions between this homonormative respectability politics and a neoconservative agenda that works to rip apart families that do not reproduce the white supremacist normative settler nuclear family. As Melinda Cooper argues, the 1970s witnessed a historic convergence between neoliberals and new conservatives, both of whom invested in the idea of the private nuclear patriarchal family as a means for privatizing the safety net and relinquishing the state of any responsibility to provide care for its children, elders, and disabled people.[10] This accompanied the internalization of neoliberal values within once-grassroots queer and feminist movements. Informed by this history, the trope of the good, respectable queer family overlaps with the intensification of neoconservative family values: both uphold the sanctity of the private nuclear family, rooted in the notion that the responsibility for care resides, not with the state, but with that private family. Thus, while litigants and defendants in these lawsuits vehemently disagree about who belongs within this legitimate family, its basic parameters, its violences, and its racial and colonial exclusions remain in place.

This contradiction is dramatized in queer pleas to foster and adopt children via private Christian agencies that have been subcontracted by the state. Bethany Christian Services, especially, rose to notoriety when, working within Trump's "zero tolerance" policy, it was exposed for its role in the forced seizure of migrant children and babies from their caretakers who were seeking asylum. As I ultimately argue, these cases reveal the extent to which queer litigants—once deemed unfit to participate in social reproduction through parenting—become complicit in the further enclosure of the privatized family, contributing to a broader landscape in which many communities are forcefully separated from their kin.

In foregrounding queer complicities, I draw from several decades of debates surrounding homonormativity and neoliberal multiculturalism. This literature enables us to understand the structurally impossible position in which marginalized communities are placed: though backed into a corner to participate in a neoliberal capitalist system, we must also be held to account for the oppression that we thereby perpetuate, even if unwittingly so—and we must recognize and challenge it as well. These complicities come into stark relief when juxtaposed with the history of the lesbian mothers' custody movement, discussed in the previous chapter: what was once "a fierce fight [of queers] to keep their own children in the seventies and eighties" has somehow warped into the articulation of a "'right' … to take other people's children."[11] Focusing the fight on participating more fully within the current foster-adoption system eclipses other, more radical, possibilities for truly expansive families. And it contributes to the foreclosure of conversations about the reparationsowedtocommunitieswhosechildrenhavebeenstolen—conversations that are, I contend, indispensable to queer social justice movements.

Such tensions amplify the urgency of developing a framework that would adamantly oppose the state-sanctioned kidnapping of children in all its forms. Simultaneously, they also attest to the stakes of a framework that would refuse the recentering of normative narratives that affirm the legitimacy and supremacy of the nuclear biogenetic family created solely through heterosexual coital conception and parenting. I will thus propose a theorization of queer reproductive justice that demands an end to structurally enforced forms of family separation, at the same time that it resists the tendency to pose the normative biogenetic family as a neutral and nonviolent answer to many of the problems with the foster care and adoption system. A "queers against family separation" protest, at the end of this chapter, will offer a concrete example of such a stance. In the intervening sections, meanwhile, I will discuss two key court cases: *Dumont v. Gordon* (2019) and *Marouf v. Becerra* (2018).

FAMILY VALUES: ON RESPECTABILITY AND DESERVING SUBJECTS

> Adopting a child shouldn't be about whether you are heterosexual or gay but about whether or not you can provide a loving home that provides for safety and opportunity for Michigan's foster children.
>
> —Michigan attorney general Dana Nessel[12]

Central to ACLU's rhetorical strategy in the *Dumont v. Gordon* case in Michigan was the assertion that LGBTQ+ couples could offer "good" homes that would respond to the needs of vulnerable children within the foster care system. "With 13,000 children in foster care in Michigan," stated the ACLU's Leslie Cooper, "we can't afford to have good families cast aside.... So when agencies choose to accept tax dollars to provide public child welfare services, they must put the needs of the children first."[13] This aligned with Michigan attorney general Nessel's statement, which separated a person's sexual orientation from their capacity to offer "safety" or "opportunity" to children for whom neither was a given.[14]

Both the ACLU's and the attorney general's framings thus focused on two tropes—the good queer family and the care-worthy child. And both of these framings are couched within discourses of respectability, similitude, and value. As sociologist Deborah Gould explains, respectability politics is "concerned above all with social acceptance ... entail[ing] efforts of some members of a marginalized group both to disprove dominant stereotypes about the group and to regulate and 'improve' the behavior of its members in line with socially approved norms."[15] Gould's definition is informed by the context of the avowedly antirespectability, confrontational politics of queer AIDS activists of the 1980s. It offers us analytical parameters to distinguish between homonormative desires for acceptance into a liberal rights regime from what Cathy Cohen famously theorized as the "radical potential of queer politics" to "create a space in opposition to dominant norms."[16] And it helps us to unpack the framing that surrounds notions of the "good" queer to which those seeking rights must, in turn, adhere.

Much of the Dumonts' appeal to respectability is predicated upon the divisions and privatizations that earlier lesbian and queer radicals critiqued. In their efforts to socialize reproductive labor and cultivate a sense of collective care for the community's children as "our joint responsibility and our joint hope," to quote Audre Lorde, prior movements of lesbian parents challenged the state's narrow definitions of family that informed custody law.[17] In contrast, the Dumonts reproduce the state's version of the private nuclear unit as an elite club in which only those deemed worthy of social reproduction can participate. The Dumonts' discourse is predicated upon a rejection of the radical queer reproductive justice politics embodied by movements and writers in prior chapters. Instead the Dumonts and the ACLU appeal to respectability politics that might deem them worthy of motherhood, rather than critiquing the underlying assumptions of this family form and its consequences.

These tensions are embodied in a video produced by the ACLU to publicize the Dumonts' lawsuit, which illustrates the racial, class, and gendered dimensions of this respectability politics, presenting the white-passing Michigan couple to a public audience in the effort to garner support. Shot in soft light, this video shows Kristy in a purple cable net sweater and Dana in a spring-tone, plaid button-down shirt. The two women smile as they reminisce about their 2011 wedding in Vermont, before gay marriage was legalized in Michigan. Paragons of middle-class midwestern suburbia, they are seated on their overstuffed couch in their new home. Wedding photos flash on the screen and the camera pans back to show Dana warmly greeting her dogs as she enters a ranch-style home, with its freshly mowed lawn and SUV minivans parked outside.

This narrative is carefully crafted to defy prevailing stereotypes of queers as antagonistic to children's best interest. It presents them, instead, as worthy guardians for the most vulnerable. The ACLU's framing positions the Dumonts as model citizens whose excellent comportment renders them worthy of inclusion into the liberal familial institution. The video enumerates the many ways in which the Dumonts are on par with the acceptable (and presumably heteronormative) family, reifying a powerful discourse: that of family values.

Emphasis on the responsible private family, as Melinda Cooper argues, was central to the ascendency of post-1970s neoliberalism: such a family was to serve as the "primary source of economic security" for children, elders, and those with medical needs.[18] This neoliberal push overlapped with the coalescence of a conservative backlash that centered the private nuclear heteropatriarchal family as a moralizing societal force. As a result, odd bedfellows—neoconservatives and neoliberals—emerged with a shared investment in the resuscitation of the private nuclear family. This consensus worked to "transfer ... the legal burdens of public assistance onto parents, adult children and relatives."[19] It also reinforced a moral boundary between "good" and "bad" families: those who could versus those who could not pass muster as respectable citizens, and those who could versus those who could not shoulder the financial burdens of austerity politics by assuming the care of children abandoned by the state.

The ACLU video begins by identifying the Dumonts as fiscally responsible citizens in a move that implicitly pathologizes the poor, blaming individuals for a lack of resources rather than structural conditions. As Kristy states within the first twenty seconds: "We're both really established in our careers. We're really well established in our relationship. We are very happy and comfortable. We just moved into a new house and we feel that we can provide a nice, safe environment. [Parenting] is just sort of the next phase of our life, it's the next journey for us."[20] Kristy's repetition and vocal stress on the word *established* locates the couple properly within the linear familiar progression of a normative life course in ways that undermine queer time. This reassures the audience that the couple is what it ought to be: stable, friendly, happy. The Dumonts have met all the necessary prerequisites for forming a family unit that will contribute to society: they have graduated college, established careers, pursued marriage, and purchased a home. Photos of the Dumonts' modest yet immaculate and solidly middle-class house underscore this narrative. They assert a proper subjectivity and union over and against the motley crew of queers who threaten propriety and social norms. This propriety, or so the argument goes, deems the Dumonts to be worthy of social reproduction— a right patently denied to many, but that their heterosexual counterparts of the right race and class never need to demonstrate. Bringing a child into their life is thus the next step on this path.

This discourse of respectability is consistent with the framing values that were reinforced in the landmark 2015 *Obergefell v. Hodges* decision that legalized gay marriage. This case argued that gay marriage would grant "recognition and legal structure to ... parents' relationship (thereby allowing children) to understand the integrity and closeness of their own family and its concord with other families in their community and in their daily lives."[21] *Obergefell* both reified and expanded the boundaries of who could (and who could not) be included within the privatized, enclosed, nuclear family. It thus promoted what political theorist Cyril Ghosh has articulated to be a "heavy-handed endorsement of a specific conception of the good intimate life—one that positions marriage, romantic love, monogamy, parenting, and the nuclear family as standards to which all Americans ought to aspire."[22] Underscoring normative claims, it put forth moralizing notions of proper subjects and lives, ones rooted within compulsory monogamy as the unquestionable expression of the good life. This good life is decidedly white and colonial in its disavowal of all other kinship forms and modes of organizing families. It directly contradicts the aims of earlier feminist and queer liberationist movements to dismantle the nuclear family system and transform it into an inclusive, communal, and egalitarian institution.

In addition to demonstrating respectability, the Dumonts' rhetorical strategy also hinges upon proving their moral value as gendered maternal subjects. As Daniel Rivers historicizes, contemporary tropes of children's "maternal preference" are rooted within Victorian notions of gender and femininity, centering the image of the "virtuous mother," who is implicitly "white, middle-class, [and] of European ancestry."[23] To assert their proximity to this idealized figure, then, Kristy and Dana mobilize their middle-class status, their light skin, and their capacity to exude maternal love as something that can override their sexual difference or slight gender variance. Kristy and Dana are successful in their careers, the story goes, but they will also be good mothers. They are nurturing, loving, and fun. Despite their sexual difference from heterosexual couples, they are not *too* different. They retain gendered maternal value that their sexual orientation, presented as mere sidenote, doesn't quite upend.

The couple's proximity to normative life comes through as the couple explains how they decided to adopt a child through the foster care system. As a state employee, Dana first felt called to foster after receiving an email with photos of children sent out by the Department of Health and Human Services (DHHS). She and Kristy chuckle and sweetly coo at the computer screen, presumably taken by some adorable child's image. "I think we have a lot to offer: love, affection, caring," Dana follows up, while Kristy chimes in to add: "Security, place of belonging ... there's a lot of love to give here."[24] This capacity for maternal love is expressed as the couple giggles together at a screen.

Legal strategies for inclusion, as Dean Spade elaborates in his critique of rights discourse, most often rely on "a strategy of similitude in arguing 'we are just like you; we do not deserve this different treatment because of this one characteristic.'"[25] The Dumonts fit the bill: they are productive, friendly, and well comported, cisgender—and thus potentially maternal—women. They are financially stable, married, and monogamous. The Dumonts' resemblance to heterosexual couples is further underscored in Kristy's framing of her social and professional experience as typical, devoid of discriminations that would mark her as Other. As she states:

> I am very lucky, I have very supportive friends and family, and I work in a very supportive environment, so I really have not faced any discrimination over being gay, so calling agencies and being told that it is our policy to not place kids with same-sex families was pretty hard to hear. I mean, they didn't even know us! They only made the decision solely based upon who we are married to. It made me angry.[26]

This statement asserts similitude. The Dumonts are the *same* as other good couples, "close and ... [in] concord with other families"—short of the additive detail of their sexual orientation.[27]

This framing positions their rejection as potential foster parents not as a function of the system but as an exception. Accordingly, the Dumonts' exclusion can be pinpointed as a discrete and finite moment, not the symptom of an inherently violent system that routinely rips poor, migrant, Black, and Indigenous children from their families and communities. It is an aberration falling upon worthy, undeserving victims. This, in turn, remains consistent with rights-based quests for inclusion, which, as Spade puts it, "often focus on deserving ... [individuals], often people whose other characteristics (race, ability, education, class) would have entitled them to a good chance ... were it not for the allegedly illegitimate exclusion that happened."[28] By depicting the Dumonts through this frame, the ACLU's narrative does not locate the injustice at a structural, systemic level but rather presents it as an isolated incident.

Even as this approach seems to work for the Dumonts, it fails to promise any measure of protection or support for multiply marginalized subjects. This is because "laws created from such strategies, not surprisingly, routinely fail to protect people with more complicated relationships to marginality."[29] Such laws are never likely, for example, to provide protection to Black mothers, who are defined under the law as the antithesis of innocent victims who deserve support. As Dorothy Roberts argues in her recent book, *Torn Apart*, approximately 85 percent of children who are removed from their families' custody and put into foster care are not taken from their homes because of physical or sexual abuse.[30] Rather, these children are removed according to a capacious definition of *neglect* that includes inadequate shelter, not enough food, or a lack of clean clothes—all resources that families lack because of poverty, and that are very rarely deliberately withheld.[31] Thus what social workers, courts, and judges interpret as "neglect" is most often a result of poverty and systematic racism in a context marked by "deep income inequality, predatory banking and real estate policies, residential segregation, and dearth of affordable housing," as parents are punished for poverty's negative effects.[32] This is particularly acute in the case of Black families because state institutions have always misrecognized and disrespected Black kinship forms.

Within this context, the system of child welfare effectively functions as an arm of the prison-industrial complex, drawing Black children and caretakers into a carceral web of surveillance, punishment, and control through Child Protective Services and other state agencies.[33] As Roberts makes clear, those targeted by the family regulation system cannot appeal to individual rights as worthy victims of the system; their pathologization frames ideologies of "good" versus "bad" parents upon which legal cases like the Dumonts' depend. While "good" white affluent parents are celebrated for "free-range parenting" as a way to encourage independence, Black mothers are accused of neglect for an inability to afford childcare.[34] While the state does not bat an eye when "good" white affluent parents drink alcohol in the company of children, this can be the grounds for the removal of a Black child from a loving home.[35] Black parents are often accused of child abuse for bringing an injured child to the hospital, while this is rarely the case with white affluent parents.[36]

By reifying a respectability politics through the trope of the good mother, the ACLU's discourse fails to address these fundamental questions of systemic racism and resource maldistribution. Instead, the ACLU's articulation of rights frames the Dumonts' access to these children as the fundamental justice issue. By implication, the daily violences interwoven with the terrors of settler colonialism, racial capitalism, xenophobic nationalism, or poverty need not be engaged. Nor do the grievances of those for whom heteropatriarchal violence cannot be so neatly pinpointed as an aberration deserve a response. All of this, in turn, siphons precious energy away from the cultivation of collective movements that would respond to the reproductive injustices embedded in daily life under a white supremacist, settler-colonial, and patriarchal state. It prioritizes the short-term goals of an elite few over more just kinship relations for all. This, in turn, obfuscates the kinds of structural transformation that a true platform of queer reproductive justice requires.

VALUE'S UNDERSIDE: SOME HISTORIES AND CONTEXTS

ACLU's discourse upholds a bootstrap narrative that effectively, if inadvertently, blames the vast majority of "undeserving" individuals for their collective conditions. This narrative relies on problematic notions of value that often exclude even the most normative and privileged of LGBTQ+ subjects, while they actively disenfranchise those who cannot even aspire to conform.[37] This forecloses other, more radical imaginaries of family. Furthermore, the assertion of this kind of subject requires a historical amnesia surrounding the alternative queer families that have long animated queer intimacies and political movements. And yet, despite the ethical compromise of conforming to this worldview, rights are still no guarantee, even for the most privileged of queers.

Fatma Marouf, a queer litigant in another case sponsored by Lambda Legal, obscures the limitations of rights-based frameworks as she responds to her and her wife's denial as potential foster parents: "We're both highly educated, stable and we have a lot of love to give."[38] Doubling down on respectability narratives, Marouf ends up reinforcing the hierarchies of value that, predicated precisely on the devaluation of those unlikely to ever be included, underlie inclusion strategies. This brings home a key point made by Lisa Marie Cacho: that value relies upon its opposite. That is, under neoliberal democracy, there is always a denigrated opposite to the rights-worthy and deserving subject: the socially dead subject, rendered surplus, who remains permanently locked out of capitalist, colonial, ableist, and anti-Black measures of value.[39] By appealing to the script of a "good parent," the queer case for adoption reifies the devaluation of the mass majority; this script is also predicated upon privatization, policing, and militarization. This, in turn, further exacerbates deep rifts between mainstream LGBTQ+ subjects who aspire to fit the mold and communities that are further abandoned by a state that has long engaged in multiple forms of extraction, exploitation, and theft of their labor, resources, and land.

This appeal to existing hierarchies of value, moreover, ignores the very recent histories in which queers were defined precisely in opposition to children's best interest in the era of the lesbian moms' custody movement and beyond. "From the earliest days of homophile, lesbian, and gay organizing," as Liz Montegary writes, "activists, regardless of where they stood on the issue of homosexual parenting, have been forced to engage—whether to refute, to accept, to embrace, or to reimagine—queerness's antithetical relationship to reproductive futurity."[40] Throughout the twentieth century, queers were constructed as pedophiles, child molesters, and just plain bad for children, culminating in Anita Bryant's infamous 1977 "Save Our Children" crusade that spurred attempts to keep queers away from children—be it in the classroom or in the pediatrician's office—as well as the effort to ban gay foster parents in the Democratic stronghold of Massachusetts in the 1980s.[41]

Only within the latter part of the twentieth century were the most privileged of queers constructed as a "safety valve." LGBTQ+ families, Laura Briggs argues, were allowed to adopt only to provide stopgap, crisis services for a state that disavowed responsibility for systemically impoverished and exploited families and children.[42] In a society that refused to attend to the material needs of children, middle-class and upwardly mobile LGBTQ+ desiring parents would became a resource for the state to care for children hailing from communities plagued by decades of aggressive policing, systematic impoverishment, and the harsh criminalization of poverty.[43] The pairing of so-called hard-to-place kids with queers as "second-rate" parents speaks to the brute hierarchy of human life.

With the conferring of fostering and adoption privileges, predominantly white queers with citizenship and wealth could thus ostensibly be converted from pedophiles to saviors. But they could do so if—and only if—they adhered to and upheld values of respectability and could shoulder the financial burden the state pushed onto them. Importantly, this acceptance of particular queers over others linked newfound mainstream notions about the "respectability of the upstanding, coupled, well-educated, and middle-class gay folk" with a widespread, and long-standing, consensus regarding "the immorality of the poor," to quote Briggs again.[44] This consensus on the immorality of the poor has had dramatic results for children and families, especially in the late twentieth century, when, as Dorothy Roberts bluntly puts it, "the central mission of the child welfare system transformed from providing services to intact white families to taking Black children from theirs."[45] The unraveling of the welfare state and the draconian expansion of incarceration have since led to the widescale separation of children from their families, communities, and kin of origin, resulting in a context in which an estimated one-third of children under state custody are African American.[46]

A queer politics of reproductive justice must raise questions about why the system that now relies upon predominantly white and middle-class LGBTQ+ parents to perform reproductive labor does so at the expense of those who are defined as being outside the newly drawn parameters of respectability. It must also be cognizant that queer communities will never entirely be secure and that even among the most privileged, the provisional inclusion within the category of respectability is highly conditional. "Historical depictions of gay men, lesbians, bisexuals, and transgender people as unfit parents," contextualizes historian Daniel Rivers, "intersect with those that pathologize parents of color, poor families, and single women," often defining racial and sexual minorities as "unhealthy to children and to the very stability of society itself."[47] However, in seeking guardianship of a new population of children—often from the homes of

queer, queered, and non-normative, non-nuclear families—
LGBTQ+ desiring parents with enough social, economic, political, and moral capital now repurpose notions of child welfare.
This transformation accompanied other large-scale shifts in
what Jasbir Puar famously dubbed a "homonationalist" order
that drew (particular) queers into the US security state in a time
of heightened war.[48] By recruiting respectable queers, the state
attempted to pink-wash widescale crusades of terror that targeted Muslim, Black, immigrant, and Indigenous populations
and sought to rebrand militarism, imperialism, and war. Cru-
cially, this transformation enabled the state to more effectively
kill those queer, queered, and feminized populations who
remained pathologized, criminalized, and rendered enemies of
the state. Moreover, these practices were accompanied by less
spectacular attacks on communities perpetrated by the state's
more benevolent agencies—such as the DHHS, which routinely
removed children from communities subject to the "low-
intensity" terrors of poverty, the war on drugs, and wholesale
abandonment.[49]

Thus, taken as a whole, LGBTQ+ mainstreaming worked in
tandem with the expansion of diffuse technologies of captivity
and punishment—migrant detention centers, prisons, and refugee camps—to criminalize, entrap, and kill those deemed surplus to the neoliberal economic order.[50] All the while, "Gay people with sufficient financial wherewithal ... [could be] seen as a
resource for the state to avoid supporting children" when this
abetted larger neoliberal goals of militarization, privatization,
criminalization, and US nationalism.[51] This placed the figure of
the "good queer" within a larger global biopolitics of race that
(provisionally) embraced particular LGBTQ+ families, so long
as they helped to facilitate the "transmission of biological and

economic assets—that is, children and wealth" through marriage.⁵² By a sleight of hand, (certain) LGBTQ+ people could (sometimes) adopt, but only when they were brought into the moral order of neoliberalism and its practices of war, prisons, militarization, homonationalism, capitalist expansion, and more.

This assimilation of the most privileged queers into the fold of parenthood coalesced with the austerity state, which, bluntly put, needed well-to-do and mainly white, monogamous, cisgendered, wealthy queers with capital and US citizenship to assume the cost of reproductive labor. Accordingly, as political theorist Tamara Metz argues, the legal rationale for gay marriage worked to "[sentimentalize] individuals and their families ..., plac[ing] all responsibility on them for caring for each other ... [and thus serving] the neoliberal order by simultaneously securing and obscuring the radical privatization and deeply flawed distribution of the costs and benefits of care."⁵³ The wealthiest of queer parents profited further from the rewards of neoliberal privatization, which included, but were not limited to, marriage rights. All of this happened amid "shrinking state entitlements for those who ... [could not] work" and entrenched "the role of the family as the site of the privatization of dependency."⁵⁴ Meanwhile, countless families and individuals fell deeper into poverty and criminalization in a cycle that jeopardized their ability to retain and care for children.

Couched within progress narratives, the transformation of particular queers—from dangers to saviors—thus indexed the mainstreaming of liberal LGBTQ+ rights. This played into the further privatization of the family and the shrinking of the state apparatus, especially through the reification of marriage as the exclusive site for the allocation of care and the nuclear family as a site for the transfer of personal wealth. These violent shifts affected those for whom a nuclear family was neither desired nor possible, and further devalued those gendered and racialized subjects illegible within its metrics.

It was youth—and particular youth, at that—who bore the collateral damage of these transformations. Throughout the 1980s, tens of thousands of Black children became wards of the state, as did an estimated one-third of Native American children who were removed from their kin. And, in a history contiguous with the state-led kidnapping that accompanied the Argentine junta throughout the US-backed Dirty War, thousands of kids of (alleged) communist dissidents from El Salvador and Guatemala were adopted out by private US agencies.[55]

Thus, just as the most privileged of queers gained adoption rights, they were folded into the neoliberal capitalist project of antisocialist privatization, militarism, anti-Blackness, and US empire building. It was under these specific conditions that LGBTQ+ people were "invited to provide a safety valve to states in their decades-long wars on impoverished people and communities of color and [granted] their ability to raise their own children," as Laura Briggs perceptively puts it.[56] This, in turn, drew more diverse subjects into the fold of capital, whiteness, and imperialism via the nuclear private family, all the while bolstering mechanisms for the further disenfranchisement and killing of the mass majority.

FOR THE CHILDREN: SAVIOR
DISCOURSES, ANTICOMMUNISM, AND THE
UNACCOMPANIED MINOR

In 2019, Queer Parents, a prominent Facebook group of LGBTQ+ parents, went ablaze with controversy when a member posted an article regarding Fatma Marouf's lawsuit against the US Department of Health and Human Services (DHHS) for denying her application to foster or adopt an unaccompanied minor. Commenters fired passionate arguments about the ethics of taking in unaccompanied minors; this debate was especially inflamed in a time when children were being actively detained at the border under Trump's contemporaneous zero-tolerance policy. Marouf rebuffed these critiques, arguing that what was at stake was not simply her rights but those of the children who were being denied possible homes. "It's not just us who are being denied," she and her partner, Bryn Esplin, elaborated in official materials publicizing the case. "It's the child, or that particular sibling set who is being denied."[57]

Marouf named Christian anti-LGBTQ+ policy as harmful to children. Centered on child welfare discourses, however, this position ironically aligned Marouf—a queer Muslim of color, progressive law scholar, and refugee rights attorney—with the same right-wing, Christian foster care agencies that denied LGBTQ+ families the possibility to foster, such as Bethany Christian Services and St. Vincent Catholic Charities (SVCC). One core premise united these parties: that fostering and adoption were the ways to support, or even save, migrant children. This was an ironic convergence. Bethany had a prominent role in many neoconservative antifeminist, Islamophobic, and antiqueer causes, including rejecting prospective LGBTQ+ foster parents.[58] Bethany enjoyed a special relationship with high-up operatives of the Trump administration, specifically with Betsy DeVos, who donated millions of dollars to the agency personally and through various family foundations.[59]

How are we to understand the convergences of these two, otherwise politically diametrically opposed, parties? As Erica

Meiners has argued, the claim to be serving children's best interests has quite often united unpredictable allies. Meiners traces the discursive mobilization of child welfare, arguing that

> for the sake of the child, women—particularly poor, dis/abled, and/or nonwhite women—have been sterilized, involuntarily drug-tested, and continue to be denied access to reproductive rights (Garland-Thomson 2006; Silliman and Bhattacharjee 2002; Roberts 1997). The child's welfare continues to be used to advance a range of political, economic, and sociocultural ends: to develop and implement alternative judicial systems (Feld 1999); to expand policing and surveillance and to restrict First Amendment and privacy rights (Bernstein 2010); and to legalize and challenge gay marriage (McCreery 2008). The specter of the international trafficked child is used domestically to punish and regulate consensual sex work and non-heterosexual practices. (Bernstein 2010; Vance 2011)[60]

The rallying cry of "saving children" has historically bolstered wildly different political aims, effectively stirring up charged moral panics that are difficult to oppose. This has been especially germane in debates surrounding sex and sexuality, which always come to bear an "immense symbolic weight,"[61] serving as "vehicles for displacing social anxieties" in times of national instability in particular—to cite Gayle Rubin.[62] It thus comes as no surprise that—even given the position of certain LGBTQ+ families as safety valves for the austerity state—adoption by LGBTQ+ parents emerged as a target for political debate, bringing together moral panics surrounding sexual orientation and children's welfare.

Accordingly, all parties involved in the LGBTQ+ adoption lawsuits claim to be fundamentally motivated by the same benevolent interest: child welfare. On their end, queer desiring parents argue that homophobia limits the number of possible homes for children within the system. "There [are] 13,000 kids in Michigan that need homes, and we have some," proclaims Kristy Dumont.[63] "When there are so many kids out there who need a loving home and there is such a shortage of foster families in Texas in general," Marouf adds, "to be turned away just because of our sexual orientations seemed very short-sighted."[64] Litigants in both cases frame their true motive as being less about adults' wishes; they are doing it for the children, first and foremost. "[This issue] affects the children because there are so many other couples like us out there who want to provide a home for these kids and are being told no," explains Dumont. "Someone really needs to stand up and be an advocate!" Marouf exclaims, echoing that sentiment. Notably, they both deploy the powerful rhetoric of children's welfare in an attempt to garner mass support, with little attention to the ways that the legal claim to protect children's "best interests" has so often been an instrument of homophobia. Nor do they raise questions about racist state policies and imperial histories that lead to the separation of these children from their family in the first place.

On the "other" side of this legal debate, defenders of the Christian Right pose themselves as the sole legitimate guardians—and saviors of—youth in crisis. As their argument goes, these lawsuits harm children because they drain resources, which could instead serve children, from agencies that do not want to cater to LGBTQ+ parents. "ACLU would put children's needs last," states the law firm representing Gordon in *Dumont v. Gordon*. "Forbid[ding] the state from partnering with faith-based adoption agencies," they continue, will result in "fewer homes for children, especially minority children and those with special needs."[65]

The claim of saving children thus becomes the basis upon which opposing parties stake the righteousness of their claims.

However, just beneath these discourses of child welfare, other agendas surface. Take, for example, the position of SVCC, one of the two private Christian agencies targeted in the Michigan case. Consistent with other legal cases around the country, the Dumont case involves private Evangelical and Catholic agencies subcontracted by a vastly whittled-down state to administer services that are designated to be public.[66] These agencies purport to operate from a charitable agenda to "help save lives and show the love and mercy of Jesus Christ," as SVCC claims.[67] Savior narratives frame a "desire to comfort the afflicted and serve them with compassion, integrity and faith," and this mission encompasses not only children but also their birth parents.[68] "We feel like our first ministry in foster care is to the child, no matter what," explains SVCC foster mom Susan Hayes, "but I also feel that God has called us to a second ministry, which is to these birth parents."[69] Hayes frames adoption as a service to God, children, and even the communities from whom children are stolen.

Hayes's statement perpetuates vast hierarchies between those giving and those receiving aid—real or perceived—or, more aptly put, between those taking in and those losing children. This actively ignores the church's implication in the very inequalities and harms that lead communities to have their children taken by the state in the first place. This all crystallizes in the narrative of twenty-year-old foster daughter of color Shamber Flore, who testified against the Dumonts and on behalf of SVCC in the ACLU lawsuit. Hailing from "a rough part of town," she explains, her early life was characterized by "continual poverty, danger that was often found at the tip of a gun, and women working jobs that would be a disgrace to voice openly."[70] According to this narrative, Flore was "saved" by foster parents who afforded her material comforts and care, including "delicious food, a cozy bed, a roof over my head and beautiful clothing," and bestowed upon her "the greatest gift of all: Jesus."[71] In Flore's discourse, poverty, trauma, and violence are all attributed to the wrongs of individual actors, in this case her parents. "At the age of 5, gunshots and sirens were my lullaby," wrote Flore in an op-ed defending SVCC against the ACLU, "and I was exposed to gangs, prostitution, drugs, and abuse before most kids learn their ABCs."[72] Individual pathologies criminalize Flore's parents, framing their behavior as driven by a lack of moral values. Savior narratives such as this obscure the systemic underpinnings of poverty, racial warfare, imperialism, and more, and silence questions surrounding the reparations that would be necessary for intergenerational communities to flourish.

Thanks in part to this framing—in which no questions are asked about processes of exploitation, appropriation, and extraction that create the conditions that gravely imperil certain communities' capacity to care for their children—SVCC posits itself as an apolitical charitable entity. Yet a closer look at its work reveals a geopolitical vision aligned with US imperial aims. SVCC uses explicitly anticommunist language to describe its refugee resettlement work, which lays the foundation for their charitable mission. Materials explaining SVCC's refugee resettlement assure the churchgoer that the organization indeed supports US national interests in fighting communism and terrorism, and in molding hardworking American citizens. In particular, the SVCC website frames early Vietnamese refugees as victims of communism—and communism alone—with no mention of the imperialist war or imperialism itself, both of which lead to devastation to this day. Laotian refugees are guaranteed to belong to "the Hmong ethnic minority, who worked for the United States military and CIA during the Vietnam War," and are thus humanized by having supported the US government in opposition to communism.[73] Poles, Russians, and Cubans fleeing communism are also worthy of church assistance, according to SVCC. The list extends in more recent years to include refugees from Afghanistan, Syria, and elsewhere who have fallen prey to Islamic terrorists and thus cannot be enemies of the US state.[74]

Facile narratives of good versus evil from the Cold War and the war on terror offer reassuring explanations of an external enemy that absolve the US of any responsibility, putting SVCC volunteers and donors in a position to serve refugees and country alike.[75] The destabilizing imperialist role of the United States—be it through the abetting of repressive governments, economic warfare, outright bombing, genocide, imperialism, or all of the above—is obscured. Meanwhile, SVCC literature assuages the fears of potential donors. A video on the website assures congregants that refugees "contribute to the economy as a whole ... by providing employers with hardworking individuals [and] ... invest[ing] in the community."[76] Here selected refugees are presented as unthreatening, pliable workers who will support the US national interest. "Refugees ... stimulate the economy," the website continues. "They open new businesses, tend to be very hard workers and take pride in their work."[77] This framing of the refugee as a compliant, dutiful worker reinforces dominant values and hierarchies of human worth: as grateful recipients of aid, they are never to challenge the US state. Nor will they question the generous do-gooders who work for their salvation.

Importantly, the promotion of the American way of life shuts down any discussion about the role of the church or the state in the creation of unlivable conditions for entire communities.

This reproduces a fundamental division between good and bad people: between those capable of generating value and those who are illegible within these rubrics and therefore disposable. And it resonates, ironically, with the case for gay adoption, as all parties converge in the belief that those too poor to present the optics of a stable life should not have children under their care.

The question of complicity, moreover, is also obscured. No party is held accountable for perpetuating global systems of inequality, plunder, and war that constantly throw children and families into crisis.[78] Since everything can be boiled down to individual actions and pathologies, families and children are not in crisis because of US imperial warfare, slavery and its afterlives, or colonial extraction. Instead, poverty is endemic and charity is the solution. All of this reifies notions of the private, responsible child-serving family, even as the church and LGBTQ+ parents battle to define the limits and parameters of who gets to inhabit this family.

ZERO TOLERANCE, FAMILY REGULATION, AND THE CASE OF BETHANY CHRISTIAN SERVICES

SVCC and other Christian adoption agencies thus promote a political agenda that supports US imperial aims but are cloaked in discourses of charity. Invoking child welfare, they highlight the fates of vulnerable youth in order to carry out their missionary agenda. This draws from the child-as-proxy logic that is especially effective in times of moral panic and national instability. Furthermore, it converges with the core assumptions of queer prospective adoptive parents, who also position themselves as benefactors to children (albeit generally under the aegis of a benevolence that is not explicitly driven by missionary zeal).

This for-the-children rhetoric uniting both parties obscures the deeper changes that would be necessary to deliver justice to children and their families. While seemingly opposed, these parties overlap in several key domains. Neither calls for immediate family reunification of wrongfully separated children and their kin. Neither challenges the US migration policies that shift the blame for collapsing political and ecological systems onto those who bear the brunt of imperialism and that punish those who have been made into refugees by US imperial policies and broader structures of racial capitalism and extraction.

Nor is either party critical of the war on drugs that has led to the mass dispossession of majority-Black communities from their children through the prison-industrial complex. Eliding the root causes that inform which families routinely lose their children, both parties play rhetorically and materially into the politics of mass incarceration, border imperialism, and ongoing colonization that sustains the child welfare system. Both the liberal and conservative positions retrench the nuclear private family as a privileged institution for the reproduction of the powers that be under racial capitalism. The opposing camps simply diverge over who belongs within the inner circle of this nuclear family unit in the context of a highly privatized racist economy and a moralizing family form that punishes the poor.

Despite these overlaps, however, it is the Christian Right that more actively embodies the explicitly imperialist, neoconservative, and white supremacist agenda at play. As the largest adoption agency in the country, Bethany, in particular, has been a strong arm of the antichoice movement, typifying the ways that Evangelical churches have increasingly mobilized biblical concepts of caring for "orphans and widows" as the highest form of service and as a means of demonstrating one's allegiance to God.[79] Leading up to the *Dobbs* decision, Bethany supported networks of antiabortion crisis pregnancy centers that lure vulnerable pregnant people under false pretenses and encourage them to relinquish their babies for adoption in lieu of abortion, targeting especially pregnant people without access to forms of support such as healthcare or community care networks.

Bethany thus deploys Christian values of service to children as the moral front for a deeper agenda that is decidedly political. Importantly, this is consistent with a larger Evangelical project that, as historian Kristin Kobes Du Mez argues, ties together a series of seemingly disconnected political issues by mobilizing "culture war" issues of gender, family, and reproduction to reestablish a "father's rule in the home[, which] is inextricably linked to heroic leadership on the national stage."[80] This agenda centers the evisceration of reproductive rights and an attack upon transgender youth, also embracing adamant opposition to gay marriage, divorce, contraception, and advanced reproductive technologies (ARTs).

Moreover, this Evangelical paradigm holds a key contradiction: it strongly supports adoption—and thus the removal of children from their original kin—when the children in question hail from BIPOC and low-income communities. Simultaneously, they stress the importance of DNA and biological family in cases of donor-assisted conception, pushing for the parental rights of gamete donors and the delegitimization of non-biologically related queer parents, as chapter 3 will elaborate. Thus DNA matters for Evangelicals when non-normative families assert kinship rights, whereas it is discounted entirely when it comes to the breaking apart of the families of anyone beyond white Christian heteronuclear families. Or, as Du Mez sums it up, "What evangelicals mean by 'family values' always comes down to white patriarchal power."[81]

This plays out insidiously in Bethany's work on international private adoption. Bethany participates in nefarious means of securing children abroad: adopting out children from communities devastated by poverty, the impacts of climate change, and political instability from Haiti to Ethiopia, who generally enter into white Christian US-based families. This was most notoriously brought to international attention after Haiti's 2010 earthquake, as children (many of whom were not actually orphans) were stolen en masse by US-based Christians, including the Far Right Supreme Court justice Amy Coney Barrett (who has also cited adoption as a justification for the *Dobbs* decision).[82]

Such investments also frame Bethany's long-standing work with unaccompanied minors at the US border, and the agency's role in permanently adopting out migrant children expands well beyond the Trump years. Bethany has helped to facilitate foster placements and permanent adoptions of migrant children not only during but also prior to the Trump administration.[83] The agency has admitted to facilitating foster placements and permanent adoptions of migrant youth since the 1980s, playing a hand in family separation long before it was an official policy.[84]

Bethany was well positioned to play a role in the administrative support of Trump's "zero tolerance" policy, which specified that all noncitizen adults attempting to enter the US outside of official ports of entry would be detained, criminally prosecuted, and separated from any children in their guardianship. Under this policy, upwards of five thousand children, hailing primarily from Central America and separated forcefully at the border from their caregivers, were stolen from their kin.[85] This includes the eighty-one children Bethany has admitted to have had in their custody—a number that is likely higher in reality.[86]

Importantly, the removal of Central American children from their families did not occur in a vacuum; they were contiguous with earlier histories of US involvement in the removal of children from communities as a strategy of attack on socialists and the poor throughout the Cold War.[87] With the rise of Trumpism, however, the political agenda behind state-sponsored kidnapping was laid bare: the US state kidnapped children with explicit political xenophobic goals in mind. Kidnapped children became pawns in the frenzy to feed into Trump's populist base and consolidate a larger power grab. Meanwhile, blame was displaced onto migrants themselves, who were depicted as irresponsible for seeking refuge with their children in tow. As Jeff Sessions chillingly put it, "We need to take away children."[88]

Bethany thus became part of a broader chain of institutions that helped to kidnap and torture migrant children and their caregivers. Amid widespread criticism and outrage, however, the agency still clung to the justification of being driven by children's welfare—a claim that grew all the more unbelievable amid leaked audio recordings of crying migrant toddlers begging for their parents, and videos of children clandestinely ushered to foster care agencies under the cover of night.[89] As the American Association of Pediatrics decried "zero tolerance" as a form of child abuse, Bethany claimed innocence, arguing that they were merely offering a service to vulnerable kids.[90] Bethany stated simply that the agency was "committed to providing unaccompanied children with the best care possible" and insisted that children could be appropriately cared for in their facilities.[91]

Testimonies of Bethany employees on the inside, however, told otherwise. One employee, Alma Acevedo, denounced the agency's complicity in the harming of migrant children by facilitating their prolonged separation from their families. Acevedo told *New York Times* reporters that she would cry in her car each day before entering the office. Tasked with soothing inconsolable youth who had just been ripped from their caregivers, she grew particularly distressed every time a new child would enter the office bereft. With each new trauma, the other babies, toddlers, and kids would relive traumatic memories of the moment they were taken from their loved ones. Ultimately, Acevedo quit her job, unwilling to so actively play a part in causing extreme harm, which she could no longer justify.[92]

As an Evangelical arm of the neoconservative Right, Bethany epitomizes the ways in which the discourse of child welfare has served as a smoke screen for many cruelties and contradictions—particularly in the Trump era, when US and white supremacist agendas were laid unabashedly bare. This prompts critical questions of LGBTQ+ prospective parents, like the Dumonts, who sued to adopt specifically through Bethany, as well as those wishing to take in unaccompanied minors, like Fatma Marouf and Bryn Esplin.

Moreover, it is helpful to take a step back to consider the complex work of a child welfare system that has been rightfully criticized for wrenching marginalized children from their kin. Indeed, as critics of the zero tolerance policy were apt to point out, this policy—despite the attention it garnered—was not an aberration. Rather, it formed part of a larger "racialized haunting [of] generation upon generation of children who have lost parents, and parents, children" that has been at the heart of the US state enterprise.[93] This includes the experiences of lesbian mothers who routinely lost custody of their children from the late 1960s through the 1980s—a history that chapter 1 connected to deeper racial and colonial histories of state-sanctioned kidnapping in which the US state has continually engaged. Zero tolerance must be situated amid myriad histories of natal alienation and separation that have long separated poor children, immigrant children, and children of color from their families as a critical function of the state regulation of race, sexuality, and family.[94]

This critique of the state-regulated foster care system aligns with a large body of work by Black and Native feminist reproductive justice scholars who argue that the US state's child welfare apparatus has continually stolen children from their communities in order to expand the US settler state and maintain whiteness as property.[95] Attempts to remove Native children from their communities bookends a longer process of the weaponization of the adoption system to target Native children and families, including the infamous "sixties scoop" that led to the mass removal of Indigenous children from their families and their placement in the foster system in Canada. As Joseph Pierce argues, "Native children were never meant to become Native adults," especially given "the ongoing intent [of the settler state] to remove, displace, steal, and, ultimately, exterminate Indigenous people."[96] In all of these examples, the forced removal of children emerges as a mainstay of colonization.

Contemporary critics also link DHHS to a larger history of slavery's regulation of Black reproduction. Roberts's watershed 2003 text *Shattered Bonds* powerfully located the child welfare system as an extension of the prison system.[97] Roberts's subsequent work offers a devastating critique of the entire apparatus of family policing that simultaneously exploits and scapegoats historically impoverished communities. As Roberts elaborates, the "foster industrial complex" feeds poor and BIPOC parents and children into a larger carceral web, criminalizing and surveilling Black mothers in particular from the moment of conception.[98] This ignores research that shows that children caught up in the system would be much better served through a fair distribution of wealth and the provision of basic services than through the breaking up of their families.[99] As Roberts concludes, the abolition of the family regulation system is necessary because it is so rooted in the destruction of Black families in particular, and Native, poor, and communities of color more broadly.

These connections—between US state interest, racial capitalist extraction, prisons, and state-sanctioned kidnapping—are also elaborated upon by abolitionist Erin Miles Cloud. As Cloud writes:

> Unlike the criminal legal system, the foster system is often excused from rigorous critique, in part because it is framed as helpful, supportive, and well-intentioned rather than punitive and retributive. Yet it is incumbent on society to interrogate all systems that disproportionately impact Black people, even those that supposedly protect us.... If we can agree that implicit bias and racism are at least part of why our society is more likely to shoot a Black person, call the police on Black people, or profile a Black body, why do we believe that there are more noble reasons for the disproportionate reporting of Black mothers and removal of Black children? The reality is that both the criminal legal and the foster systems are rooted in deeply violent historical narratives about Black bodies that do more to promote punishment than safety.[100]

Cloud demystifies the tropes of child saviorism that grease the wheels of DHHS. She joins Roberts in arguing for the abolition of the child welfare system among prison abolitionists. This aligns with the work of organizations such as the Movement for

Family Power, which calls for an abolition of systems of racialized family surveillance.[101]

As these scholars and activists argue, the child welfare system ought to be renamed the "family regulation system," premised as it is on the "regulat[ion] and punish[ment of] black and other marginalized people."[102] This lays bare the ways that child welfare works to "regulate and destroy the very families deemed expendable by the US state in the name of child protection," and it makes the important case for the abolition and reconstitution of child welfare as we know it.[103] For, as unconscionable as the separation of unaccompanied minors at the border has been, it cannot be disarticulated from a broader system determining the fates of the more than four hundred thousand children who are currently in the US foster care system. Nor can those invested in justice mobilize unnuanced notions of "children's best interest" without attention to deeper issues of what reproductive justice, collective care, and support for the proliferation of truly diverse kinship formations might look like.

THE CASE OF *MAROUF V. BECERRA*: NEOLIBERAL MULTICULTURALISM

The discussion above problematizes discourses of the child's best interest that have framed the arguments both for and against LGBTQ+ adoption. In these arguments, neither party takes it upon itself to transform a xenophobic immigration system or the deep racism at the heart of the settler colonial state and anti-Black prison binge. Nor does either party address the systemic conditions leading to the creation of refugee populations and family separation under relentless imperial violence and terror. Instead—armed with the virtuous language of

service, welfare, and even social justice—they further naturalize assumptions of which families should be the ones to receive
other people's children.

This context casts new light on *Marouf v. Becerra*, a case that
nuances our analysis of the collusions between homonormative
respectability politics and the neoconservative family-values
agenda. In this case, a married queer couple in Texas fought for
the legal right to foster unaccompanied minors. They argued
that this benevolent work would best help children traumatized
by a migration system that separated them from their kin.
Marouf's argument parallels the Dumonts' in key aspects, particularly as the litigants work to adhere to tenets of mainstream
gendered and economic value. What distinguishes the Marouf
case from that of the Dumonts, however, is the appeal to the
neoliberal value of multicultural diversity through which the
couple seeks to present themselves as the perfect candidates for
adopting unaccompanied minors. They imply that they can
resolve the deeply systemic and structural crisis befalling so
many isolated and houseless migrant youth as a result of horrific
migration policies, border imperialism, xenophobia, and racial
capitalism.

Marouf and Esplin first argue that they are capable of being a
"good family" who display economic and gendered value. As the
Lambda Legal video publicizing the case makes clear, it is not
too difficult for Marouf and Esplin to argue that they pose no
challenge to the austerity state, given their elegant facade. Their
standing as professors of law and bioethics at a major US university puts them squarely within a respectable, highly educated
stratum of society.[104] Shots of the two in their modern kitchen
preparing an organic pizza, chopping vegetables, and strolling
through tree-lined residential streets, hand in hand, visually

reinforce this. They are positioned as the sophisticated corollary to the Dumonts, their more humble midwestern counterparts.

Nor is it challenging for the couple to present as caring, maternal, and appropriately gendered subjects, despite Marouf's racial and religious positionality. Both she and Esplin are well dressed, conventionally attractive, thin, and able-bodied cisgender women in a monogamous marriage. Both repeatedly display a playful tenderness toward each other, lighting up when extolling each other's maternal virtues. Marouf speaks lovingly of her wife's exemplary ability to connect with children, who seem to be "drawn to her by some magnetic instinct."[105] Photos of Marouf's nephew playing the guitar with Esplin and of Marouf reading to a child accompany this narrative, alongside images of them both clad in white wedding dresses amid a sea of family and children. Esplin reciprocates the compliments; she smiles and recounts how fun Marouf is. Even Bryn's Mormon grandmother fell in love with Fatma, she declares. "Every baby or child that we have ever met loves Fatma!"[106]

With this value established, the video next turns to the added special feature of this couple: diversity. This is delicately balanced so as to position Marouf as an appropriate immigrant, one who poses no threat to the prevailing order. This comes through particularly as she argues that she will mobilize her own difference to serve society. As she explains, many facets of her identity uniquely qualify her to help diverse children in distress.

> As an attorney who works with refugee kids and unaccompanied minors, I know that a lot of these kids, and especially the unaccompanied minors coming from Central America, have gone through hell to get to the US. And, I have seen first-hand their need to find families here, how they have often been separated from their parents and entire families . . . [Our rejection] doesn't take into account

the diversity of refugees that are coming in, what their religions are, what their cultural backgrounds are and how we might actually be a pretty good fit for some of those kids.[107]

Marouf's witness to the plight of unaccompanied minors makes her an empathic character who is credible as a potential advocate and parent. Generic notions of difference undergird Marouf and Esplin's claims that they will serve the needs of children torn from their families—despite profound cultural, linguistic, religious, racial, class, and national differences between them and these children's families of origin.

While these claims are rooted in the presumption of a shared experience between Marouf and migrant children, the only thing they hold in common is their lack of proximity to whiteness. The claim of commonality thus re-entrenches the normative white Christian heteronuclear family as the norm against which all else is judged. Flattening heterogeneity under the banner of a streamlined "diversity," Marouf and Esplin hold fast in their belief that they have what it takes. "Refugee children have been through enough trauma to last a lifetime," Marouf said. "They need love, stability, and support, which Bryn and I have in abundance."[108]

An appeal to neoliberal multiculturalism positions the couple as appealing candidates to help resolve the enormous problem of the unaccompanied minor; they offer a palliative for the conditions that lead to mass migration. Yet however sympathetic Marouf and Esplin appear, they must appeal to a neoliberal multiculturalism, which, as Jodi Melamed has argued, functions through its capacity to proliferate oppression through prevailing notions of racial, sexual, and cultural difference. Importantly, neoliberal multiculturalism promotes generic and dematerialized notions of cultural difference that remain amenable to the workings of racial capitalism, US empire, and white supremacy. Meanwhile, this system stigmatizes those who cannot appear to be "multicultural, reasonable, law-abiding, and good global citizens," and whose disposability is justified through their lack of access to capital that defines the neoliberal multicultural elite.[109]

Under neoliberal multiculturalism, difference—in its most elite form—becomes a niche market and selling point that renders US empire more flexible. This, in turn, shores up white supremacy, making it more durable, more immune to critique and thus to systemic transformation. This all works in tandem with a homonormative politics that promotes "a privatized, corporatized 'gay rights' agenda" at the direct expense of "any revolutionary and redistributive yearnings that would challenge the foundations of the U.S. state, capital, and racial relations."[110] By promising a brand of diversity that won't disturb mainstream definitions of gendered maternal value, Marouf and Esplin conform to these ideals, all the while offering the allure of privatized care as a fix for the structural crisis at the border. In so doing, they shield the state from further critique, if only unwittingly so.

By promising privatized solutions to the crisis of unaccompanied minors, this case individualizes structural crises, eclipsing the role that the US imperial security state plays in creating unlivable conditions for migrant youth and their families in their countries of origin. Furthermore, Marouf and Esplin put forward another dominant narrative—that of family values—as they proffer their affluent but also religious family as the proper site of care. In particular, Marouf and Esplin draw from the multifaith nature of their marriage to promote themselves as particularly qualified to instill values in their future children.

As Marouf continues in the Lambda Legal video: "People probably don't think of Mormons and Muslims as very similar, but I think that they are both very family focused. We are very lucky that our families were able to adapt to our both being gay. I don't think that our families really anticipated that."[111] With no irony, the couple appeals to a religiosity couched within a conservative family values argument. By stressing the "family-focused" nature of each partner's religious community, Marouf seeks to align marginalized faiths—first Mormonism, and, more strikingly, Islam—with mainstream Christian sects, and namely with the tendencies of Catholicism and Evangelicalism that are denying her case. Wedding photos of the two, clad in white amid beaming grandmothers, underscore the key point that Marouf and Esplin are united by an abiding monogamous love that moralizes them as the kind of lesbians who are still family centered and religion abiding.

Marouf's narrative, finally, also adheres to a central tenet of neoliberal multiculturalism: a stress upon the individual. This bears out the legal case through which Marouf and Lambda Legal asserted that as taxpayers and thus as part of a broader collective, the couple had their rights violated. They argued this because they were forced to fund Catholic Charities of Fort Worth's discriminatory, and therefore unconstitutional, policies.[112] However, the court dismissed this and determined that "Plaintiffs Marouf and Esplin [did] have standing not as taxpayers" but rather as aggrieved individuals, which was all that was legible to the law.[113] Thus, instead of understanding the couple as part of a collective, the court found "that Plaintiffs Marouf and Esplin ... [had] sufficiently pleaded individual standing" because they were able to demonstrate "individual injury" and "redressability."[114]

The law can rarely grasp collective subjects and can therefore read violations of the individual rights of particular individuals only in very specific terms. The collective cost of allocating state care to private subcontracted agencies is excluded from the discussion, as is any conversation about the dire impact of adoption policies upon these children and their families of origin. Left out entirely is also any discussion of what it means for specific, privileged LGBTQ+ people to claim what Laura Briggs calls the so-called "'right' to take other people's children"—a "right" that Briggs contests—as a matter of justice for themselves, the children, and society at large.[115]

RECONCEIVING PARENTHOOD, QUEERING REPRODUCTIVE JUSTICE: QUEERS MELT ICE!

This chapter has critiqued the ways that privileged queer desiring parents get drawn into legal battles that reinforce a violent racist classist system of family regulation. This stands directly in stark contrast with previous queer struggles to forge family on our own terms. Despite this dominant trend within mainstream LGBTQ+ movements, however, the history I told represents just one possibility when it comes to thinking about queering parenthood and family in the twenty-first century.

In this section, I turn to counternarratives advanced by those positioned in communities in which children are routinely separated from their families—who push back upon the US state's power to define who and what constitutes family. I begin with one contemporary manifestation of this alternative praxis: the 2019 series of "Queers Melt ICE!" protests in San Francisco. This precedes a discussion of radical Black and queer feminist-of-color retheorizations of motherhood.

Organized in the early days of the zero tolerance policy, Queers Melt ICE! brought together three queer organizations with a broader coalition to voice collective opposition by occupying the ICE headquarters in San Francisco for an entire month. These groups were Queers Undermining Israeli Terrorism (QUIT), Gay Shame, and Lesbians and Gays Against Imperialism, groups that had their roots in the queer anti-imperialist and antiracist Left. This coalition came together in a time when many were experiencing shock and disorientation over images of children in cages. They can thus be read as an alternative queer response to the politics of zero tolerance and state-sanctioned kidnapping at the heart of US statecraft more broadly.

Queers Melt ICE! offered leadership to a broader Month of Momentum that convened activists addressing overlapping issues—ranging from Indigenous sovereignty, to tenants' rights, to the rights of adoptees of color, to challenges on the Muslim ban. All speakers stressed a politics of solidarity to build movements strong enough to radically transform state and economic structures that oppressed all parties involved. "Solidarity knows no borders and it's important to remember that queer people are everywhere," stated Kate Raphael, cofounder of QUIT and key organizer of the Month of Momentum.

Speakers also refused to treat the zero tolerance policy as an exceptional moment in US history. Japanese internment camp survivor Chizu Omori argued that this was not the first time the US had locked up and detained young children.[116] Zahra Billoo of the Council on American-Islamic Relations drew out the irony of "advocating for civil and human rights" on stolen Indigenous land.[117] Racism, Islamophobia, and settler colonialism were directly confronted as systems and structures in which no social justice movement should ever take part.

In a particularly poignant speech, Pennie Opal Plant of Idle No More addressed the crowd to speak of her grandmother's journey by foot across the artificial border dividing the US and Mexico with two small children in tow. Her voice rose as she concluded:

> The United States government has been detaining Brown children's people since they first got here. They were stealing Indigenous children from our families; they were putting them into boarding schools where they were abused the way that these children are now being abused. If you are a mom, a dad, a grandma, an aunt, an uncle who loves your child, who loves the neighbor's kids. If you are a healthy adult, then there is no way that you should not be disobeying these laws. We are done with it![118]

By invoking the boarding schools and their connection to the current migrant detention, Opal Plant made it clear that no one is safe when any child can be locked up. She appealed to anyone who loves a child to underscore our obligation to disobey these policies as a means to securing a future for all children. This articulates a queer politics of reproductive justice that is founded in a fundamental commitment to the wellness of all youth, and a refusal to comply with the subjugation of the least institutionally protected.

Read together, these moments of protest converged to articulate an unabashed praxis of radical care. This puts into practice what Karma Chávez has argued is a politics that "challenge[s] the national social imaginary that figures queers and migrants as threats to family values and the good citizen."[119] The very act of coming together emerged as an alternative practice of making kin and creating family, otherwise.

By adamantly rejecting these conditions of death, Queers Melt ICE! decried the torture and child abuse of family separation under zero tolerance in the context of a broader politics of refusal. This, as organizer and Mother Frankie Free Ramos put it, was absolutely necessary in a time when what felt "the most demoralizing" was a widespread sense that she and others "didn't know what to do" as children were being put into cages in plain sight.[120] This praxis of kin making works powerfully against the further entrenchments of racial violence and imperialist economic warfare put forward by the mainstream LGBTQ+ rights movement for adoption. It moves us away from compromised framings of individual rights, to a broader discussion of how our families and movements fight for the abundant harmonious futures that generations to come deserve. It also challenges the reification of family as a static structure that is ordained, sanctioned, and disciplined by the law and—as the next chapter shall explore—biogenetic ties. Instead, this protest, and the larger movement to which it contributes, opens up the terms of what it means to create family as a practice of radical love.

RADICAL MOTHERING AS A PRACTICE OF QUEERING FAMILY

The protest above enacts a praxis of radical motherhood that emerges out of Black feminist and queer-of-color mothering movements. Writing on organizing with Latinx migrant mothers, for example, scholar-organizer Verónica Vélez poignantly shares the lessons she has learned from mothers, many of whom are separated from their children through migration or who come from political struggles of mothers of the disappeared in Latin America. As Vélez argues, migrant activist mothers offer us a definition of motherhood that refuses the parameters put forth by the state to legitimize or delegitimize certain kinship formations. This definition, she argues, is capacious and rooted in a political commitment to share in the fight *"para los mismos sueños."*[121] Here motherhood is a relation that is forged through political praxis.

Activist migrant mothers offer us a reconceptualization of a motherhood that "honor[s] mothers and their relentless struggle for their children and families in a patriarchal society" while also "extend[ing] its reach to include others who, despite falling outside of motherhood's traditional definition ..., [stand] in solidarity with and [work alongside movements for justice]."[122] This radical idea of motherhood is beholden to neither gender nor biology—a point that will become increasingly important in the next chapter on the ascendency of biological categories of parenthood within LGBTQ+ discourses. Nor is it delimited by legal categories—a fact that is particularly significant given the mothers' immigration status, as well as their direct experience with movements of the disappeared in Central America prior to immigrating to the US. Rather, motherhood emerges as an action and a verb: as a practice in love and radical care in service of the community's collective survival. It is a practice, a commitment, *"a political identity* ... a movement committed to challenging ... institutions that marginalize families."[123] This motherhood is fundamentally de-privatized, nonexclusive, and severed from both biogenetic and legal, state-ordained definitions.

This theorization complements the argument of Black Lives Matter memoirist and journalist Ma'ia Williams for an alternative "practice of mothering [that is] ... fundamental to creating co-liberatory revolutionary movements and societies."[124] Writing from the front lines of different political struggles—Ferguson, the Democratic Republic of Congo, and Black midwives' movements—Williams identifies a collective motherhood praxis that centers "an interdependent ethic of care ... that will affirm and nourish life" in our movements and all that we do.[125] Motherhood is anything but participation in elitist, private, nuclear, state-sanctioned structures. It is, rather, the evisceration of these very structures. "The work of mothering, of affirming life," writes Williams, "is creating morally liberatory worlds and movements ... [and] communities strong enough to resist the powers of colonization, enslavement, of evil."[126] These radical visions of mothering demand a praxis of deep love and collective care—one that is grounded in respect for all life because it centers an ethic of interdependent freedom: not freedom *from* but freedom *with*.[127]

This aligns with the work of Alexis Pauline Gumbs, who, as I elaborated in the Introduction, theorizes the work of Black mothering in the face of neo-eugenic assaults of the Reagan era onward that materialized everywhere, from policies of population control to tropes of the welfare queen. Gumbs contends that, under these conditions of death, Black feminists reappropriated the terms of motherhood as a creative queer insistence on collective life. This required a de-privatization of motherhood whereby the community was responsible for the futures of all children.[128]

CONCLUSION: MOTHERHOOD BEYOND FAMILY AS QUEERING REPRODUCTIVE JUSTICE

The above redefinitions of motherhood displace the core assumptions on which the case for LGBTQ+ adoption rests. Vélez's reconceptualization of motherhood moves us away from something that can be granted or taken away: it is a commitment to resisting state violence in all of its forms. Williams highlights mothering as a practice and as a form of collective action that interconnects all justice movements. Both writers challenge state institutions that pathologize and punish families through exclusive notions of citizenship, selfhood, kinship, and humanity.[129]

These forms of motherhood are the antithesis of state violence, responding to conditions of death with a demand for collective intergenerational life. "Is it any wonder," asks Ruha Benjamin, "that black people, whose meta-kinship threatens the biological myth of white supremacy, have had innovative bonds that can withstand the many forms of bondage that attempt to suffocate black life? Cultivating kinfulness is cultivating life."[130] Thus the most brilliant articulations of survival emerge from communities that have always been marked by reproductive insecurity, violence, genocide, and intergenerational assault.

These examples offer important antidotes to the mainstream narrative of LGBTQ+ adoption, anchoring us back into imaginaries and practices of radical care and queering family. This enacts a queer reproductive justice praxis that stresses radical interdependency and mutual liberation with a deep reverence for generations past and those to come. It also joins with other radical practices of queering family that have, historically and in the present, put into practice an ethic of solidarity and love that future chapters shall take up.

Put simply, queer reproductive justice cannot be rooted in regimes of destruction, exploitation, or plunder. Instead, the act of making family more broadly emerges as a praxis that transgresses the bounded family unit to stand by and with all youth. Here caring for kin challenges systems of dominance by insisting upon the futures of those whose lives are never guaranteed as a matter of collective survival.

By offering these examples, I have highlighted the fight for communal self-determination in response to all forms of reproductive injustice, eugenics, reproductive surveillance, disciplining, kidnapping, and other cruel practices that a queer politics of reproductive justice must oppose. Unlike the mainstream LGBTQ+ adoption efforts that this chapter has critiqued, queer reproductive justice thus rejects both the deadly constraints of a neoconservative homophobic and a neoliberal homonormative politics. It refuses the strangleholds that both place upon our capacity to imagine and enact radical futures. This forms part of a larger commitment to building queer abolitionist, decolonial, and antiracist feminist futures that are rooted in collectivity and care.

CHAPTER THREE

Your Children Are Not Your Children

Queer Investments in the Biogenetic Turn

> Bionormative families are taken to have something
> that other families lack—a particular parent, or set of
> histories, or genetic web—and implicitly become the
> model for completion, even wholeness. And then, it's
> still easier for "lacking" to slide subtly into "less
> than."[1]
>
> —Alice MacLachlan

In 2019, the sensationalist headline "Lesbian Couple First to
Carry Baby in Both of Their Wombs" told the story of Donna
and Jasmin Frances-Smith, a British couple who underwent a
new medical procedure called "shared motherhood."[2] The procedure of reciprocal in vitro fertilization (IVF) had long allowed
one parent's egg to be gestated in the second parent's body. But
"shared motherhood" went a step further, by placing the fertilized egg back into the egg-originating partner's uterus for
eighteen hours before transferring the embryo into her partner's
body.[3] The technology of "shared motherhood" thus promised

to enable both parents to "carry the same child."[4] As the mission statement of the biotechnology firm that patented the procedure claimed, it would "bring fertility treatment as close as possible to the circumstances of natural conception."[5]

"Shared motherhood" is part of a constellation of biogenetic beliefs that depart from earlier practices of queer family making that previous chapters have explored. Chapter 2 politicized the struggle for queer foster care and adoption—raising questions that might lead one to conclude that the most ethical way to create a family is through the creation of biological offspring. This chapter investigates the tensions embedded in the turn to biological family, especially within queer communities. While chapter 2 thus problematized adoption, this chapter raises questions about biological family, which is itself a much less stable category than it might initially appear to be.

"Blood does not a family make," the Ballroom queen Hector Xtravaganza once famously said. "Family are those with whom you share your good, bad, and ugly, and still love one another in the end."[6] As Daniel Rivers traces in his 2013 history of lesbian and gay parenthood, queer people have long created families in ways that subvert bionormative understandings of parenthood and have challenged the idea of family as exclusively biogenetic with alternative notions of chosen and found family.[7] Queer family movements have also critiqued the collapsing of biology and family. This has been the case even, and often especially, with respect to biological procreation. For example, when in 1982 the Oakland Feminist Women's Health Center (OFWHC) established the first queer insemination services in a clinical setting, they did so under the slogan that "biology is not destiny. Social conditioning is."[8] OFWHC differentiated between sperm donors and fathers. They stressed that openness was important so that children could shape and define their own relationships with their donors. This stance aligned with their larger feminist reproductive justice values of self-determination, empowerment, and the queer ethos of defining family on one's own terms.[9]

Xtravaganza, Rivers, and OFWHC join LGBTQ movements that challenged ideas of fixed biological heredity that earlier chapters have chronicled. However, with the increasing geneticization of life in the late twentieth and early twenty-first centuries, queers have become more and more imbricated in a biological determinism that expresses itself everywhere: from the conflation of sperm, egg, and embryo donors with parents, to emerging technologies to fuse the reproductive materials of lesbians as the route toward an ostensibly more authentic motherhood, to the implantation of uteruses into those born without uteruses, to the popularization of donor "sibling" registries and kin networks, to practices such as "race matching" that attempt to biogenetically engineer "pure" bloodlines through gamete (sperm and egg) selection.[10]

Such biologically determinist practices are part of a larger turn toward "biogeneticism" in queer family making that this chapter takes up. As defined by legal scholar Michael Boucai, biogeneticism is the "uphold[ing of the] biological relation to be the truest and most unquestionable form of family."[11] By undertaking an expensive complex medical procedure, Donna Francis Smith aspires to a more biogenetic family, reasoning that "you get a lot of same-sex couples where one person is doing the whole thing, ... whereas with this we're both involved in a massive way ... [creating] a special bond with ... [our baby]."[12] By deploying "shared motherhood" as a way to mimic heterosexual coital reproduction, moreover, Smith is reinforcing the notion of nonbionormative family as one defined by inherent lack—and claiming equivalency as an answer to this lack.[13]

Interestingly, this recent revalorization of the biological has often conflated and moved between various signifiers of biological relatedness—what Jenny Gunnarsson Payne calls "kinship grammars"—that serve to establish a relationship between parent and child.[14] These include blood or DNA in varying combinations, which are also taken to be quantifiable, authentic, and fixed. "Shared motherhood" stands out because it values the process of gestation, however fleeting, as a signifier of authentic motherhood, even while it adds further uncertainty—and extra financial cost—to the already challenging process of conception.[15]

However, as this chapter chronicles, the current dominant kinship grammar is not gestation. Rather, I focus predominantly on what is the most popular of these markers—the gene.[16] I trace the ascent of an ideology that I elsewhere call "gamete personhood" that posits kinship as inherent to gametes. This ideology, which has been embraced by many LGBTQ communities, "increasingly attributes everything—from one's IQ and proclivity toward crime, to one's sexual desires—to the essence of the gamete itself."[17] This has largely been facilitated by the advent of commercial DNA testing, which, in the year 2000, changed the landscape of gamete donation, making anonymous donation essentially impossible. Simultaneously, "gamete personhood" has surfaced through organizations like the Donor Sibling Registry (DSR), which emerged as the first online database to allow donor-conceived children to locate their donors and other children conceived with the same donor, in "the conviction that it is healthiest for donor-conceived children to connect with those who share genetic material through a sperm donor."[18]

This chapter reads *Donor Family Matters*, the 2020 memoir of DSR founder Wendy Kramer, alongside other DSR texts to unearth the story that DSR's discourse produces about family. I examine the implicit racial, colonial, and gendered projects embedded in the renorming of family as biological to probe the implications. As I argue, DSR's discourse reveals the popularization of a "biomedicalization" of life through which the "emergent molecular gaze" comes to discipline ideologies of true family and parenthood.[19] Far from being neutral, a unitary model of biological heredity rest upon notions of queerness as pathology and lack, also reproducing troubled racial and colonial histories and epistemologies with which we must contend.

The first section of this chapter examines the tensions between notions of human difference that are grounded in biology and those anchored in antiracist queer feminist genealogies. I unsettle the one-to-one correlation between biology and parenthood that underlies the biogenetic turn in queer parenting. Next, I analyze Kramer's *Donor Family Matters* and *Finding Our Families*, another text coauthored by Kramer, with particular attention to the racial and colonial implications of the stories they tell about family. I end with a critical discussion about the nuclear biogenetic family as a cultural form, raising questions about what the contemporary queer embrace of these ideas means.

Ultimately, this chapter queries the privileging of definitions of family structured through DNA in particular, and biogenetics and patriarchal bloodline more broadly. What does it mean to attempt a (simulacrum of) a normative model of nuclear family through biotechnical intervention? How does this serve as a barometer of shifting queer sensibilities in an age of homonormativity? What is gained and what is lost?

BIOLOGICAL FACT, DNA, AND KINSHIP

A brief turn to queer feminist theoretical interventions into essentialist understandings of biology gives context to the current uptake and popularization of genetics in debates surrounding LGBTQ family. This section reads several canonical texts that unsettle the taken-for-granted truths surrounding biology, facts, and parenthood. I end with a discussion of the multiple grammars of kinship that challenge unitary models of heredity.

"Scientific Racism and the Emergence of the Homosexual Body"—a watershed 1994 text by Siobhan Somerville—refuted historical notions of race and sexuality as scientific categories of an intrinsic and immutable selfhood. Tracing late nineteenth- and early twentieth-century scientific constructions of "the sexual invert," "the mixed body," and "sexual perversion," Somerville argued that the homosexual body had emerged as a category of medicalized personhood in ways deeply entwined with scientific racism. What Foucault had famously called "the emergence of the homosexual body," she argued, coincided historically with efforts to repolice the color line in the wake of emancipation. Just as newly emancipated people needed to be tracked and identified so as to be kept separate, so did divisions between the homosexual and heterosexual need to be mapped as discrete categories in need of policing and segregation.

By implication, race and sexuality—reified within medical discourse and enshrined as "biological facts"—could not be disaggregated from one another. Turning to her contemporary context at the close of the piece, Somerville raises questions about the resurfacing of sexual orientation as a biologized category. Referring to then-nascent efforts, in the early 1990s, to locate homosexuality within chromosomes and the brain,

Somerville issues a warning to those who might see "political efficacy in these new scientific studies" that naturalize queer sexuality as biological and hence fixed.[20] Instead, she sees in them the danger of igniting "cultural anxieties and desires about racialized bodies."[21]

Somerville's text aligns with a radical political critique of the biogenetic nuclear family, highlighting the political consequences of racial and sexual essentialisms that emerge out of these troubled histories. "Scientific Racism and the Emergence of the Homosexual Body" offers an important context for our inquiries about the ever-powerful prominence of the bionormative within contemporary debates about all things queer, remaining very relevant to a queer reproductive justice politics. Sommerville's words proved prescient in the face of subsequent work that focused on the human genome in scientific explanations for homosexuality, and the embrace of this position by the mainstream LGBTQ movement.[22] Her thesis continues to be borne out in current debates surrounding donor conception and advanced reproductive technologies (ARTs), particularly when the racial classification of the intending parents differs from that of gamete donors or surrogates.[23] More broadly, Somerville undermines one side of the construction of bionormative family: biology. Emerging alongside a queer and feminist critique of the family, Somerville's work troubles the veracity of scientific truth as closed, fixed, and ahistorical.

Amade M'charek, another feminist scholar of science, problematizes the authority conferred upon biological facts without attention to the social processes and conditions that grant authority to these facts. "The factness of facts," M'charek brilliantly writes, "depends upon their ability to disconnect themselves from the practices that produce them."[24] Drawing from her experience in the lab studying mitochondrial DNA, M'charek refutes the dichotomy between fact and fiction that often animates nature/culture debates. As "nature-culture hybrids," M'charek theorizes, "facts are heterogeneously configured from diverse material (theoretical hypotheses, specific methods and technologies, available biological material, scientific networks, etc.)."[25] Facts are not pregiven objects to be discovered; rather, they are an effect of specific cultural, social, political, and scientific practices that are fluid, complex, and always in the making. This brings into stark relief the modes of bionormativity and gamete personhood that, as the rest of this chapter will examine, gained traction at the turn of the century.

M'charek's framing is especially helpful in light of the ways that DNA becomes collapsed with the category of parenthood—a notion that itself is complicated by ARTs that open up the many ways to conceive a child (even if one remains attached to biogenetic kinship). The proliferation of new technologies, as Daniela Cutas and Anna Smajdor argue in their work on paternity, has troubled assumed equivalencies between DNA and fatherhood. As medical ethicists, Cutas and Smajdor run through ten possible scenarios for two hypothetical parents, "Mary" and "Billy," to conceive a baby. These include the insemination of Mary with the sperm of Billy's identical twin and the possibility of Billy being a trans person who has retained their uterus to gestate a baby with one of Mary's eggs inseminated with donor sperm. In the former scenario, Billy's identical twin would transfer identical DNA to the child; in the latter, Billy would gestate and deliver the baby, while the child would not carry the same DNA as Billy.[26]

Here the ascription of authentic parenthood is informed by which "biological facts" carry more cultural weight, when, and for whom. The cultural contingency of scientific facts is borne out concretely as ever-evolving ARTs open up different ways to conceptualize what counts as "biological" heredity. Ultimately, Cutas and Smajdor contest the assumption that "shared biology" is a necessary prerequisite for parenthood. As they argue, the idea that "the special worth of a child to a parent lies in their biological connection" falls apart if one does not buy into the hierarchical and possessive notion of "children as belonging to the adults who have made them—literally made them."[27] Cutas and Smajdor destabilize simple one-to-one relationships between biology, kinship, and genetics, underscoring M'charek's point that biological facts—in this case the "facts" of parenthood—are multiple, constructed through social practices, and always informed by context. Challenging fatherhood as a universal category and fait accompli, Cutas and Smajdor show how power informs *which* biological facts end up being valued.

Tensions surrounding which "biological" facts count do not only apply to paternity, as discussed above. They emerge in discussions of surrogate and gestational motherhood. With the advent of IVF in the late 1970s, it became possible to split the "biological" process of gestation from "biological" materials of eggs, gametes, and DNA, raising new questions about "biological" motherhood. In particular, IVF highlights the ways that the conferring of biological motherhood is informed by power relations. Class, citizenship, gender, and racial asymmetries weigh heavily, particularly among intending parents who use the outsourced gestational labor of those who have few other economic options or who reside largely in the Global South and the former Soviet Union.[28] This has been highlighted in legal cases in which contracted surrogate laborers were denied custody after wishing to retain the babies they had gestated and birthed.

Among these are two highly watched cases, from 1986 and 1990, in which white and Black surrogate mothers, respectively, were unsuccessful in their attempts to gain custody of the children they had gestated, carried, and delivered.[29] In these cases, credence was given to the "owners" of "genetic materials" over those who had performed the reproductive labor of gestation, birth, and breast- or chest-feeding.[30] Shared blood flow through the placenta and the lifelong, multigenerational influence of epigenetics were valued less than DNA shared via eggs, sperm, or embryos. At the same time, it is worth noting—for those who have the financial means to procure donor eggs or embryos— that gestational parenthood is legally protected by contract. Moreover, the value placed upon gestational labor versus genetic materials differs from the context of reciprocal IVF in which one partner gestates the egg of another partner.

Parenthood as biological fact cannot be abstracted from larger power relations and cultural values, as well as the social processes that infuse the creation of scientific facts. Race, nationality, citizenship, gender, sexuality, and class inform when one mode of biological motherhood is granted more credence than another. Furthermore, social and legal factors inform a hierarchy of truths that privilege certain scientific facts over others.

Additionally, surrogacy arrangements never take place outside of a racialized context that has been deeply etched by slavery and its afterlives. As Alys Weinbaum argues, the separation of gestational mother and child through natal alienation is, precisely, a product of chattel slavery. For Weinbaum, surrogacy is a racializing process that effectively creates a hierarchy between the gestational laborer and the socially defined "mother" whenever these two roles are separated. This holds regardless of the racial identities of the individuals involved. As such, what Weinbaum calls "slavery's episteme" cannot be disentangled from current surrogate economies.[31]

Weinbaum's argument raises key questions of queer family-making processes that do not default to coital reproduction as the norm. This underscores this book's larger claim that a queer reproductive justice praxis must always draw attention to the larger racial, colonial, and economic context to ask whose bodies, gametes, and labor bring children into the world. Weinbaum's work prompts a key question: If surrogacy as a form of alienated reproductive labor is always overdetermined by racial slavery, how should we think about other technologies like egg, sperm, and embryo donation? What are the consequences of holding heterosexual coital reproduction as an ethical and political standard against which all other modes of conception are judged?

KINSHIP'S MULTIPLE GRAMMARS AND
THE PLURALIZING OF BIOLOGICAL
RELATEDNESS

In response to the questions above, Jenny Gunnarsson Payne offers an important formulation of the varying "grammars of kinship," which opens the discussion to multiple kinds of biological motherhood that can further nuance this discussion. Payne lays out three dominant grammars that have, historically, shifted over time: "the grammar of blood," "the grammar of genetics," and "the grammar of epigenetics."[32] Whereas blood had been conceptualized as the primary mode for the transmission of inheritance in Europe since ancient Rome, it was overtaken by genetics when the clinical gaze of the eighteenth century gave way to the "emergent molecular gaze of today."[33] Currently naturalized as the dominant grammar, "the grammar of genetics" hinges on the idea that heredity is locked into a static genetic code that can be discovered through DNA.[34]

Payne draws from research on epigenetics that posits that the environment surrounding the genes greatly informs how, if, and to what extent genes are read and expressed. This is because the genome is "an extremely dynamic entity, constantly changing its properties in generally adaptive response to its environment," and because, "far from being an eternal substance, ... it is much better seen as a process, a highly complex set of dynamic activities ... [and] relations [that are] are bi-directional."[35] Contextual factors such as stress, nutrition, or trauma affect which genes are transcribed into RNA, and this is passed down across multiple generations. As historian of science Nathaniel Comfort explains it:

> The more we study DNA, the more ... the ... notion of an isolated, protected germ line seems to melt away. The genome proves to be highly dynamic, with gene activity and even gene structure changing over the course of a life. Further, our genome isn't ours alone: studies of the "microbiome" show that the genes one inherits are supplemented by those of the dozens, perhaps hundreds, of different kinds of microbes that live in our bodies. To cap it all, "genetic" no longer necessarily means "innate." ... The more we learn, the more difficult it becomes to formulate a strict genetic definition of "me."[36]

As Comfort argues, genes do not operate in isolation. Nor do they hold a static deterministic relationship with the essential self they supposedly produce. Genetic expression is fluid, shifting, and part of a larger ecosystem, influenced by environmental factors both inside and outside the body.

Prevailing notions of genetic determinism attest to, returning to Comfort, the "ever-widening gap between science's understanding of genetics and the public's understanding of science."[37] Thus, as Natali Valdez puts it, epigenetic factors influencing the embryo are understood to stem from "*exposure* from inside the body, including cells, organs, as well as the microbiome and *exposure* from outside the body, including the natural built environments."[38] It is precisely this "gap in understanding" that fuels a cultural fascination and fetishization of DNA in popular culture and discourse of which queer reproductive justice movements must be mindful.[39]

Here it should be noted that the framework of epigenetics itself is not inherently a feminist intervention. Epigenetics can also be mobilized as a discourse in order to pathologize pregnant people (and generally poor pregnant people of color) for not cultivating the "proper" environment for their fetuses to develop, conflating responsibility with social conditions.[40] However, epigenetics usefully moves us beyond fantasies of the gene as all-determining in ways that complicate the bionormative understandings. This reframes genetic heredity as variable, helping to account for the influences that multiple kin and caregivers have upon a child for generations to come.

A "grammar of epigenetics" thus opens up the possibility of multiple forms of biological inheritance, lineage, and kinship. As Payne elaborates:

> A grammar of epigenetics helps us to understand the contingent character of biological kinship: the biological mother is no longer one but can be several. This means, for example, that we could understand the kinship relationship between a child, a gestational surrogate, a genetic parent, and the social parents in a way that opens up another model of understanding biological inheritance ... [in order to] rethink the notion of what it is that can be "passed down" between parents and children.[41]

The environment in which a fetus, a baby, and a child grows and is nurtured has a deep impact. By interpreting the environment to encompass a variety of settings beyond the uterus, Payne acknowledges how others shape a child's biology throughout the course of their life. This values relations of intimacy and care, refuting narrow and exclusionary bionormative ideas about parenthood as a self-evident, preordained fact.

Payne's analysis joins other queer efforts to "[decenter] genes and instead … [highlight] intercorporeal connections that are produced through 'interaction, intimacy, or companionship.'"[42] Resonating with geneticists who debunk popular understandings of DNA—ranging from an oversimplified understanding of the relationship between traits and genes, to a lack of understanding of what DNA tests actually measure—this conversation dislodges bionormativity's stronghold.[43] This allows for a much more contextual understanding of what family is and can be. It also honors multiple traditions of kin making, neither silencing the importance of "the biological" (or its prevailing definitions) within particular cultural and historical contexts nor disciplining those for whom it is not contextually appropriate.

The pluralizing of biological motherhood further problematizes notions of a singular scientific truth, pushing back against what Donna Haraway has called a genetic fetishism. "A gene is not a thing," writes Haraway, "much less a 'master molecule' or a self-contained code." Rather, "The term *gene* signifies a node of durable action where many actors, human and nonhuman, meet."[44] Haraway unearths the larger webs of relationships, actors, and contexts that all need to be obscured for the gene to be endowed with its magic-like qualities. This informs anthropologist Kaushik Sunder Rajan's concept of genomic fetishes, which, far from operating outside of a political-economic context, "have everything to do with both the scientific and the market frameworks within which they are generated," such that "life, in the techno-corporate world of biocapital, is always already a business plan."[45]

What is it, then, that grants the gene so much societal and symbolic power in the popular imagination? What is congealed there? To attend to some of these questions, I turn to Wendy Kramer's *Donor Family Matters* and to subsequent queer uptakes of her discourse.

DONOR FAMILY MATTERS AND THE "SOCIAL LIFE OF DNA"

Donor Family Matters is the self-published 2020 memoir of Wendy Kramer, who cofounded the Donor Sibling Registry (DSR) with her son, Ryan, in 2000. As the first public mother-son combination to take on the cause of donor-conceived (DC) children, the duo gained fame through early appearances on *Oprah* and *Good Morning America*, eventually advising MTV's *Generation Cryo*, a reality-style show in which a young woman seeks out her "donor siblings" ("diblings"). Kramer has also coauthored multiple studies on donor families with credentialed academics, founded a popular Facebook group for DC children and their parents, and cowritten the DSR guidebook, *Finding Our Families*, with legal scholar Naomi Cahn.[46]

Donor Family Matters equates sperm donors with fathers and treats DC children of shared donors as half siblings. This philosophy is visually represented in a color-coded diagram from the DSR website titled "Donor Conceived Person's Parents."[47] A blue circle labeled "child" is at the center of the diagram. Arrows point to four boxes. "Biological mother" and "biological father," also in blue, appear on either side of "child." "Non-biological mother" and "non-biological father" are printed in orange below. This diagram is clear in its definition of a "biological" parent: this person is a "50% DNA contributor." In contrast, a "non-biological" parent is a "raising/legal" parent and, in the case of a gestational mother, a "sometimes birth" mother. A color key further shuts down any room for multiplicity or heterogeneity. In blue, "biological mother and father" are "always parents," whereas "non-biological" parents, in orange, are only "sometimes parents."

Clear-cut and resolute, this taxonomy enforces normative gender categories within a two-parent monogamous family as the empirical picture of health. However, in its attempt to corral families back into proper form, it performs another interesting operation. Superimposing an imaginary of proper kinship upon a wide swath of situations, it marks non-normative families as aberrant—even as it simultaneously claims similitude. If donor-conceived families are defined by "lack," there is a corrective for this lack, at least partially so, in (re)establishing connection between the gamete donor and child.[48] This affirms what Sarah Franklin has dubbed the "curious" relationship between IVF and reproduction.[49] As Franklin theorizes, IVF reinforces the idea that kin is best created through the biological joining of egg and sperm, while simultaneously redefining what it means to create life through technological intervention. No longer can "natural" and "technological" be held separate as dichotomous categories. The biological purity that the chart works so hard to reassert is destabilized.

This "curious" relationship carries through in the awkward application of normative biogenetic categories to all donor families, as an entire "order of things" is read back onto a diverse set of contexts.[50] As boxes and lines rein in families, we witness an attempted erasure of a vicissitude of kinship arrangements across cultural contexts. Additionally, as Black feminist bioethicist legal scholar Kimberly Mutcherson points out, this model is not only ideologically laden but also factually incorrect; despite the fact that the biogenetic connection between parent and child is most valued, emergent technologies involving mitochondrial DNA make it possible for a child to have three genetic progenitors, even within the biogenetic paradigm.[51]

In the case of queer conception, moreover, the inherent differences between coital reproduction and conception through ARTs cannot be so easily smoothed over. This is Black feminist Emily Owens's argument, as she reflects on her decision to select a shared sperm donor so that she and her white partner may carry biogenetically related babies. Owens unpacks the complexities that trouble her "proximity to the heteronormative ideal of familial belonging," despite the legitimacy she may gain through both gay marriage and a biogenetic relatedness between her future kids.[52] "By tying our children together as biological half-siblings through the use of a shared donor," Owens reflects, "we were looking to produce a likeness that could cover over [an] illegitimacy," in an attempt to "resolve the nonbiological relation of . . . queer family."[53] And yet, by premising a legitimate familial relationship between siblings on a shared donor, the broader stigma of illegitimacy of nonbiogenetic kin is reinforced, undercutting the authenticity of all such familial relationships.

Wendy Kramer's *Donor Family Matters* offers a case study of the making of this taxonomy and helps understand what makes it stick, even in the face of its many contradictions. One resounding theme in the text is that of reconciliation and repair. A white heterosexual woman, Kramer entered a fertility clinic when she and her infertile then-husband, Dan, decided to have a child. Kramer witnessed Dan's discomfort over sperm donor selection, so she hastily left the decision up to a clinic employee.[54] After Dan's alcoholism took hold, Kramer left him furtively in the night, remembering her own violent, alcoholic father.[55] She gained full custody of Ryan and raised him as a single mom.

As an answer to this loss, *Donor Family Matters* chronicles the duo's search to locate "donor 1058." Kramer's narration of family comes to be riddled by multiple fractures, the first of which is the "devastating news" of Dan's infertility, to which Kramer feels the need to respond to with "urgency."[56] She openly states that donor conception was a last resort, once she realized that Dan's substance abuse would make them ineligible to adopt.[57] Compounding this, Dan never establishes a parental relationship with Ryan, relinquishes his parental duties while still married,[58] and gives up all legal rights after their divorce.[59] This triggers Kramer's familial memories, as she realizes that she does not want her child to suffer the way she did at the hands of an alcoholic father. This all leaves her feeling as if her "life [has] blown up … [and she can] only wait and hope for the pieces to settle down to earth."[60]

Kramer's experience of brokenness thus brings together several compounding factors. Dan's infertility, his inability to parent, and his substance abuse, combined with her own traumatic childhood memories, create a sense of disarray to which Kramer must respond. Having internalized the ideal of the heteronormative nuclear family, she asks herself, "[Is] no father better than a bad father?"[61] Looking for the source of her woes, Kramer conflates serious issues of patriarchal violence and substance abuse with her inability to create a bionormative family as the source of her problems.

Kramer's fantasy about the curative role of reestablishing genetic continuity feeds into powerful cultural scripts through which, as Alondra Nelson puts it, "DNA has become an agent in the politics of repair and reconciliation."[62] DNA, Nelson continues, "is sought after as a communal balm and social glue, as a burden of proof and a bridge across time."[63] Nelson is speaking about the turn to commercial genetic genealogy among African Americans seeking to address the transgenerational traumas of slavery. Despite the specificity of context, however, Nelson's research also pinpoints a larger dynamic through which technological innovation—in this case, the turn to DNA via consumer-based genetic testing—is seen as a quick fix for an array of societal and political problems.[64] In Kramer's narrative, this logic emerges in the quest to connect donor and child, which is held out as the answer to lack. "Perhaps because so much had been broken within my own family," writes Kramer, "it became crucial for me to try and repair the gaps within my son's unknown family so that it, and he, would be somewhat less broken or incomplete."[65] Here the "social life of DNA," as Nelson aptly describes it, is put to work: DNA is held up as "a portal to the past that yields insights for the present and future."[66] Reinforcing a genetic essentialism, DNA's reparative function is central to Kramer's quest to heal from the past and make her family whole.

This discourse of brokenness that emerges in *Donor Family Matters* also informs a shifting discourse among queer parents, who, as I have argued elsewhere, have come to embrace notions of biogenetics and gamete personhood.[67] This is reflected in the DSR website, which reports that a third of the parents who use it are LGBTQ.[68] A shoddily assembled series of first-person testimonies uploaded on the website drives this point home, as queer parents speak to the deficiency of their families and their desire to connect with donors to fill the holes. In order to rectify this brokenness, they follow suit, working to include sperm donors as "fathers" and reinforcing the inferior position of "non-biological" parents within the family.

One such testimony, titled "Non-Biological Perspective," underscores this position. The mother of a three-month-old recounts intense feelings of jealousy over her partner's pregnancy, including her own fears that, if she ever gets pregnant, "her" baby will receive less attention.[69] Insecurities over her inferiority as the "non-biological" mother haunt her.[70] Reinforcing capitalist competition and scarcity, as well as the idea that children belong to parents, this narrative further naturalizes the family as an exclusive, enclosed unit. Eventually, she warms up to the idea that the sperm donor ought to be included in the child's life, despite her own feelings of inferiority. As she resolves, her three-month-old's eventual (and presumedly inevitable) desire "to know her biological father can't take away my love for her, or her love for me."[71]

Such narratives of conversion and redemption reinforce the hierarchies inscribed within biogenetic understandings of self and family. The unquestioned language of the "biological father" belongs to the narrative of the broken family that Kramer's story universalizes: a "fatherless" family will never be enough. Reifying the idea that relatedness can be quantified by DNA, this discourse naturalizes the moralistic message that it is best for the child to connect with the sperm donor as "biological father." This performance of penance, in turn, serves as a kind of corrective to the original sin of using donor conception, responding, more fundamentally, to the constructed deficiency of failure (or lack of desire) to reproduce through coital hetero-sex.

This didactic language effectively disciplines the reader, repackaging Kramer's message for a queer audience. This is typified in the write-up of another lesbian mom, who advises others to select their sperm donors wisely, just as she did. After explaining her process of selecting a donor who would want to play a central role in her child's life *as a parent*, she instructs others to do the same. "Our babies are real people," she writes, "[and] we have to realize that some of the choices we made for them when they were small are choices that they will have to live with … [living] on for generations [and affecting] our children's children and their kids after that."[72]

The pathologization of the two-mom household is repeated in a *Boston Globe* article in which queer mother and Brooklyn-based journalist Stephanie Fairyington processes feelings regarding her child's relationship to three other children conceived through the same sperm donor whom she has never met.[73] Fairyington describes the bewilderment her four-year-old expressed when she was told, one day, that she had "half-siblings." While Fairyington admits how her own confusion played into unclear communication with her child, she resolves that this ambiguity is good: it allows for "a queer kinship of sorts" with these families and is, ultimately, a lesson for her daughter as she is confronted with a disjuncture between society's definitions of "siblings" and her lived reality.

In arguing that her family holds lessons for all families, Fairyington suggests that queer kinship upends other, normalized and naturalized, relationships. In the same breath, however, she confesses her fear that her family is riddled with deficit, rooted in the lack of a father for her daughter. A main reason that she wishes for her child to connect with "donor siblings," she states, is so that they may commiserate over "the unique challenges of growing up in two-mom households and, more importantly, exchange thoughts and feelings about their common paternal absence."[74] Fairyington's words resuscitate notions that a two-mom household is a liability and that fatherlessness is an inherent problem, also suggesting—oddly, given her geographical location—that her daughter may not have any other peers from non-normative families.

This narrative of lack and shame multiplies across social media, as queer social media influencers stress it, performing public penance for the ways they went about forming their families. Lawyer Gena Jaffe, who runs the LGBTQ parents' organization Connecting Rainbows, urges other queer parents to "connect [their children] with their other bio family."[75] Speaking to her huge social media following, Jaffe apologizes for her prior statements that her children had no father.[76] She performs public penance, having been convinced by activists who admonished her for failing to consider what they deemed to be her children's inherent need to recognize and know their fathers.[77] Likewise, "sterlingmoms," another lesbian Instagram influencer, "comes out" by admitting, regretfully, that her children are not "biologically related."[78] This is a fact, she writes mournfully, with which she will have to "make peace" through much "hard work."[79]

Remorse, regret, and shame are the dominant emotions in all of these posts, as queer and lesbian mothers apologize for failing to initially recognize that it was within their child's best interest to honor and connect with "biological" fathers, edging toward apologizing for their mode of conception itself. "We need to do the work for our kids," Jaffe writes, "because it's not about us."[80] Within this narrative, any assertion of family outside of bionormativity is simply a result of parental narcissism, vanity, and a need to protect parents' feelings. The gamete emerges as the prime source of a child's identity, self, and family. Without a connection to the originators of the gamete, a child is presumed to be incomplete, and the parent negligent.

With no irony, these queer mothers assume Kramer's tragedy of "fatherlessness" as their own, warning others that a failure to bring a patriarch into the family is a selfish act that will irrevocably and inevitably harm their children—and for generations to come. Rehashing worn tropes of the queer as a danger to children, both propose a way out to those who follow the rules, to form appropriate relationships with their donors and/or children conceived through the same donor. In these narratives, an insidious heteronormativity creeps back into the family, while the narrators never need to account for their queerphobic and transphobic implications. If gametes hold an undisputable truth about the self and the family, this discussion is taken outside the domain of politics. According to this story, nonbiogenetic and queer families are bad for children, not because queers are unfit parents, but on the grounds of *genetic deficiency*. In short, if you cannot provide sperm, you have failed from the outset. This, in turn, repackages homophobia, albeit under the presumably apolitical artifice of scientific empiricism and the presumed objectivity of the gene. Following these scripts, the stories of DSR's LGBTQ families above conform to the regeneticization of the sperm donor as "father." They perform a type of repentance, conversion, and reform, all under the banner that this, like so many other political agendas that prior chapters have traced, is best for the children.

QUEER FAILURE, QUEER LACK

In *Donor Family Matters*, Kramer longs for the restitution of her broken patriarchal family unit. Fearful of raising a fatherless child, she mourns this loss for both herself and Ryan.[81] She works to fulfill the fantasy of her lost husband, coparent, and arguably father. However, what does this mean for the queer parent for whom the psychic romance of heterosexuality does not hold? What happens if one does not want to repent? What if failure to achieve the "right" family is not something to run from but rather something to embrace?

Debates within queer theory have engaged centrally with notions of lack and failure to which queerness is always tethered.[82] Initially grounded in the nonreproductivity of the (white) gay male body, canonical figures such as Lee Edelman and Leo Bersani argued against a queer politics of futurity—or a politics in general—and rejected valorizing narratives through which one might lay claim on progress and the future.[83] This nihilism was challenged by feminists and queers of color such as José Esteban Muñoz, who famously pointed out that in Edelman's and Bersani's thought, the innocent child whose interests aligned with the state's pronatalism was decidedly white.[84] These thinkers did embrace the shame[85] and the "impossible desires"[86] stemming from what Heather Love calls queer desire's "long history of association with failure, impossibility, and loss."[87] But they also embraced the potentialities of a yet-to-arrive queer utopia that could never be contained within a desire for the normal.[88] In other words, this cohort rejected the death-of-politics thesis even as it also embraced failure. Or, as Jack Halberstam summed it up in *The Queer Art of Failure*, "To live is to fail, to bungle, to disappoint, and ultimately to die ... [and thus] rather than searching for ways around death and disappointment, the queer art of failure involves the acceptance of" such failures and all that they entail.[89]

This critical context problematizes the rebiologizing of queer family,[90] and it directly challenges the oft-made DSR assertion that "very few of us would have chosen to have a child this way."[91] By embracing lack, queer frameworks resist the call to correct the nongenetic family. However, the pull toward fixing is strong, particularly given the prominence of biomedicine and the clinic as a primary site for queer conception from the end of the twentieth century to the present. As Laura Mamo argued in her groundbreaking 2007 ethnography of lesbians wishing to conceive, biomedicine had effectively pathologized queer parenthood.[92] After the fertility industry overtook DIY, at-home donor inseminations in the 1990s because of a slew of factors—significantly HIV among queer men—seeking pregnancy became a medical condition requiring outside expertise and intervention.[93] Constructing the queer body as broken, this underscored Foucault's dictum that illness, pathology, and queerness would remain forever entwined.

Lack materializes in Kramer's narrative, where it applies to all families who are "queered" through their failure to expand kinship through coital reproduction (or through their lack of desire to do so). Queer conception as lack conflates a deviation from the "gold standard" of biogenetic family with an illness that must be rectified.[94] *Finding Our Families*, a text coauthored by Kramer and Naomi Cahn, also builds from the starting point of nonbiogenetic family as lack. Addressing infertile heterosexual couples, authors counsel parents to expect their children to experience disappointment akin to these parents' own displeasure at being forced to come to grips with their infertility or their inability to find a (heterosexual) coparent within a two-parent monogamous formation.[95] Universalizing one family form, the book defines all who stray from the norm as broken and forever in need of a cure.

In seeking a cure, Kramer recentralizes the donor as the second parent within a two-parent family, regardless of context, and thus perpetuates what sociologist Abby Lippman dubbed the "geneticization of life."[96] While this model is sometimes appropriate, a wide array of situations problematizes it. As anthropologist Kath Weston famously wrote in 1991, gays and lesbians created kinship structures that were rooted primarily in loyalty, commitment, and love and that—while drawing on the metaphorical language of blood—did not correlate kinship directly with biological ties.[97] This emerged from dreams of and praxes toward a world in which procreation, both literally and more expansively defined, could be delinked from the patriarchal family. As prior chapters have argued, while the dominant narrative of childbirth within a two-person couple has gained prominence since, especially in the wake of the "gayby boom" of the 1990s, this certainly has never been the only mode of kin making. It has never been the most prominent among Latinx queer families, as Juana María Rodríguez points out.[98] Nor, as Mignon Moore adds, is this model predominant among Black lesbians, who are much more likely to become mothers by entering relationships with women who have children or to come out after already having a child.[99] Bionormative family also excludes what Ruha Benjamin has called a "Black kinfulness" that values relatedness "not only *beyond* biological relatives" but beyond the bounds of the physically living as well.[100] All of this presumes a monogamous two-parent biogenetic unit as the superior—and only legitimate—family form.

This chapter's analysis so far only scratches the surface of the ways in which kinship is porous, contextual, and laden with power—a topic that has been taken up with much substance and care within critical kinship studies. In their introduction to *Relative Values: Reconfiguring Kinship Studies*, Sarah Franklin and Susan MacKinnon summarize kinship debates, arguing that "the same substance (blood, genes, eggs, sperm) that is mobilized to create kinship ties in one context, will in different institutional contexts—given different historical, political-economic and religious forces as well as different individual perspectives—be made to create other kinds of relations, or no relation at all."[101] As Franklin and MacKinnon conclude: "Kinship is not a preexisting thing but rather something 'congealed.'"[102] By characterizing kinship as "congealed," they point to all of the contextual forces—political, historical, epistemological, and scientific—that allow certain markers of kin to hold meaning while others vanish from view.

FAMILIES LOST, FAMILIES SEVERED, FAMILIES THAT MATTER

The notion that nonbiogenetic family must be corrected is not a universal truth; rather, it is a colonial ideology that carries with it powerful histories and cultural politics. Here I examine a potent assumption that anchors this claim: that any family departing from the biogenetic family is wounded. As I argue, the biogenetic family is itself a cultural form that is reinforced through the DSR.

One of the bibles of this movement, *Finding Our Families*, is coauthored by Kramer and subtitled the "First-of-Its-Kind-Book for Donor-Conceived People and Their Families." Framed as an objective how-to resource, *Finding Our Families* offers step-by-step advice for parents who have used donor gametes. The underlying message of the text is that one must be open with one's children about their origins—a position that emerges out of a history of advised secrecy that was (arguably) driven by a desire to protect the masculinity of fathers within heterosexual couples when coital reproduction did not result in conception.[103] A short postscript at the end of the book recounts the "sense of peace [and] of wholeness" that first came over Ryan after he met "his biological father and grandparents,"[104] and offers a parting wish that the reader, too, gain an "enlarged ... sense of family and the preciousness of life" that can come through such connections.[105] It instructs the (parent) readers to choose the best interest of their children or—following the name of another organization—to place "them [the children] before us [parents]" by privileging a familial connection between those who share gametes.[106]

On the surface, then, advising truthfulness with DC children about their genetic origins is one key purpose of *Finding Our Families*—a goal that I wholeheartedly support (and that has not generally been a contested issue within queer families).[107] Written as a pedagogical resource, the text relies largely on anecdotes to support its argument, weaving authoritative advice with highly compelling stories of DSR-affiliated children and parents. This reinforces what philosopher Kimberley Leighton calls the "authenticity paradigm," which presupposes a "bionormative understanding of identity as pregiven, natural, biological, or genetic," and as rooted in a true self that can be known (and therefore liberated and healed) only through biogenetic information.[108]

Rooted in the assumption that "severance" from one's DNA is a necessarily harmful condition regardless of context, DSR's discourse silences the substantive differences between and within circumstances of adoption, donor conception, and other means through which a child comes to be raised by nonbiogenetically related parents.[109] Leighton gives this slippage a name: geneticization. Importantly, Leighton differentiates between *genealogy* and *genetics*, distinguishing a static biogeneticism that argues ardently against anonymous gamete donation[110] and the "continuous and open-ended process of identity-making" that can be created in the search for "genealogies of the ways in which we become related to others."[111] Primarily a philosopher of adoption, Leighton values the desire to know that may (or may not) inform a child's identity formation. However, she is keen to scrutinize the erasure of the many different circumstances through which a child comes to lack that genetic information—namely, the differences between donor conception and adoption.

Leighton thus makes visible the operations through which the DSR asserts that dislocation from one's DNA is an intrinsic harm. In drawing unabashedly on the language of adoptees' movements, DSR discourse assumes "that adoptees and donor-conceived people (DCP) share many of the same issues and struggles" as those addressed by the "DCP Bill of Rights," a document uploaded on the DSR website.[112] This is inspired, in turn, by Articles 7 and 8 of the UN Convention on the Rights of the Child, which include "the right from birth to a name … the right to know and be cared for by his or her parents" and "the right … to preserve his or her identity … name and family relations," and from which contemporary DC movements to highly regulate and end anonymous—and in some cases all[113]—gamete donation draw.[114]

Importantly, the history of these articles has nothing to do with donor conception. Born out of the Cold War, they were initially drafted in response to a situation in which an estimated five hundred children were stolen and thirty thousand people were disappeared by the state amid the brutal Dirty War (1976–83) in Argentina and the Southern Cone more broadly.[115] The children separated from their families (genetic or otherwise) were primarily stolen from leftists who opposed imperialism. These separations were part and parcel of state-sponsored acts of torture against revolution in the region and against a broader spate of Third Worldist movements of the oppressed across the hemisphere. Several decades later, interpretations of these articles have shifted. What was initially written in response to the mass-scale kidnapping of children as a weapon of state terror took on entirely different meanings.[116]

In the 1980s, this language was put to different ends as adoptees drew from it to press for an end to closed adoptions, referring specifically to the "right to know" one's genetic origins vis-à-vis their birth certificates. Most recently, a small but vocal contingent of donor-conceived children have lobbied the UN to stretch this even further. Calling for "the right to preserve relations with biological, social, and gestational families, regardless of when or where they were conceived or born," they interpret these articles to call for pre-and postbirth screening, the outlawing of out-of-region donations, the outlawing of anonymous gamete donations, and criminal sanctions for anyone who defies the rules.[117]

These claims typify what Leighton calls "geneticization" because the only thing tying these disparate situations together is the idea of the gene, which—as I have argued—is not a stable entity. Geneticization silences the very different circumstances through which nonbiogenetic families come to be. This is dramatized in the publication *Severance*, a "magazine and community for people who've been separated from biological family."[118] The magazine's editor, B. K. Jackson, is a writer who, after taking a DNA test, discovered that her parents were not who Jackson thought they were (because of an affair). Jackson universalizes her experience to propose a theory of "severance" that posits a dislocation from one's DNA line to be an intrinsic violence.

As the magazine proclaims, "Severance from family may occur due to adoption, abandonment, or an NPE (non-parental event or not parent expected)—a term pertaining to misattributed parentage resulting from situations such as formal or informal adoption, kidnapping, undisclosed step-parent adoption, paternity fraud, donor-assisted conception, nonconsensual sex, and, most commonly, an extramarital affair."[119] Regardless of the circumstances, severance is essentialized as trauma such that the emotional realities of the very disparate groups named above can be yoked in one breath. Here the act of severing is universalized across a wide variety of contexts to equate wildly differing scenarios. While they are not all named, many very heterogeneous scenarios—from state-sanctioned kidnapping, to an abusive family regulation foster system with roots in the carceral state, to donor conception, to rape—would fall under their definition of "severance."

Severance thus draws from assumptions of brokenness similar to those that animate DSR discourse, overlapping with a constellation of DC organizations, as well as the DSR, that share the founding belief that separation from one's genetic lineage is necessarily traumatic.[120] However, as this chapter has argued, much is congealed within the idea of DNA as the intrinsic key to self and family. More to the point, the discourse put forth by *Severance* silences the dramatically different power relations and conditions that lead to the "severing." It erases, in particular, the racial, imperial, and colonial histories that give rise to the forced removal of children of color from families and communities en masse through the adoption/prison system or to the removal of Indigenous children from community through residential boarding schools, to the family regulation system examined in chapter 2. In a breathtaking sweep, those who suffered the mass kidnapping, murder, and disappearance of loved ones as a weapon of war are understood to be "the same as" the children of families queered by their process of family making that did not center coital heterosexual reproduction.

However, we must draw out the racialized implications of the drawing of such equivalencies. The history of adoption in the United States, as I have already argued, has been riddled with the theft of Indigenous children, Black children, children of color, and poor children from their families of origin.[121] It is also imperative to question the implications of likening pregnancy and childbirth that result from rape to all other family-making efforts that move beyond the biogenetic nuclear two-parent family.[122] In these instances, the legitimate grievances of children and their caretakers are appropriated in the service of a wholly different purpose: to argue that any family that falls outside the heteronormative script poses inherent harm to children.

Appropriation is thus a landmark operation of the discourse of "severance," as the latter draws on the labor of prior movements of oppressed groups is in order to decry donor conception and to reinforce the heteronormative family as the only kinship unit. However, in addition to drawing heavily from those movements, DSR discourse draws from yet another discourse—that of Black freedom struggles—to prop up its moral and ethical currency. Take, for example, a series of didactic epigraphs by African American writer Alex Haley that frame two key chapters of *Finding Our Families*. Opening the first chapter, an epigraph by Haley counsels the reader that "in every conceivable manner, the family is a link to our past, a bridge to our future."[123] Here Haley's original reference—the forced removal of peoples of African descent from their homelands and their enslavement—is conflated with donor conception. This analogy sets the terms for the intrinsic goodness of genetic relatedness (or badness of the lack thereof); within this formulation, there is little room for this dichotomy to be nuanced. This prompts the question: What does it mean to liken donor conception to slavery?

This analogizing grows even more heavy-handed in a chapter called "After the Telling," describing the turmoil that donor-conceived children may confront when they learn about their conception. Prefacing stories of children's pain, Haley's words instruct the reader that "[in] all of us, there is a hunger, narrow and deep, to know our heritage, to know who we are and where we have come from. Without this enriching knowledge, there is a hollow yearning. No matter what our attainments in life, there is a vacuum, an emptiness and a most disquieting loneliness."[124] This passage speaks forcefully about the need to know one's own cultural origins. But here too, Haley is speaking to a wholly different context. Derived from his highly influential book *Roots* (and the even more popular television series), Haley's words encourage descendants of enslaved Africans to reconnect with their ancestral genealogy in an attempt to memorialize the forced removal of enslaved Africans from their communities of origin via the transatlantic slave trade—a position that itself has been widely nuanced and stretched by Black scholars and movements.[125] In Kramer's appropriation, however, we see the familiar discourse of lack and emptiness applied to nonbionormative families—a lack already presumed by the book's title, *Finding Our Families*.

By drawing from Haley, *Finding Our Families* appeals to the fears of parents, issuing a grave warning that their donor-conceived kids might experience the same staggering "vacuum," "emptiness," and "disquieting loneliness" as the one described by Haley. Black studies scholars have rightfully critiqued the more general appropriation of the rhetorical, affective, and ethical appeals of Black freedom struggles, arguing that one of the lingering aftereffects of slavery is that Black lives are assumed to be always available for all.[126] In *Finding Our Families*, this tired strategy is employed once again.

This is not the only time that DSR discourse relies upon Black movements to do its rhetorical work. Published in 2020 alongside the burgeoning Movement for Black Lives, *Donor Family Matters* directly appropriates the rallying cry that "Black Lives Matter." But the language of "whose life matters" has been stolen far and wide—from the reactionary call that "All Lives Matter" to the equally noxious propolice slogan "Blue Lives Matter"—and Kramer is not the only person within her milieu to use it. "Them Before Us," headed by a neoconservative, born-again Christian (and disgruntled child of lesbians), Katy Faust, has made it its mission to decry donor conception—and to outlaw any kind of family beyond heterosexual married couples. Arguing against gay marriage, divorce, and transgender people, Faust's website features a series of articles with subtitles that borrow from that language: "Gender Matters,"[127] "Marriage Matters,"[128] and "Biology Matters."[129] A click on any of these headers leads the reader to one basic conclusion: families that fail to conform to the heteronuclear married family are inherently harmful to children.

While Kramer and Faust differ in their stated political positions, similarities abound. Both rely on the curated testimonials of DC children to make their case, drawing from the language of whose life matters while circulating decidedly anti-Black messages. Both draw authenticity from claiming to speak in children's unmediated voices in their quest to "put children first." This calls up an older discourse of protecting childhood "innocence" that has historically centered white children as the ones deserving protection, while it criminalized many other communities of children and adults alike (and particularly queer and transgender adults, constructed as pathological).[130] This move to advance fundamentalist ideas of family under the banner of children's interest serves as another example of the child-as-proxy logic that earlier chapters have critiqued.

Recently, further similarities have materialized, as Kramer has partnered with Jennifer Lahl and her neoconservative Center for Bioethics and Culture (CBC) to promote the DSR.[131] A big opponent of surrogacy, "super-straight Lahl," as she calls herself on Twitter, has also recently taken to attacking transgender people, as the title of her recent film, *Trans Mission: What's the Rush to Reassign Gender*, makes painfully clear. One need only look to the CBC's funders—which include the Witherspoon Institute, the Heritage Foundation, and multi-billion-dollar Terra Novae Institute—to understand the Center's explicitly transphobic, antifeminist, racist, and homophobic policy positions. All of this combines in a moment of heightened moral panic over children to further outlaw all forms of family that fall outside of white, heteronormative ideals, implicating Kramer and her DSR in the consequences of genetic essentialism when it is taken to its furthest logical conclusion.

These connections are not mere side points. They surface in Kramer's story, particularly when it comes to the subtle yet ever-present assumption that families and children require patriarchs (and white ones, at that). This alignment with white, heteropatriarchal ideals is even more direct when race, and specifically Blackness, surfaces in the texts. For example, the only time that race is explicitly invoked in *Donor Family Matters* is when Kramer has placed a classified ad in a newspaper searching for her donor. Kramer receives a collect call from a jail from a man who is "clearly African American," in her estimation.[132] Taken aback, Kramer assures herself that "[she] can handle" this when she hears what she is certain is the voice of a "black inmate."[133] Her anxiety is resolved quickly, however, when it becomes clear that it is a wrong number. She "breathe(s) a sigh of relief" over the "mix-up," never again reflecting on the incident.[134]

Donor Family Matters, like much of DSR's discourse that also includes the discourse of *Severance* and the CBC, thus functions by appropriating the labor of Black movements at the same time that it advances an overt anti-Black racism. What does it mean to champion the Eurocentric nuclear private bourgeois family while relying on the moral and ethical righteousness of movements for Black freedom? In what follows, I locate the biogenetic, two-parent, heterosexual nuclear family as itself a cultural form—and one that has been historically associated with settler colonial expansion, extractive nation building, heteropatriarchy, and the passing down of private property.

BIOGENETIC NUCLEAR FAMILY AS CULTURAL FORM

Building on long-standing feminist critiques of the heteropatriarchal family, Black, Indigenous, and queer-of-color scholars have carefully demonstrated that the private, two-parent, reproductive family is a culturally contingent kinship arrangement that is rooted in slavery, conquest, and the creation of whiteness as property. As Joey Mogul, Andrea Ritchie, and Kay Whitlock summarize it: "From the first point of contact with European colonizers—long before modern lesbian, gay, bisexual, transgender, or queer identities were formed and vilified—Indigenous peoples, enslaved Africans, and immigrants, particularly immigrants of color, were systematically policed and punished based on actual or protected 'deviant' sexualities and gender expressions, as an integral part of colonization, genocide, enslavement."[135] Importantly, these genders and sexualities were not free-floating. They were rooted within the institution of the family, which colonizers identified as the prime site of aberration to be managed, controlled, or eliminated.

Thus, as Kim TallBear elaborates, white settler nation building in the United States and Canada was contingent on the naturalization of a monogamous nuclear family form that brought together marriage, property rights, and citizenship. By ensuring the expansion of the white settler population, this family form privatized property rights for white settlers. At the same time, colonizers lorded a set of sexual standards "over Indigenous peoples as an aspirational model and used these standards to justify curtailing their biological reproduction and the stealing of their children."[136] While the reproductive private normative family was accessible only to white settlers, those who could not (or did not wish to) mimic it were policed and punished.

An interconnected dynamic held true for enslaved peoples, as Aliyyah Abdur-Rahman illuminates. The very idea of the monogamous heterosexual reproductive nuclear family was itself a lynchpin of slavery, working to mask the routine raping of enslaved peoples by the slave master.[137] While the slave master reproduced his "property" through systematic rape, this "perversion" of excessive or violent lasciviousness was projected upon enslaved peoples, who were hypersexualized. This, in turn, served as a pretext for further subjugation and domination. As such, the *story* of the nuclear biogenetic family allowed white supremacy to continue through the facade of the normative family that only white people could access while committing the ultimate transgression.

It thus becomes impossible to disentangle the "pure" white monogamous two-parent family—itself a fiction—from anti-Black sexual violence. The two are mutually constitutive, as "both whiteness and heteronormativity were conceived, constituted, and stabilized through their opposition to and haunting by the specter of the black sexual deviant."[138] Thus we see how "whiteness [was] ... the requisite racial category for heteronormative qualification."[139] The normative family was, by definition, the domain of an elite few, while those who could not access this normativity were simultaneously punished for it.[140]

Slavery and settler colonialism thus form the mold of private nuclear family that, in bionormative discussions, is naturalized and moralized as the norm. These imprints also linger in the metrics used to construct life as quantifiable through measurable blood and bodily substances, taking us back to histories of craniology, which infamously used measurements of the human skull as meaningful scientific evidence of character, virtue, and intelligence. In her lucid reflection on her family-making process, Emily Owens untangles notions of a measurable heredity that haunts her own selection of a shared donor to impregnate both her, a Black woman, and her white partner. Interrogating their desire to bear biogenetically related biracial "half-siblings," she reflects that

> the quantification involved in figuring out who belongs to one another as siblings has everything to do with the same kind of counting that produces race. The phrases "half-sibling" and "step-sibling" quantify just how related to one another two people are.

This quantifying language mimics nineteenth-century language of blood quantum that lingers in contemporary racial consciousness: the counting of ancestral lines that produced the "mulatto," "quadroon," and "octoroon." ... Categories that define sibling relation by asking how much of a relation two people share—"half-" or "step-siblings"—resonate with terms like "mulatto," "quadroon," and "octoroon" (as well as the now more colloquial and euphemistic "mixed-race" and "biracial").[141]

In drawing from the ostensibly race-neutral metrics of relatedness, Owens confronts a "mathematical calculation of racial genealogy" that cannot be disentangled from our systems of quantifying relation through the measurement of bodily substances.[142] Conversations about shared donors carry anxieties about legitimacy and belonging that reinforce hierarchies of race, value, and life, regardless of the racialization of the parties involved. This, in turn, fuels what Michelle Murphy has called the "economization of life" that "continue[s] the project of racializing life—that is, dividing life into categories of more and less worthy of living, reproducing, and being human," often under the banner of a race-neutral neoliberalism.[143]

Moreover, the model of the human genome undergirding DNA itself is premised on colonial and Eurocentric notions of population, so that "notions of ancestral populations, the ordering and calculating of genetic markers and their associations, and the representations of living groups of individuals as reference populations all require the assumption that there was a moment, a human body, a marker, a population back there in space and time that was a biogeographical pinpoint of originality," as TallBear puts it.[144] Reified as fact, this imagined population is a product of the Western colonial imagination, often leading to a recursive relationship between preconceived tax-onomies and genetic "findings" about human populations.[145] And yet, without the stabilization of this imagined originary moment, body, and population, the entire classificatory apparatus under-girding the mapping of individual relations through DNA falls apart.[146]

Rather than existing in a pure state of nature to be discov-ered, then, genetic and biological markers of identity are informed by social and political hierarchies and value systems. Rajan has proposed the term *epistemic fetishism*, which is useful in the further unpacking of DNA as a human-mediated formula-tion. "The irony—and power—of epistemic fetishism," he writes, "is that probability statements start operating with deter-minate legitimacy."[147] Rajan names the political economic forces that naturalize the gene as both property and scientific fact in the context of genomic labs and drug companies attempting to market pharmaceuticals to discrete ethnic groups. He locates the slippage between scientific hypothesis and truth that, in the popular imagination, comes to endow the gene with definitive meaning through the speech acts of experts and authorities. We see how the ideological forces of settler colonialism, taken out-side of the laboratory, also come to structure the ways that our prevailing genetic determinisms acquire so much power. Bio-genetic discourses that reproduce the model of the reproductive nuclear family as the norm are further stabilized by the rubrics and logics through which these families and selves are meas-ured, evaluated, and accorded value. All of this underlies the model of the biogenetic family rooted in gamete personhood, which flattens all of these histories and power relations in its assertion that DNA, and the gametes that carry it, dictate per-sonhood, parenthood, and family.

DATA COLONIALISM: THE MEASURING AND DISCIPLINING OF LIFE, SELF, AND KIN

The aforementioned histories of geneticism offer a context for thinking critically about our current juncture, in which biometric data serves as the prime arbiter of Truth. Here it is vital to linger on the material implications of this. As Simone Browne argues in *Dark Matters*, the disembodied gaze of surveillance technologies—of which blood quantum and the DNA test are examples—has long worked to enforce a kind of "digital epidermalization" that dictates the truth about Black bodies based upon bodily data "despite subjects' claims."[148] Browne traces various technologies, including "facial recognition, iris and retinal scans, hand geometry, fingerprint templates ... and, increasingly, DNA," all of which extract information as a way of identifying, classifying, and controlling Black communities.[149]

Brown's thesis is borne out with the increasing reliance of the state on DNA databases in order to manage Black and other racialized populations via migration policies and policing. For example, Trump's border policies included the mandatory drawing of DNA samples from migrant babies, children, and adults imprisoned in border camps.[150] This is elaborated upon by Ruha Benjamin, who writes about the ways that UK border surveillance also relies upon DNA to police migrants in particular. Benjamin documents the forced collection of saliva, hair, and nails from African asylum seekers, in particular, as part of UK policies to prevent supposed "nationality swapping," in which, according to DNA fingerprinting experts, immigrants claim false nationalities in order to have a better chance of asylum; these practices, Benjamin notes, are rooted in "huge and unwarranted assumptions about population structure in Africa."[151]

Here the "epistemic fetish" described in the previous section endows a false truth to harmful practices of racism and xenophobia through the state's speech act.

Such border policies accompany the increasing reliance on DNA databases by police in identifying crime suspects, leading Nelson to conclude that "the growing number of African American samples in genetic databases and disproportionate racialized surveillance makes DNA genealogy databases ... a risky proposition for African Americans."[152] This holds true because it takes the genetic profiles of a very small percentage of the population to deploy DNA surveillance across a group of people.[153] Claims to empirical neutrality are trafficked in, despite well-founded critiques of the conflation of race and geographic origin of ancestry used in racial phenotyping. We also know that a suspect's face cannot necessarily reveal their racial origin and cannot, therefore, be used as a point of reference for DNA matching.[154]

Biometric surveillance forms part of a much deeper history of racial and colonial violence via data colonialism and bodily extraction. This ranges from the extraction of Native American "bone ... blood, spit, and hair,"[155] to the long-standing policing of Black life through the many surveillance technologies rooted in biogenetic data extraction that Browne details.[156] In all of these instances, the state gives prime credence to bodily "evidence" in order to criminalize, control, manage, and eradicate particular populations. This informs our current juncture in which "DNA genealogical databases are a goldmine for police, but with few rules and little transparency," to quote the headline of one *Los Angeles Times* article.[157]

This broader context of biometric surveillance informs the meaning of commercial DNA testing, even if the stated intent of the DSR is to facilitate relationships and the intent of 23andme. com or ancestry.com is simply to further personal discovery.

Taken out of context, the search for ancestry through these tests appears benign; however, it can never be separated from the larger context I have described above. The handing over of genetic data to commercial genealogy databases—even with entirely different aims in mind—holds implications that reverberate far beyond "welcoming you [to yourself]," as 23andme.com promises to do.[158] Far from being race-neutral, the mapping of DNA through commercial testing has larger ramifications for already-criminalized populations and communities. This especially affects those registered by the DSR, some of whom rely on commercial genealogy tests as a starting point to map "families," and some of whom are able to connect with others through their donor's bank-granted numbers. However, on a broader level, the DSR operates according to the same logic as the personally driven commercial DNA test. By registering for the DSR, participants add their own genetic information to an ever-growing complex of database information that uses an individual's mapped DNA as a data point to connect to others. This, in turn, raises ethical and political questions for those who rely on DNA's architectures to infuse relationships with power and meaning about self, family, and kin, regardless of the reasoning or intention.

QUEER INHERITANCE, QUEER FUTURES

The numbers, symbols, unfamiliar terms on the screen were a language I didn't understand. It had taken 0.04538 seconds—a fraction of a second—to upend my life. There would now forever be a before....
My mind began to spin with calculations. If Susie was not my half-sister—*no kind of sister*—it could only mean one of two things: either my father was not her father or her father was not my father.
—Dani Shapiro[159]

Dani Shapiro's popular memoir *Inheritance* recounts the moment that a DNA test delivered her a blow to self that affected her more than all others had, leading her to eventually discover, well into her fifties, that she was donor conceived.[160] No stranger to shock, Shapiro experienced a stupor that exceeded even the dismay of learning of her parents' lethal car crash or the moment that her baby was diagnosed with a rare disease.[161] However, in Shapiro's narrative, these moments of shock do not come close to the impact of her DNA test results. Here we see the hegemonic power of biogenetic data to reduce her sister to *"no kind of sister"* in a mere 0.04538 seconds.[162]

This chapter has theorized the cultural power of narratives such as this; I have brought back into the frame the histories, epistemologies, and politics that can bestow such powerful meaning on alien data delivered in such a short time. While Shapiro's story is one of decades of secrecy within the paternalistic culture that prevailed in the early days of donor conception, stories like hers have, instead, been taken to be about the inherent violence of nonbiogenetic families. This chapter has questioned this presumption. What must be conflated, and erased, I have asked, in order for the diversity of circumstances that lead families to stray from the biogenetic norm to be pathologized and moralized as an inherent problem? What happens when this pathologization is internalized by queer families, who are, by and large, inherently nonbiogenetic and nonbionormative?[163] And what happens when we begin to reveal the instabilities and racial histories that inhere within the gene, the family, and biology itself?

A powerful fetishism must take hold in order for biogeneticism to stick—and one that erases the cultural, historical, scientific, epistemic, racial, and colonial contexts that stabilize and enshrine the biological, singularly defined, with so much meaning. Far from being neutral, genomes are entangled in racial and colonial histories and social processes, "constituted as scientific methods by laboratory methods and devices, and also by discourses or particular ideas and vocabularies of race, ethnicity, nation, family ... tribe," and more.[164] The rubrics, measurements, and systems of translating genomes into meaningful data hold material implications, particularly when it comes to the surveillance state and the prison-industrial complex.

Thus the biogenetic monogamous nuclear family is a racial, settler colonial, and national project as much as it is one of gender and sexuality—and it is constituted through the many erasures that must take place in order for the story of this family as universal and natural to hold. Such erasures take place on multiple scales, from the molecular level at the site of the laboratory to the broader context, where power relations influence which studies are funded, which truths are valued, and who has access to the pristine family form in the first place. In its assertion of what families ought to be, DSR discourse brings along with it all of these cultural values; this also reifies long-standing narratives of queerness as lack.

To be clear, this chapter has not argued against the desires that children may hold to know, connect with, or forge meaningful relationships with those who share their DNA. Everyone has the right to negotiate and forge relationships over time, in open ways that can lead to experimental and new kinship forms. Rather, I have sought to place these desires within a cultural, historical, and political context in which "all of our desires are filtered through, or suffused with, the culture (the norms, the values, the practices) they are located in."[165] As philosopher Daniel Groll argues, we must acknowledge that the discussion about the meaning of DNA does not take place in a "vacuum ... [but] in a society that takes the traditional family structure— a mother and father who are genetic progenitors of their children—as the gold standard of what a family should be."[166] This leads to facile pseudoscientific notions of genetic inheritance, and to a "culture [that] tends to treat genetics as destiny," that this chapter has unpacked.[167]

There is nothing inherently right or wrong about the meanings that individuals create in their quest to forge a sense of self and family. Rather, this chapter has tracked the ascendence of one particular form of biogeneticism, its naturalization over time, and how its hegemonization might sideline other modes of family making. This, I have contended, is a central question with which a queer reproductive justice politics must contend. The reinscription of biology carries with it racial, gender, colonial, and sexual histories, hierarchies, and consequences that must be addressed.

What, then, does it mean on a structural level when discourses surrounding queer family come to be imbued with these ideas? The DSR website's tab for "LGBTQ Families," which features photos of predominantly blue-eyed, blond-haired children hugging one another, offers some insights on this question.[168] In *Gay Parent Magazine* and *Philadelphia Family Pride*, a series of print ads for the DSR are arranged in a timeline. One reads: "Not only did the DSR connect us [but] we became family. Val and I were married in June!"[169] The bizarre story of a couple joined romantically by a shared sperm donor underscores the main message: that the acknowledgment of shared donor gametes can bring deepened love, sense of family, and togetherness. A statement from another parent, more nuanced than this one, acknowledges the queer history of "exclusion or distance from one's family of origin, and thus the need to create our own families."[170] Its author ends on a more hopeful note, that "as gay families continue to evolve, our rainbow flag has the potential to get brighter and brighter" because, with donor family networks, "our definition of family in the queer world is expanding even further."[171]

While idiosyncratic, this collection of materials compiled on the DSR website all rests in a fundamental friction. Laura Mamo names this friction in her discussion of the simultaneous possibility for shifting queer intimacies created through the "regenerative possibilities offered through technoscience" and the normalization of "bio-ties" that comes along with a further folding into the biotechnological, social, and legal apparatus.[172] Mamo seeks a more pluralistic space where multiple meanings of family and kinship may coexist. Rather than holding these in binary opposition, Mamo valorizes the "bio-ties" while they are also upset through new technologies; the troubling of this dichotomy creates the possibility of "queer intimacies" for Mamo.

Mamo's notion of queer intimacies raises important questions that have no easy answers. Are such queer intimacies possible without the reification of the myth of the two-parent heterosexual couple as the default? What does it mean to reinforce "bio-ties" as a way to extend beyond the nuclear unit, especially given a legal panorama in which custody can only be granted to two people?[173] Are there queer possibilities for more open modes of family, gender, and intimacies that do not reinscribe biological essentialism? How does this work within a deeply racist, classist, and heterocentric legal system that only understands one to two parents and that systematically fails to move past deep biases when determining who can be a legitimate and good parent? What are the legal implications of exploring these more murky spaces amid rising movements to constrict the rights of nonbiological queer parents?

This tension was at the heart of the technology of shared motherhood with which this chapter began. It is a technology that promises a slew of "social, emotional, and psychological benefits," as the medical director of the clinic first performing this procedure reports and as the couple who successfully conceived through it agrees.[174] The director conflates intimacy and connection with individual biological experience. The eighteen-hour period during which both partners are pregnant is deemed important enough to justify increased financial costs, the lowered chance of successful pregnancy, and the medical risks of transporting the embryo twice. As the clinic reports, it "allows both women [*sic*] to feel 'equally related' and build a bond with the child, something that, while a common experience of heterosexual couples, hasn't previously been possible for lesbian couples."[175]

This tension has also manifested in the legal arena in particularly troubling ways. In February of 2023, in a much-watched custody case in Oklahoma, advocates were disturbed to see the granting of custody of a toddler to Harlan Vaughn. Mr. Vaughn's custody hinged upon the denial of custody to Kris Williams, his nongestational mother who had previously been married to Rebekah Wilson, the biological mother, and who was initially listed on the child's birth certificate. After Wilson and Williams divorced, Wilson petitioned to remove Williams from the birth certificate. Vaughn then petitioned the court for custody of the child, eventually winning, even though he had not met the child until he was nearly two years old, while Williams was parenting the child.

Williams had not undertaken second-parent adoption—a costly and at times invasive process whereby a nonbiological parent must appeal to the court to be granted custody of their child. Moreover, in an article for a local Oklahoma parenting magazine, Wilson told the story of being advised by social media donor-conceived activists to refer to Vaughn not as her child's donor but as his dad because it was better for the child—which she did.[176] Critically, Wilson's public writings on social media in which she named Vaughn as the "father" and embraced a biogenetic understanding of the relationship entered the formal legal record.[177] With this relationship established, it became very difficult for Williams to retain custody of the child; as the judge presiding the case ultimate ruled, "Since Williams did not give birth to the child and did not adopt the child, she could not establish a mother-child relationship."[178] This case does not stand alone, and, unfortunately, similar rulings in New Mexico, Pennsylvania, and Idaho have denied custody to nonbiogenetic moms on the basis of parentage laws that require lesbian women either to be biologically related to their children or to adopt them in order to be considered a legal parent. These cases bring particular concerns, as the Epilogue will examine, in the wake of *Dobbs*, which raises key questions about how the conflation of gametes with personhood creates new openings for the state to police reproductive, and even prereproductive, bodies.[179]

A far cry from earlier queer and feminist visions, this schema radically departs from a political history of collective liberation struggles that earlier chapters have traced. As the normative experience of heterosexual parenthood (ostensibly) inches closer within the reach of certain LBGTQ parents, its newest participants must comply with a singular authentication of family rooted within bio-ties (and, in turn, a delegitimization of all other ties). A possessive and competitive frame takes hold whereby only some are entitled to the pleasures and privileges of kinship—and only if they can afford the experience—whereas others are decidedly not. Advancing the idea of biogenetic authentic family that consumers of ARTs may access at an exorbitant price, shared motherhood remains rooted in the "feminist heterosexual imaginary of reproduction" and in a white settler idea of the private reproductive monogamous family.[180]

In 1970, radical feminist Shulamith Firestone argued that the key to feminist liberation was the seizure of control of reproduction, including the "seizure of control of human fertility," so that "the reproduction of the species by one sex for the benefit of both would be replaced by … artificial reproduction: children would be born to both sexes equally, or independently, of either."[181] Firestone argued for the opposite of shared motherhood: she wanted to rid "women" of mandatory reproductive labors as a prerequisite for a revolution. This complements histories recounted in chapter 1, such as that of New York City's Third World Gay Revolution Collective, which in 1971 put forward a sixteen-point program that centered the "abolition of the institution of the bourgeois nuclear family" along with the abolition of other oppressive and disciplinary institutions, including the police and the court system.[182] A decade later, Pat Parker, whose writing was also analyzed in chapter 1, issued an impassioned speech linking imperialism, racism, and the nuclear family that argued that "in order for us to move to revolution, [the nuclear family has] to be destroyed."[183]

In these moments we see a radical explosion of, and expansion beyond, the nuclear biogenetic monogamous family as a starting point for the kind of world in which everyone can live and flourish—a world that does not continually rely on the expropriation of gendered and racialized labor, the privatization of society, and ever-elite notions of what makes a family. And the archive of these arguments continues. In 1990, as neoliberalism was really taking hold, John D'Emilio warned of the reprivatization of society enshrined within the biological family. Like others before him, he called for "structures beyond the nuclear family that provide a sense of belonging," rooted within a socialist vision that centered collective survival within extended networks of kin caring for one another.[184]

As history has revealed, however, instead of pushing for more and more open, public, and shared conceptions of family as collective, the homonormative turn has led us elsewhere. I write these words in a time of intense frictions between those who aspire for nothing more than the promise of assimilation (through bionormativity and other means) and those who argue that such normalizations advance a racial and colonial worldview that mires us perpetually within xenophobic nationalisms, unending imperialist wars, settler colonialism, and the prison-industrial complex, among other problems.[185] I also write these words in a time when the entwined catastrophes of global racism, climate change, genocide, and COVID-19 further reveal the deadly consequences of ever more privatized and exclusive frameworks of care. I write this in a time when entire genealogies of Palestinians and Indigenous people on the front lines against extraction are being exterminated, while First World fetuses are enshrined with life, according to the US Supreme Court. All of this has implications for which kinds of families will be able to survive in precarious times. As the already frayed safety net collapses under the unbearable weight of yet another blow to our collective well-being, we simply cannot afford to further winnow down our networks of kinship and care.

In the face of all of this, openings present themselves for undoing the forms of biogeneticism that this chapter has problematized. Against these quagmires, the next chapter offers alternative histories of the present, reengaging the radical and expansive imaginaries of family abolition born of Black feminist and queer-of-color movements of the 1970s to the present. These alternatives help to kindle sacred intergenerational life amid a war in which the most vulnerable of our children are positioned on the front lines. Revitalized in contemporary movements for mutual aid, prison abolition, disability justice, and collective care, they open space for the embodiment and proliferation of expansive definitions of kin, care, and futures, even as narrow biogeneticisms threaten to draw us back in once more.

CHAPTER FOUR

Queering Family Abolition

Intergenerational Archives of Care

An abolition feminist ecology emerges from everyday
practices, collective experiments driven by necessity,
practice, and reflection, and in sinewy networks that
crisscross time and space.[1]

—Angela Y. Davis

In *Abolition. Feminism. Now.* (2022), Angela Y. Davis, Gina Dent,
Erica Meiners, and Beth Richie chart a genealogy of abolition
feminism. They map a history that acknowledges the seemingly
small, diffuse, and peripheral political projects that cohere political imaginations and bring about abolition.[2] The authors reveal
these forgotten, small-scale, and seldom-grasped radical experiments of imagination and creativity. Their archive includes, but
is not limited to, artistic projects and writings, and "toolkits lost
on the internet, study and action groups that leaned into the
former and forgot the latter, indie documentary screenings,
small clusters of militant picketers, campus groups that erupt
and dissipate."[3] Without these peripheral projects, they argue,
the powerful calls to abolish prisons and the police that crested

to the surface in 2020 in the early pandemic would not have been possible.[4]

The authors highlight the importance of accounting for how the "rarely acknowledged and sinewy genealogies that tether movements and campaigns across time and space continue to spark freedom."[5] This chapter maps a genealogy of a less frequently considered lineage of abolition feminism—family abolition—as a movement that expands the project of queering reproductive justice. I turn to the archives of care produced by radical queer, Black, and LGBTQ feminists of color from the late 1970s through the present. In these archives, I argue, we see ongoing enactment of care that subverts and exceeds the private nuclear family form. Here I refer to abolition as a positive project that builds up systems of life-affirming care and collective support as much as it seeks to dismantle prisons and punitive institutions and ideologies of social control.[6] As transgender Marxist scholar Zoe Belinsky puts it, "Family abolition [is] ... an *expansive* rather than *reductive* process."[7] I draw from this core principle of abolition feminism: the rejection of one hierarchical, rigid, and punitive colonial and carceral institution—in this case the private nuclear family—and its replacement with more humane and sustainable structures of care. This, in turn, offers an antidote to the increasingly problematic turns that mainstream movements for LGBTQ family have taken.

Methodologically, I borrow from Ann Cvetkovich, who writes that queer history "demands a radical archive of emotion in order to document intimacy, sexuality, love, and activism."[8] Cvetkovich affirms the political importance of tending to the ephemeral traces and minor genres produced by marginalized subjects who are rarely rendered legible through the archive. I am also inspired by Saidiya Hartman, who writes that "every historian of the multitude, the dispossessed, the subaltern, and the enslaved is forced to grapple with the power and authority of the archive and the limits it sets on what can be known, whose perspective matters, and who is endowed with the gravity and authority of historical actor."[9] Hartman forges space for the "revolution in a minor key" that can be glimpsed when we listen to "the things whispered in dark bedrooms" by subjects who are categorically disregarded as subjects of history; she asks that we read for the fleeting moments when "visions and dreams of the wayward [are experienced to be] ... possible."[10] I bring together examples of different scales and registers of family abolition to reveal how earlier generations of queer radicalism served as precursors to a radical present and future.

The chapter analyzes archives of queer care of the late twentieth and early twenty-first centuries that built alternatives to the exclusive, hierarchical, privatized modes of care that characterize the nuclear family. Its first section offers a definition of family abolition. I focus on the family's reliance upon the idea of children as belonging to parents, as well as the family's privatization as the privileged site for the provision of reproductive labor and care. I also highlight critiques of the family as an institution that is required to shore up racial capitalism and settler colonialism.

The next two sections read the intergenerational writings between Audre Lorde, Cherríe Moraga, and their children, Rafael Angel Moraga and Elizabeth Lorde-Rollins, asking how these mothers and children challenge conventions of parent-child relationships bound by ownership and hierarchy. These exchanges reveal a radical rescinding of parental investment in a predictable future for their children, exemplifying what June Jordan called the cultivation of "love as lifeforce," an energy that cannot be controlled, managed, or corralled.[11] The ensuing discussion also nuances abolitionist conversations about reproductive labor by valuing the radical transformative potential of the reproductive labor of communities who have been long subject to eugenics and reproductive injustice.

The end of the chapter asks how this ethos carried through queer care activism from the late 1980s through the early 2000s. I examine a range of expressions of this work—from AIDS/HIV care work to mutual aid efforts to support lesbian political prisoners—that militated against the privatization of the queer family at the turn of the century. These acts challenge a dominant queer assimilation politics, voicing an insistence upon abiding care for the most marginalized in times of abandonment and embodying what AIDS activist Douglass Crimp called "promiscuous care."[12] This type of nurturing exploded the boundaries of the exclusive family to include the lives of loved ones and strangers alike. Last, I situate this counterhistory as a precursor to the burst of collective queer movements that erupted in the early pandemic to challenge the boundaries of the private family. This history is positioned within a broader tradition of abolition feminism, which, to cite Alisa Bierria, Jakeya Caruthers, and Brooke Lober, "constitutes a long arc of ethical life-making and everyday practice."[13]

SINEWY GENEALOGIES: DEFINING FAMILY ABOLITION

Located at the crosscurrents of Black freedom, feminist, and anticapitalist struggles, family abolition resists the abuses and inequalities that are hidden within the private nuclear family as an institution of white supremacy, racial capitalism, and settler

colonialism.[14] It throws into question what feminist theorist
Kathi Weeks calls the family "as a ... mode of social belonging
[that] *naturalizes* hierarches" through a "privatised system of
social reproduction."[15] Rooted here, family abolition is the positive, expansive process of proliferating networks of care, love,
and support that crowd out the rigid, hierarchical nuclear heteropatriarchal family.[16]

Family abolition brings together critiques of interpersonal
violence with long-standing Marxist feminist, transnational,
Black feminist, and feminist-of-color critiques of the unequal
distribution of reproductive labor under slavery, globalization,
and racial capitalism.[17] Seeking to make reproductive labor visible, it challenges the private family as the privileged site for the
provision of care. The critique of the family as an enclosure of
care has gained relevance with the state's increased abdication of
responsibility for populations under neoliberalism. Abolition
protests "the neoliberal insistence on only taking care of yourself
and your closest kin"—an idea that, according to the contemporary Care Collective, a London-based collective of academics
and activists—leads to "paranoid" modes of care that are fueled
by scarcity and competition.[18] Moreover, beyond simply offering
a critique of the private heteropatriarchal family, a queer abolitionist project also requires a destabilization of the gendered
assumptions underlying the normative nuclear family.[19]

In addition to addressing inequitable labor arrangements
among adults, family abolition problematizes the hierarchical
relations of ownership that structure the parent-child relationship—a line of thinking that has been a less considered important
dimension of queer movements of the late twentieth century. In
his famous essay "Capitalism and Gay Identity," for example,
queer historian John D'Emilio identified the ownership of

children to be an idea that "is so deeply ingrained that we can scarcely imagine [otherwise]."[20] This analysis led D'Emilio to call for the collectivization of care for the next generation, pointing to the need for inclusive structures of support and belonging, including shared childcare, housing, and emotional camaraderie, as replacements for the family as the primary site of kinship.[21] Additionally, lesbian mother activists of the 1970s and 1980s argued that children's oppression within the family further entrenched heteropatriarchy. For example, as lesbian mothers Mary Peña and Barbara Carey unflinchingly put it in 1979, "[CHILDREN [do] NOT BELONG TO THE PATRIARCHY / THEY [do] NOT BELONG TO US [LESBIANS] EITHER / THEY…BELONG ONLY TO THEMSELVES."[22] Peña and Carey decried the objectification of children as the property of parents of any gender, reminding fellow lesbian mothers that they could not simply replicate patriarchal structures and values. This position was also argued by activist Baba Cooper, who called upon fellow lesbian mothers to explode the oppressive family from within. Writing in 1989, Cooper argued that "the radical potential of lesbian mothering" lay in the resocialization of a generation—and particularly daughters—in a combined struggle against misogyny, ableism, and heteropatriarchy.[23] There would be no feminist or queer revolution as long as children remained oppressed.

Meanwhile, Black feminists critiqued the nuclear family on a more fundamental level. As early as the 1970s, Kay Lindsey argued that the nuclear family was a "white institution" upon which states and empires relied to maintain racial and gender subordination and land as private property.[24] Patriarchs sought ownership over women and children, Lindsey argued, but only after the family had been established to seize the land needed for unjust imperial expansion.[25] Lindsey's argument foreshadowed contemporary Black and Indigenous feminist arguments about the nuclear family as a lynchpin of slavery and settler colonialism.[26] She did not see a possibility for the full humanization of the Black woman until private property and the state were abolished.[27] This, in turn, would require no less than the unmaking of the United States as we know it.

These historical flashpoints reveal three key facets of family abolition. First, they put pressure on the private family as the privileged site for the provision of care. Second, they contest the ownership relations that bind child to parent, harkening back to a time during which, to cite queer historian Michael Bronski, "gays wanted to liberate children."[28] Finally, they articulate a rejection of the family as a core site for the reproduction of white supremacy, imperialism, and the settler state. In what follows, I show how the exchanges between Audre Lorde and Cherríe Moraga and their respective children both embody and expand these principles.

BEGIN THE WORLD AGAIN AND AGAIN: AGAINST THE INJURY OF DEVELOPMENT

In the 2023 reprint of Cherríe Moraga's *Waiting in the Wings*, an afterword by her son, Rafael Moraga, includes an intergenerational dialogue that challenges the hierarchies of ownership that typically characterize the parent-child relationship. Rafael responds to his mother's book about his conception and birth a quarter century later, reframing his own struggle for survival as an infant and his health struggles later in life. Rafael details the subversion of traditional familial hierarchies and the forging of relationships of reciprocal respect. This, in turn, offers insight into the work to crowd out nuclear family forms.

Entitled "One Hundred Nights," Rafael's essay anchors his reflections in the early months of his life that he spent in the NICU. While his quarantine was, by definition, isolating, Rafael holds the experience in relationship to his ancestral history. He owes his strength to his grandmother's fight to live after stomach surgery, and to the ways that his mother taught him to "use the same determination [he] ... had from birth to stand up for ... [himself] and others; to face discrimination and inequality."[29] Rafael's narrative embodies intergenerational continuity as he gathers strength to face the future from his ancestors.

Rafael's connection to family, defined expansively, comes through in his reflection upon the more corporeal knowledges that his own experience of illness has taught him—an experience that was brought into even sharper focus amid the confusion, fear, and isolation of the early COVID-19 pandemic. Rafael refers to the pandemic as a "second incubation" that triggered his memories of quarantine in the NICU as an infant.[30] It also presents an opportunity to heal. "I know now," he writes, "that I will re-emerge on the other side of this plastic void with renewed ganas ... knowing there is a future beyond the horizon."[31]

Rafael claims the genealogy of an extended family through modes of identification that span far beyond blood relations or his private family unit. He fosters a radical hope that is "cultivated," as he puts it, "with the fortitude of Chicana familial consciousness, forged by our ancestors from the deserts of Sonora and the mountains of Durango."[32] Embodying an alternative to the insular family, he argues that his identity has been formed in relation to many "Black and Brown artists, educators, entrepreneurs, and community organizers" who were always in his midst as he grew up in a home that was "refuge" for many, but especially for queer women of color.[33] Rafael thus positions himself to be as much the child of a movement and a collectivity as he is the child of an individual family.

Moreover, Rafael claims the epistemological interventions of *This Bridge Called My Back*, stating that he experiences his most important knowledges as "an emotional and physical recall."[34] This exemplifies one of his mother's most abiding collective theorizations: a theory in the flesh.[35] "A theory in the flesh," famously wrote Cherríe and *This Bridge* coauthors, emerges from a place "where the physical realities of our lives all fuse to create a politic born of necessity."[36] Rafael inhabits the body as a vital space of knowledge production and honors his precognitive memories both as an individual and as a member of multiple collectives.

Rafael also actualizes his autonomy as someone who has been freed—and has seized the space—to forge his own path because he is "in charge of defining ... [his] own existence."[37] He challenges the construction of children as property—a construction that both privatizes care for the child as the sole responsibility of the parent and strips children of their autonomy. Raised to be an active agent in his own life, Rafael is not some "formless entity" who can simply be "shaped" by his mother, as she puts it.[38] Rafael writes that he was never treated as "damaged goods" or "Bubble-Wrapped through life."[39] This challenges ableist constructions of disabled children, and especially disabled children of color, as unable to consent and exercise critical judgment.[40]

This reworked relationship also challenges what queer childhood studies scholar Hannah Dyer calls the "injury of development," which projects normative life pathways upon the figure of the child.[41] As Dyer elaborates, childhood is "queered" insofar as the figurative child represents radical unpredictability and "epistemic uncertainty," thus spurring adult anxieties and attempts to assert control.[42] Cherríe resists this injunction to control, respecting Rafael's capacity to, in the words of queer childhood studies scholar Kathryn Bond Stockton, "grow sideways." As Stockton argues, "The child from the standpoint of the 'normal' adult is always queer," precisely because "the child is who we [adults] are not, and never were."[43] Stockton and Dyer theorize a queering of the parent/child relationship that occurs when parents consciously resist the pull to direct children along a unilinear path toward an idealized maturity and instead dwell with the child in a space of uncertainty and unknowing.

Instead of seeking to corral Rafael, Cherríe embodies this stance. In the original memoir, Cherríe sees her premature infant in acute condition with an intestinal infection that threatens his life. She finds herself deep in prayer, begging her baby to choose survival. Quickly, however, she is struck with the knowledge that she must allow Rafael to make his own choice—a realization that she arrives upon after feeling the presence of her dear departed friends, including Audre Lorde and Tede Matthews.[44] Cherríe takes solace in the fact that her son is not alone in the liminal space between life and death. As Cherríe describes it, she knows that if she does not allow her son's spirit to choose his own direction, she will "crush him" with the weight of her own heart.[45] Therefore, she opts to "release him"; in so doing she feels Rafaelito move "toward life" of his own accord.[46] Cherríe challenges the basic ownership relations that animate the nuclear family, subverting the objectification of children as merely "a piece of the future lodged in and under the controlling influence of the present."[47] Rafael's life is entwined with hers, but it is not for her exclusive benefit. Cherríe thus clears the space for Rafael to author his own future, writing that her son "has his own story to tell and live."[48]

This act exemplifies what June Jordan calls the practice of love as a "lifeforce" that is cultivated when parents trust the intrinsic power of children.[49] Jordan develops these ideas in her 1977 essay on children's literature, which was brought into circulation by Alexis Pauline Gumbs in the 2016 anthology *Revolutionary Motherhood*.[50] "Unequivocal in [their] ... commitment to [their] moment of being," children are, as Jordan argued, the clearest embodiment of a radical life force of change, which adults must lovingly kindle in order for us to survive.[51]

For Jordan, the most important thing any adult can do is to "nurture a child into his or her own freedom" as the most authentic act of love.[52] As she elaborates:

> When we run on love, when we move and change and build and paint and sing and write and foster the maximal fulfillment of our own lives, as well as the maximal fulfillment of other lives [of children] ... that look to us for help, for protection ..., then we make manifest the creative spirit of the universe: a spirit existing within each of us and yet persisting infinitely greater than the ultimate capacities of any one of us.[53]

Jordan places children as a counterforce against destruction; children emblemize "the ways that the world begins again and again."[54] They represent our only possibility of surviving on "a planet long defiled by habits opposite to love."[55] Cultivating children's inner brilliance is therefore necessary to maintain a habitable planet.

This radical philosophy politicizes the unlearning of the generally unquestioned "tyranny" that Jordan believes characterizes the child-adult relationship.[56] To receive children on their own terms is a sacred act. "Tell me what you think and what you see and what you dream," writes Jordan, "so that I may hope to honor you."[57] This honoring work can be understood in

Cherríe rescinding control through a renunciation of the stranglehold on the future. This is also present in the writings between Audre Lorde and Elizabeth Lorde-Rollins.

USES OF THE EROTIC: DEATH AND LIFE
IN THE MOUTH OF THE DRAGON

In her 2022 book, *Abolish the Family: A Manifesto for Care*, queer feminist socialist Sophie Lewis lays forth a case for family abolition and dedicates a section to children's liberation within queer movements of the 1970s.[58] She highlights radical care economies between young adults and elders in formations like Street Transvestite Action Revolutionaries (STAR), also citing Alexis Pauline Gumbs's reclamation of queer-of-color radical lineages of mothering, as well as the spate of experiments in collective child-rearing among 1970s radicals.

Lewis is most concerned with how the family structure works to "privatize that which should be common [through] ... proprietary concepts of couple, blood, gene, and seed."[59] However, she does not elaborate upon concrete practices of intimate intergenerational care of actual children. Rather, attention is shifted back to the adult in response to the exploitation of the reproductive laborer and the sexual drudgery of monogamy.[60] This section furthers her line of inquiry through an engagement with Audre Lorde's concept of the erotic as a means of social reproduction.

As Amber Musser argues, "The maternal is a central, often-overlooked component of Lorde's black lesbian feminist erotic," which is organized around the creation of a future with "less suffering."[61] To understand the connection between the erotic and the maternal, we must unpack Audre's theory of the erotic. In "Uses of the Erotic: The Erotic as Power," she describes the erotic as "a resource within each of us [that is] ... firmly rooted in the power of our unexpressed or unrecognized feeling."[62] Audre implores those around her to refuse the mediocrity that oppressed people internalize in a world that continually dampens their power.[63] To tap into the erotic is to claim a different relation to one's labor—for one's creative capacities to manifest themselves and transform the world.

Audre is consistent with the movement of nonmonogamous sex radicals of the twentieth century who also believed in family abolition.[64] As biographer Alexis De Veaux describes it, Audre practiced "loving without boundaries—a philosophy and behavior she found consistent with rebellion against heterosexually scripted models of monogamy."[65] However, despite her nonmonogamy, Audre opposed the conflation of the erotic and the sexual, decrying the "relegation" of the expansive power of the erotic "to the bedroom alone."[66] Instead, she enticed her readers to commit to the erotic in pursuit of nothing less than total revolution.[67]

In this way, the erotic lines up with theories of "living labor" that postcolonial feminist critic Neferti Tadiar defines as "labor which is still objectifying itself, labor as subjectivity."[68] Tadiar draws from Marx to identify one's unalienated labor as a "*living source* of value" that has yet to be objectified by capital.[69] Rather than understanding labor as something that is already objectified and owned by the capitalist, this opens up the space for the worker to reclaim the creative power and energy that fuels labor in the first place. Audre holds open the potential awe and fulfillment that is attainable through one's own creative labor prior to its objectification and capture. Because one's erotic power is so dangerous to the status quo, she argues, patriarchy seeks to "[rob] work of its erotic value, its erotic power and life appeal and fulfillment," and thus its living quality as a source of awe-some power.[70] She claims this unbridled potentiality within, calling upon her readers to refuse to hand over "the erotic's electrical charge" in a world that seeks to continually "psychi-cally milk" them and convert their labor power into profit.[71]

This intervention is concretized in Audre's speech to the graduating class of Oberlin College in 1989, in which Audre challenges young graduates to take responsibility for the "surge of power inside [them]"—a power that does not belong to their "parents or professors," and that they can elect to either "own" or waste.[72] Audre invites youths to honor their inner erotic force—and to seize their unobjectified labor, power, and creativity. This is a task that she also assigns to parents, imploring the queer community, in particular, to "make a commitment to [all] … children within our communities, to a future for them which will be free from oppression and abuse, as well as starvation."[73] Lorde thus argues that the raising of youth must be a shared responsibility for the betterment and survival of all.

Accordingly, Audre argues that parenting requires no less than radically transforming the world. In her essay on lesbian-of-color parenting in the 1980s, she writes:

> I believe that raising children is one way of participating in the future, in social change. On the other hand, it would be dangerous as well as sentimental to think that childrearing alone is enough to bring about a livable future in the absence of any definition of that future. For unless we develop some cohesive vision of that world in which we hope these children will participate, and some sense of our own responsibilities in the shaping of that world, we will only raise new performers in the master's sorry drama.[74]

Audre entwines the work of envisioning a different world with the practical day-to-day care of children toward the realization of this vision. She theorizes the imaginative work that is necessary to dream up the kind of world children will need for a "livable future."[75] She prefigures modes of kinship that rewire society at the most intimate level. This entails seizing one's erotic energies in order to replace oppressive familial structures—"the master's sorry drama"—with new relations of integrity and care.[76]

Everything must change for Audre. "If we do not grow with our children," Audre writes, "they cannot learn."[77] She opens herself up for reexamination in the hopes that her children will learn to "be who [they wish] to be," not for their parents, but for themselves.[78] This challenges what literary theorist Gabrielle Owen argues is a construction of the adult as finished, a notion that is secured only in contradistinction to its corollary: the pliable adolescent, whom adults must steer away from "degeneracy."[79] By arguing that parents must grow alongside their children, Audre resists this call to police the adolescent. The adult, like the child, is in a perpetual state of becoming and always beholden to the necessity to change and grow.

Audre thus invites parents to grow *with* their children "in the mouth of a racist, sexist, suicidal dragon" as a matter of collective survival.[80] This challenges the link between degeneracy and adolescence, instead allowing the fluidity of selfhood to seed the ever-present possibility and necessity of transformation in adults and youths alike. Embracing the radical openness and epistemic uncertainty of both childhood and adulthood, Audre lays bare her own challenges so that she might model growth for her children. This comes through in Audre's discussion of her own temper and of the work that she does to stare down oppression. "If I [do] ... not learn to handle my anger," she incisively asks, "how [can] ... I expect the children to learn to handle theirs in some constructive way?"[81]

Responding to her own question, Audre demands from herself an unflinching commitment to confront that which most challenges her: the "rage of Black survival within the daily trivializations of white racism."[82] She encourages her children to grow beyond her in their political analysis—and thus to "choose their own battles."[83] Audre must, as she puts it, show her children the contours of the larger war for survival, while teaching them that they will need to take responsibility for their own battles, even if their weapons are alien to Audre.[84]

Audre thus commits to her children's actualization while encircling them with support, understanding her mothering practice to be deeply entwined with the revolutions she wages in all spheres of her life. In this way, Audre departs from family abolitionists Lewis and M.E. O'Brien, both of whom integrate Black feminism into broader communist histories of family abolition through the uniform category of abstract labor. Voicing a keen suspicion of Black feminist reclamations of motherhood, Lewis and O'Brien argue that Black feminist reclamations of the family as a site of resistance eclipse gender and sexual oppression.[85] Complicating these terms, Audre understands reproductive labor as a site of both oppression and radical reclamation. She states that "the aim of each thing which we do [must be] ... to make our lives and the lives of our children richer and more possible."[86] She resists the complete subsumption of social reproduction to relations of total domination to position parenting as part of a labor toward interdependent futures.

Audre underscores child-rearing as political practice, especially among those who have been subjected to eugenics and reproductive injustice. This expands upon Black feminist theorizations of social reproduction, in particular Angela Y. Davis's foundational 1971 article, "Reflections on the Black Woman's

Role in the Community of Slaves," in which Davis positions the slave's living quarters as a site of contradiction and revolutionary potentiality. "In the infinite anguish of ministering to the needs of the men and children around her," writes Davis, the enslaved mother "was performing the *only* labor in the slave community which could not be directly and immediately claimed by the oppressor," and this is the site where the "thrust toward abolition" is kindled.[87]

Valorizing Black reproductive labor on her own terms, Audre joins Davis to articulate a politics of Black reproductive labor that nuances the abolitionist conversation. Audre, like Davis, does not shy away from the contradiction that reproductive labor is exploitative. However, she remains cognizant of the strategic possibilities of reappropriating reproductive labor, especially among those who have continually been subject to eugenics and reproductive injustice. This mirrors the analysis of Saidiya Hartman, who argues that a recognition of the perpetually unrequited labor of the Black mother does not preclude a recognition of her "brilliant and formidable labor of care."[88] Hartman clarifies that even though this labor is inherently exploitative, it amounts to more than simply exploitation. Love and creation are thus never "reducible to, or exhausted by" racial capitalism.[89] Similarly, Lorde is not willing to conflate social reproduction and domination: she knows that she cannot afford to, nor does she wish to, rescind the political power she arrives at through her mothering practice. She implores others to tap into their erotic potential as a "*living source* of value" that one must refuse to hand over to a racist, capitalist, patriarchal system.[90]

These lessons are put to the test as Audre watches Elizabeth's teenage rebellion grow, remarking that "it is really scary when your children take what they have learned about self-assertion

... and decide to test it in confrontations with you."[91] Audre's poem "Progress Report" examines her emotions as she becomes the recipient of the rebellions that she herself has kindled in her child. Instead of clamping down, she heeds Jordan's call to "honor" her child through a belief in the world that Elizabeth creates.[92] She raises her children as "their own [people]"—and with the ultimate confidence that they will live their lives "in the service of all of our futures."[93]

Elizabeth's poem "Second November," which is about Audre's untimely death from breast cancer, responds to the question of what kind of future Elizabeth would build. In this poem, Elizabeth continues to cultivate radical love across what is perhaps the ultimate boundary: life and death.[94] An ob-gyn, queer mother, and cancer survivor herself, Elizabeth is no stranger to the simultaneity of death and life. She stares squarely in the face of that which scares her most: what it means to continue in her mother's absence.

The poem is structured through a set of contradictions, which Elizabeth allows to coexist. She opens with a discussion of Audre's idiosyncrasies: the incredible stubbornness that accompanied her openness to change, and a harshness that was rivaled only by her generosity and warmth.[95] Elizabeth roots contradiction within the confluence of life and death that she witnesses every day in hospital "rooms where women die and bring life."[96] She resists penning Audre into the space of death as an absence. Instead, Elizabeth tends to her mother's transformed presence amid the unsurmountable heartbreak of loss.

"Second November" comes to a head in the penultimate stanza, as Elizabeth writes searingly of the unrecoverable loss of her mother. "The world is full / of motherless children and now /," she writes, "I am one of them."[97] Grief wails as Elizabeth mourns the loss of her "children's grandmother" and the fact that she will never hear Audre's commanding voice through the telephone receiver.[98] And yet, Audre is still here, her "smile sit[ting] on the … face" of a twin baby that Elizabeth delivers in the hospital room where others go to die.[99] Death in life and life in death entwine, as Audre's call to inhabit fluidity lives on.

Here the practice of fostering the other's freedom is extended back from child to mother, as Elizabeth releases Audre to follow her own course. She thus gifts her mother the space to follow her own "sideways" path.[100] Ultimately, Elizabeth ends with the lesson of her mother's enduring presence, allowing Audre to transgress boundaries in death just as she did in life.

LIVING TOGETHER: QUEER "PROMISCUOUS CARE" AT THE TURN OF THE CENTURY

The intimate practices of care that I've discussed unsettle hierarchies between parent and child, challenging the linear telos of life span, pushing past the family as a privatized site of care to embody a praxis of family abolition. This cuts against the grain of dominant trends of LGBTQ politics of the turn of the century, by which time the radical intersectional grassroots activism of queer parents decades prior gave way to large-scale, mainstream legal efforts oriented around assimilation, rights, and recognition.[101] These trends, as chapters 2 and 3 argued, raise fundamental frictions between official LGBTQ movements for inclusion and larger struggles for decolonization and abolition. However, despite the trend toward mainstreaming, and queer imbrications within marriage and official bio-legal ties, the period was also accompanied by everyday efforts toward family abolition. This section takes a step back to sketch the contours of the broader cultures of "promiscuous care" that encircled micro-interactions.[102] It reads promiscuous care as a queer formulation that challenges the boundary between stranger and relative in our accountability to another's well-being.

Promiscuous care makes visible the many webs and circuits of reproductive labor that enable everyone's lives, insisting upon the value of the disenfranchised in times of wide-scale abandonment by the state and racial capitalism. The term itself comes from ACT UP AIDS activist and queer theorist Douglas Crimp, who argues, in his 1987 essay "How to Have Promiscuity in an Epidemic" that gay promiscuity is not the cause of the epidemic; it is the solution. Crimp credits queer communities with inventing safe sex—and thus engaging in the "psychic preparation [and] experimentation" necessary to survive in ways that heterosexuals were not.[103] Crimp tenders an ethos of care that rejects exclusive notions of sex and love, defining a queer mode of radical care that "proliferates outwards to redefine caring relations from the most intimate to the most distant," to cite the contemporary Care Collective.[104] Emerging from these conditions, promiscuous care responds to the wide-scale abandonment of entire populations and the collapse of any pretext of a social safety net. With a radical embrace of the other, it rejects a politics of expendability to argue that everyone's lives are sacred and worthy. Moving beyond ideologies of the private individual or insular nuclear family, it also voices a commitment to the collective well-being of the entire community.

Promiscuous care is a specifically queer formulation that presages contemporary formulations like Hil Malatino's trans ethic of care that "doesn't rely on the family, one's intimate circle, or an abstraction of community as its locus of distribution and circulation"; instead, it centers care between "all those folks with whom we're interdependent, many of whom we may not know intimately or at all."[105] Malatino disrupts the devaluation of the lives of those whom we do not personally know, voicing a commitment to strangers whose labors and lives buttress our own. This ethic calls us into accountability with the social whole, challenging, for example, the inequalities perpetuated in the mainstream fight for LGBTQ adoption and narrow bio-genetic framings of family. A trans ethic of care further stretches theorizations of queer reproductive justice to challenge the hierarchies between those whom we know and those whose lives and labor shape our own in invisible ways.

Horizontal nonexclusive care is also theorized by Dean Spade in his contemporary formulation of "mutual aid" as a radical political practice that ruptures "social isolation and forced dependency on hostile systems."[106] Spade refuses ideologies of the isolated individual to instead forge modes of reciprocal care outside both the state and the private family. Once again, we are called upon to consider the intimate ways in which strangers shape our lives, as well as to consider our responsibilities toward those with whom our direct interactions are either invisible or fleeting. Taken collectively, these formulations offer a de-privatization and de-hierarchization of care across diffuse spaces, forging a decidedly queer legacy of care at the crosscurrents of multiple radical traditions.

Promiscuous care stresses an abiding insistence upon the value of the devalued, fashioned through a new way of living together in the face of abandonment. It articulates a way of living with and for one another that originates from the vantage point of marginality, which Cathy Cohen imagines as "a politics where the nonnormative and marginal position of punks, bulldaggers, and welfare queens" converges.[107] Cohen articulated a political solidarity that brought communities facing increasing precariousness together across their difference to demand a shared space for everyone to live. This vision was concretized by sociologist activist Nancy Stoller, who wrote in her 1998 book on early AIDS activism, *Lessons from the Damned*, that "out of death and difficulty," those surviving the epidemic would need to "find the promise of change and the possibility of developing new ways of living together."[108] Central to these acts of "living together" were emergent modes of horizontal care, such as needle exchange programs and sex worker–run organizations, which combined peer-to-peer services and community control with movement organizing. Here the language of "living together" was significant because it called for a reestablishment of collective social relations that were being frayed away under austerity politics and the increased criminalization of marginalized populations. As an inherently political practice, these forms of communal organization and service provision emphasized the inherent value of all lives, naming everyone as worthy of the resources to live and thrive.

Additionally, promiscuous care challenged the hierarchical relation between those receiving and those granting services that was being reified through an increasingly privatized professional nonprofit sector characterized by charity. Rather, as a mode of promiscuous care, practices of "living together" entailed the goals of nonhierarchical service provision. Here the line between service provision and movement mobilization was blurred. As Stoller argued, transformation and survival would be created only through community-controlled movements led by "the damned" themselves and toward their political empowerment.[109]

Notably, this fierce determination to care for others rendered expendable by the state was also a prominent theme of both

Moraga and Lorde's work. Framing *Waiting in the Wings* as "a story of one small human being's … struggle for survival / for life in the age of death / the age of AIDS," Moraga's parenting practice was informed by her work within movements navigating the confluence of neoliberal austerity politics, AIDS/HIV, gentrification, and more.[110] Cherríe writes of Merle Woo, Audre Lorde, and Pat Parker's struggles with cancer as integral to her understandings of birth and death. She also names recently departed AIDS activists, including Rodrigo Reyes, the director of the first Latinx AIDS organization in San Francisco, and Tede Matthews.[111] As a leader in the efforts named by Stoller, Matthews is of particular significance: as I elaborate in my reading of the initial publication of *Waiting in the Wings* in chapter 1, Cherríe intuits that Tede's spirit has crossed with Rafael's in the liminal space between life and death, and Tede's poetry connects to Rafael's middle name, Angel.[112]

Likewise, for Lorde, the divide between care and revolution was nonexistent, particularly with regard to her cancer.[113] As she famously stated, care for the self was "not indulgence."[114] Rather, it was an act of "self-preservation" and "political warfare," especially for the institutionally forgotten surviving the crossroads of multiple attacks.[115] Audre extended this hard-earned lesson to others, counseling comrades like Pat Parker who were struggling with cancer to understand themselves as survivors of multiple wars. "You are a survivor, Pat," she movingly wrote in 1988 upon Pat Parker's diagnosis, "and that battle on a physical level is now braided into our lives, but the war is not alien, now, is it? You and me we've been fighting all our lives."[116] By contextualizing cancer as one more manifestation of oppression, Audre sought to kindle Parker's erotic power and direct it toward her survival as she had done to combat other manifestations of injustice. Audre's commitment to the erotic as a hallmark of social reproduction extended to the fight for one's very life.

As something that she freely and graciously shared with others, Audre's pathbreaking work to politicize her illness pointed toward *political* solutions, inspiring women with cancer and many lesbians who had been involved in the movement against AIDS but who did not enjoy the same level of support themselves.[117] Here the gender and race politics of breast cancer were critical, especially in a time when many had come to accept that AIDS/HIV was a political illness but would not extend the same analysis to the many queers and women of color who were diagnosed with cancer. As a "harbinger of public breast cancer conversations," Audre politicized previously naturalized violences, spurring collective action.[118] She played a particularly critical role among feminists who had previously been politicized in the women's health movement and through their care of gay men with AIDS, inspiring them to demand the same level of community care for their illnesses that they had provided for others.

As an expression of collective intimacy, promiscuous care also challenges the increasing stress upon the private home and state-sanctioned family as the privileged place to receive life-sustaining care that marked the neoliberal turn. Steven Vider's book *The Queerness of Home* further theorizes this by documenting a range of ways that well into the 1980s and 1990s queer communities resisted the privatization of home, instead working to remake "domestic spaces into spaces of community."[119] His chapters open up the home as a communal site, through efforts such as in-home buddy programs for those living with AIDS/HIV, radical collective living experiments, queer shelter activism, and group homes created for queer homeless youth.[120] As Vider illustrates, rather than simply acquiescing to privatized norms of conservative or homonormative family, communities worked to "realize new expressions of care and coalitional intimacy" by forging a "wide range of queer domestic forms."[121] Vider gives powerful examples of the ways that communities responded to John D'Emilio's plea to "dissolve the boundaries that isolate family" through the creation of collectively framed networks of belonging and kinship.[122]

In addition to refusing the terms of expendability, promiscuous care troubles the binary between service and organizing. As Ann Cvetkovich argues in her work on histories of ACT UP's lesbians, part and parcel of the work of lesbians caring for gay men dying of AIDS was the creation of an affective community.[123] Sociologist Deb Gould argues that one of the greatest legacies of ACT UP was its capacity to create "queer" emotions that did not dichotomize affects like rage and love.[124] Historian Christina Hanhardt offers a vivid example of this through late AIDS activist Rod Sorge, who argues that while the sharing of clean needles is lifesaving, equally vital is the trust and possible friendship that is formed in the respectful "interaction between the giver and the receiver of the needle."[125] These accounts all recast the realm of care as collective and central to the creation of a different world. By naming care work as something that is at once profoundly collective and political, they show how social movements challenged the state's attempts to consign the labor of reproduction to the private sphere in the face of an epidemic and, in so doing, to abdicate any responsibility for the public.

This entwinement of affect and politics courses through Audre's work toward intergenerational revolution. Audre understood that it was only through the love of children, one another, and ourselves that one could seed a radical livable future. As she writes, while "we know that all our work upon this planet is not going to be done in our lifetimes ... if we do what we came to do, our children will carry it on through their own living."[126] Audre understood that her reproductive labor in the home was in the service of the community as well; this lives on in Elizabeth, whose research involves HIV prevention and who credits her mother with her understanding of how to be an activist physician.[127]

PROMISCUOUS CARE AS ABOLITION IN PRACTICE

In all the examples above, promiscuous care explodes the so-called private domain of the family. This rejects the hyperindividualization of neoliberalism, decentering the private home as the privileged domain of care—a point that is particularly germane for queer communities, for whom, as Malatino reminds us, the family often functions as "a site of rejection, shunning, abuse, and discomfort."[128] Malatino urges consideration of that which happens in "the intricately interconnected spaces and places where trans and queer care labor occurs: the street, the club, the bar, the clinic, the community center, the classroom, the nonprofit," and so on.[129] By drawing attention to the intimate sphere outside the private home, Malatino challenges a framing of familial care that continually obscures the forms of trans care that may be precluded from the nuclear family proper.

Because it brings new worlds into being, promiscuous care can be seen as an example of "practicing new worlds" that abolitionist scholar and social justice lawyer Andrea Ritchie argues is vital for abolitionist movements.[130] As Ritchie argues, the work of abolition "calls upon us to practice new ways of relating, new forms of governance, and new ways of being that enable the worlds we want to emerge."[131] Promiscuous care exemplifies what Ritchie describes as an effort to "seek out new ways of thinking, doing, and being in everyday actions, with the intention of shifting large and complex systems and relations of power."[132] As a nonmonogamous practice that subverts the individualization of social relations, promiscuous care moves beyond the domain of the exclusive home. It thus offers us a concrete example of what it looks like to practice the kinds of social relations that are paramount to abolition—and a more just and livable world.

This shifting of the locus of care away from the private home also allows us to broaden understandings of family abolition to include the work of prison abolitionist groups like the Out Of Control Lesbian Committee to Support Political Prisoners (OOC), an organization that was formed in 1987 to support women political prisoners and oppose control units and supermax prisons. As community historian Brooke Lober and early member Jane Segal argue, OOC is particularly significant as a force against "the turn to neoliberal inclusion" and the continued expression of "a queer and feminist politics of racial and economic justice and in opposition to US imperialism at home and abroad."[133] While the mainstream arm of the LGBTQ rights movement was solidifying and agitating for the goals of inclusion, OOC-organized routine prison visits mitigated against the psychological torture of literal isolation and abandonment, forming vital lifelines of care that former political prisoner Susan Rosenberg credits with keeping her alive.[134]

By including actions like prisoner support as a mode of promiscuous care, this analysis refuses to forsake the revolutionary lives and dreams of movement protagonists such as political prisoners. This is especially important at the turn of the century, a time of the intense criminalization of dissent on a global scale. OOC's care work was vital to face the attempted erasure of radical possibility and the locking away of those who troubled the dominant order. Extending the accountability to support those who were pushed out of both the private home and public society, OOC practiced a form of promiscuous care that honored the lives of those who were quite literally thrown away by the state and much of society.

This insistence upon solidarity with the forgotten pushes back upon the "intimate investments" that, as I argue elsewhere, more privileged LGBTQ communities came to have in the prison-industrial complex in the 1990s and early 2000s.[135] OOC therefore challenged not only the state's attempts to erase an antiracist and anti-imperialist queer movement but also the mainstream LGBTQ community's increasing buy-in to this whitewashed world. Moreover, this sustained commitment to the creation of a world for all traces back to Cherríe and Audre. One of OOC's annual events was a fundraising and cultural event called "Sparks Fly" that featured comrades such as the Menominee Two Spirit poet Chrystos, who was an original contributor to *This Bridge.*

In creating networks of support and care, OOC contributed to expansive understandings of family abolition by facilitating mutual aid projects that crossed movements and prison walls. One prime example of this was the peer-to-peer AIDS education programs that Rosenberg organized along with Linda Evans, Marilyn Buck, Silvia Baraldini, and others behind bars— an initiative that engaged ACT UP and inspired prison solidarity programs outside the prison.[136] In her autobiography, Rosenberg also writes of the influence of African nationalist Dr. Mutulu Shakur within Black and Puerto Rican community acupuncture detox clinics in New York for shaping her under-standings of care.[137] Different strands of radical care thus con-verged to pose a challenge to the locking up of dissent—and the attempted erasure of radical consciousness—while articulating a continued radical queer politic of solidarity against US empire and the private family.

Last, it is important to consider the explicitly queer-of-color abolitionist practices that Shira Hassan's book *Saving Our Own Lives* gathers under the rubric of "liberatory harm reduction"—traditions that descend directly from these lineages at the cross-currents of prison and family abolition. Hassan's work coalesces at the intersections of disability justice, healing justice, and lib-eratory harm reduction, all of which carry forth the tenets of promiscuous care. As a survivor of childhood sexual abuse, Has-san owes her life to harm reduction efforts and describes the grassroots needle exchange program that helped her as an unhoused teenager in the 1990s.

Hassan pays homage to the Lincoln Detox Clinic, which was started by Dr. Shakur and where Rosenberg worked, thus locat-ing her work within a larger abolitionist genealogy. These efforts kept her alive, she writes, as a young person who used drugs and often lived on the streets outside her family's abusive home. Abolition as promiscuous care also informs Hassan's intergenerational work, and her eventual leadership, at the Young Women's Empowerment Project, an organization for young people of color in the sex trade, which is carrying the work forward to the next generation.

At the heart of Hassan's narrative are the horizontal lifesav-ing practices formed in activist peer-to-peer networks turned queer family. As she writes:

I owe my life to sex workers, to drug users, and to people called "mad" and "criminal" by much of the world. I owe my life to Black and Brown trans women, who worked daily to survive sometimes bone deep violence. Through their commitment to themselves and to community building, they led and mentored us and all of the crooked and wounded and glorious children who were dancing and clawing our way to safety through fashion and family. I owe my life to the House community whose Balls and club scenes were places where I felt my body was safe.... I owe my life to queers, to queens, to dykes, to butches and studs, to weirdos, to the community who knit family and meaning into the sacred and mundane, like meals and bathing.[138]

As an inheritor of and contributor to different care and mutual aid lineages, Hassan forms part of contemporary BIPOC queer disability justice frameworks, which claim the legacies of figures like Audre Lorde and Aurora Levins Morales, a contributor to *This Bridge*.[139] Exemplifying and reinterpreting these ideals, Hassan unabashedly celebrates the queerness of youth, and especially queer youth of color, whose ability to survive intense marginalization testifies to their strength and beauty. Bringing together prison abolition and family abolition, she resists the criminalization and pathologization of the survival strategies of the marginalized.

For Hassan, promiscuous care happens explicitly outside the bounds of the private nuclear family to challenge the criminalization and pathologization of communities that have been left behind. Here queer reproductive justice as radical bodily autonomy is practiced among those who are both directly targeted and surveilled by the state and rejected by the private family. Promiscuous care courses through family and prison abolition as a practice of collective survival and a continuation of prior radicalisms. This work is indispensable, especially in a time when, as Angela Davis puts it, a large class of people come to be classified as "human detritus" and thus "fodder" for prisons.[140] It is also indispensable in times when, as prior chapters have argued, central strands of LGBTQ movements have left behind the precise communities that Hassan addresses.

Hassan offers an alternative to this politics of expendability that begins with the inherent value and worth of the most socially marginalized as protagonists of a new world. Sharing in the daily rituals of living like meals, bathing, and dancing, her queer family cherishes and celebrates one another's "crooked" beauty, offering an embodiment of what it means to support youth to grow in whichever direction they must.[141] Hassan names the queer Ballroom scene, yet another example of the vibrant forms of queer family produced in the face of the extreme racism, homophobia, transphobia, and poverty of neoliberalism's reign.[142] What emerges instead is the generation of alternative family in the face of abandonment—and hence a family abolitionist praxis.

This rejection of expendability holds particular importance among LGBTQ communities in a time when, as Melinda Cooper reminds us, the dividing line between the in-group and the marginalized came to center upon whether one could conform to the values of "private family responsibility" and "claim the economic and public health protections of married monogamy."[143] Here Cooper names a further race, gender, and class stratification within LGBTQ communities at the turn of the century that was determined by one's ability to conform to the mandates of the private family. This only deepened the rift between those who had the resources and the gendered and racial privilege to play the part and those who did not. This racial and class divide has been mapped in earlier chapters that have traced more privileged sectors of LGBTQ movements, who have come to embrace forms of private nuclear family that rely upon hegemonic bionormativity, as well as the workings of the state to sanction only particular families as legitimate. In the face of this realignment, however, the movements that this section has traced emerged to insist upon the value of the so-called throwaway class by revalorizing the lives of those who either could not or refused to acquiesce to dominant norms.[144]

This scattered and diffuse geography brings us back to a core premise with which I started this chapter: that mapping the "sinewy" genealogies of abolitionist struggle can anchor us, especially in moments when struggles crest to break the surface of the present.[145] Generally held in silos, all of these efforts cohere to refuse a politics of respectability against the grain of homonormativity and queer domesticity and toward the abolition of the family, and the police, that erupted in 2020. In the concluding section that follows, I briefly examine how these histories reverberate into the present through Robyn Maynard and Leanne Betasamosake Simpson's book *Rehearsals for Living*.

REHEARSALS FOR LIVING

Rehearsals for Living foregrounds a vision of home and family that is rooted in reciprocity and care. The text is composed of a series of letters between two comrades that commenced in the early pandemic. In the book, Maynard and Simpson do not simply critique the multiple disasters that their respective Black and Michi Saagiig Nishnaabeg communities have borne. Rather, they articulate dreams of a different present and future that emerge from the ongoing acts of survival, world making, and care that their peoples have continually waged in the face of impossibility.

Throughout, the authors stress the importance of their children, offering other examples of honoring children's knowledge and freedom as integral to a collective future. They locate their hopes for a different present and future in the worlds that their children embody and inhabit. As Robin D. G. Kelley writes in his beautiful "Afterwor(l)d," Maynard and Simpson teach us just how much "our very survival depends on turning dreams of decolonization and abolition into action. They know this largely because of their children.... These children run, not for their lives, not out of fear, not to stake out territory, but because they are free."[146] Yet to be socialized into the violent rhythms of anti-Blackness and coloniality, these children access the other worlds that cannot be subsumed by capitalist progress, whiteness, and modernity. Children run as an act that taps them into their bodies, the land, and the activity of inhabiting freedom as a practice. Children are the source of knowledge and the portal into the possibility and necessity of a different world.

Maynard and Simpson also underscore the racial and colonial politics of the private family as a form of enclosure that must be opposed toward the realization of this future. In one letter, Simpson writes against the notion of home as enclosure. She draws from Black theorist Fred Moten to theorize the home and family as that which is constantly given away.[147] This reworked conception of home directly contradicts the ways that "the church, the state, and broader Canadian society" have "worked .... to surveil and confine Indigenous bodies and intimacies into Euro-Canadian heteropatriarchal marriages," and thus to force "monogamous relationships designed to reproduce the building blocks [of settlement]."[148] Simpson directly theorizes the enclosure of the private family and home to be an act of colonial conquest that must be resisted, transformed, and finally, abolished.

Additionally, *Rehearsals* chronicles the struggles that coalesced in 2020—a time when genealogies of family abolition crested the surface, taking form everywhere from experimental family "pods," to mutual aid networks, to disability justice work that challenged the expendability politics of the pandemic, to widescale protests against racist police violence—and the existence of prisons writ large. *Rehearsals* reflects a moment when many of the movements that this chapter has traced came to the fore; Maynard and Simpson speak in real time from the front lines of struggles on the streets and in the home. Maynard takes part, for example, in Black Lives Matter Toronto protests to abolish the police, only to be submerged within her memories of Ferguson of 2014, Idle No More, and the historic Oka revolt of Mohawk people in 1990.[149] Maynard understands these different events to be entwined, building upon one another and leading to the present in highly visible ways. She remarks that she and her comrades never thought that they would live to see the day when the word *abolition* hit the *New York Times*, and yet it is only so because of the painstaking labor of comrades past.[150] This brings to mind a point that began this chapter: it is only in the wake of a million struggles past—most of them invisible—that revolutions bubble to the surface, taking palpable form in ways we never could have anticipated.

Rehearsals therefore brings many of the genealogies of queer care to the present, bringing to mind the words of radical geographer and trans parent of color Jin Haritaworn, who argues that, in order to contribute to a world in which our children might be free, we would need to develop "methods [that are] ... as queerly expansive as our dreams ... [thus requiring] us to be both safe and promiscuous."[151] As Haritaworn elaborates, in order get to the world we need, we must both teach and learn from our children "how to take down drones and hate pages *and* grow food that withstands droughts"—an act that requires us to live far beyond the "privatized moulds that capitalism has designed for us," including family, racial capitalism, and nation.[152] Haritaworn rightfully attributes the activism that was popularized in the pandemic such as the formation of mutual aid networks and the creation of family pods to generations of BIPOC queer activists who invented these practices out of a long-standing attack that did not begin with the Covid pandemic. They also root this acknowledgment in a commitment to both listen to and teach our children. We must not only refuse the current world but also step into a new way of being that produces abundance in the face of wreckage.

Similarly, *Rehearsals* engages in prefiguration as a core of abolitionist and decolonial life. It is, at its core, a practice of literally crowding out our current bankrupt order with expressions of intimacy, care, and love. Through their care for one another, their children, and all their relations, Simpson and Maynard build "a society that turns towards, rather than away from, its forgotten places," so that it "stands to produce new ways ... of understanding 'public' and health'" in the throes of a pandemic.[153] Ultimately, these radical acts of imagining and acting out these other worlds open doors; Kelley muses that perhaps Maynard and Simpson's children have already "discovered the 'portal, a gateway between one world and the next'" that is needed to cross over into a place where all the earth's inhabitants can truly flourish.[154]

Ultimately, Maynard and Simpson invite us to work collectively as we all face "the end of the world[, which] ... promises nothing except a chance to make the world anew."[155] Against this history, Maynard and Simpson dream of a world in which their "kids and theirs grow old … free from nation-state, enclosure, private property, and all of the carceral mechanisms in place to protect it."[156] Here children's dreams offer us insight into the world we must build. Beyond the enclosure of the family, whiteness, and empire, the child runs free.

Dreams and Nightmares

Reproductive Dystopias, Reproductive Utopias

A Google search for "LGBTQ fertility and conception" in October 2021 yields a wide array of websites for venture capitalist–funded companies that promise to attend to the needs of marginalized communities. One of the top search results is Modern Fertility, a San Francisco–based firm that is especially savvy in its marketing. Featuring diverse physicians, mental health professionals, and fertility specialists, its website recognizes and validates the pains that are suffered by people who are trying to conceive. It also invokes the concerns of marginalized communities as a central strategy in its marketing of in-home hormone tests that can, as the website promises, measure fertility.

Finessed through queer-, feminist-, and trans-affirming rhetoric devised by "branding mastermind" Carly Leahy, the company is strategic in its acknowledgments of structural oppression.[1] While Dr. Nataki Douglas, a Yale PhD and MD, advises fellow Black women to empower themselves to "have positive, productive engagement with healthcare providers," another page dedicated to LGBTQ fertility advises queer, transgender, nonbinary, and gender-variant people how to navigate the fertility industry.[2] A heartfelt blog features LGBTQ+ couples' stories about overcoming medical discrimination, prohibitive cost barriers of ARTs, climate anxieties facing prospective parents, the overall challenges of trying to conceive during the COVID-19 pandemic, and more.[3]

With open discussions of climate anxiety, LGBTQ conception, and medical racism, Modern Fertility promises to respond to existential questions about family and parenthood in uncertain times, offering a solution to a relatively diverse group of people with non-normative pathways to parenthood. It also promises to ensure a more secure future, claiming to detect "silent issues" that might cause problems years down the line and offering a "customized dashboard [that tracks individual] ... reproductive timeline(s) compared to others [of the same] ... age."[4] In its marketing materials, cofounder Afton Vechery, a stylish, white, thin, heterosexual woman in her thirties, adds a personal touch, sharing the story about her struggle with polycystic ovary syndrome, a condition that can affect fertility. This positions her as sympathetic character with whom potential customers might identify—even across considerable differences of power and wealth.[5]

Despite the veneer of friendliness and inclusivity, shadows lurk behind the scenes. Modern Fertility's main blood test measures anti-Müllerian hormone (AMH)—a test that is often covered by routine insurance panels. It is now widespread medical consensus that this test is not a reliable marker of fertility.[6] The company also collects genetic data from its customers—which is not surprising given that Vechery is a former employee of 23andMe.[7]

Moreover, a financial history of the company reveals another twist: Modern Fertility was recently acquired for $225 million by Ro, a digital health company whose first products were erectile dysfunction and male hair loss medications.[8] Modern Fertility's product line is now featured on Ro's main webpage, which markets beauty and fertility products to women—and medications for men to improve sexual pleasure and performance. An icon reading "Better Understand Your Fertility" on the website's main page is positioned in a banner that also includes pills to help women to "Lose Weight with a Weekly Shot," "Grow Longer Lashes," and "Meet [their] Skin Goals," while men are enticed to "Have Better Sex" and "Last Longer in Bed" by simply clicking "purchase."[9] The articles written originally by Modern Fertility's health team have been "reviewed" and verified by Ro's physicians, whose names link to articles such as Ro's very own guide to penis enlargement.[10] Behind the slick ad copy, Modern Fertility's social justice credentials give way to its bottom line, reasserting a rigid gender binary that is rooted in heteronormativity, cisnormativity, and patriarchy. The acquisition of Modern Fertility by Ro lays bare the inherent contradictions of a "FemTech revolution" that aspires to merge the world of finance capital and unmet health needs of "women" within the confines of a neoliberal feminism.[11]

Modern Fertility allows us to pause to reflect back upon the core tenets of a queering reproductive justice praxis that this book has theorized. By manipulating LGBTQ+ people's desperate desires to have children, Modern Fertility's rhetoric feeds into the expansion of cis-heteronormative, neoliberal multiculturalist extractive economies. While Modern Fertility puts forward its fertility treatments as a route to "success," "feminism," and even "justice," it actually masks the kinds of inequalities and injustices that it reproduces.

Rooted in a commitment to intergenerational survival, however, queer reproductive justice offers alternative approaches, prioritizing the vantage point and needs of the most systematically disenfranchised—a group that lies outside Modern Fertility's customer base entirely. Queer reproductive justice entails a commitment to the abolition of harmful structures. It calls us toward the proliferation of promiscuous care as a means of de-privatizing the exclusive monogamous, wealthy, bionormative family—valuing the lives of those deemed surplus to the dominant global political order. It is a race and class politics that decenters US white life. Queer reproductive justice also challenges facile narratives of assimilation as progress—a principle that directly contradicts Modern Fertility's promise to bring desiring parents into the neoliberal market as a route toward nuclear private family. As such, queer reproductive justice orients us toward alternatives to the facile solutions to systemic reproductive injustices that Modern Fertility and venture capitalist–funded entrepreneurs promote.

FERTILITY BIO-CAPITALISM AND THE QUICK TECH FIX FOR A WORLD SPLIT OPEN

The story of the woke feminist and queer-affirming fertility technology sold to the highest bidder—a company initially created to market its own Viagra and help women lose weight—veers into self-parody. The logic of capitalism explodes as the reproductive-body-to-be is further converted into a site of wealth extraction within an industry that, as *The Economist* puts it, largely "plays on fear."[12] By seeking a diversified customer base, Modern Fertility exploits the desperation of aspiring parents, homing in on those for whom child-rearing and—a faith in the future in general—is often furthest away. As Vechery stated herself in an interview with *Fortune Magazine*, the idea of the company came together when she realized that so many millennials were waiting until their thirties and forties to have children because of an unstable economy, also adding that 20 percent of millennials identify as LGBTQIA, thus creating a perfect market for her brand.[13] Here Vechery understands structural insecurities as an opportunity for profit maximization, thus further obscuring a critical analysis of the needs, perceived and real, for fertility medicine. This dynamic plays into what feminist political theorist Jennifer Denbow calls the fertility frontier of bio-capitalism, which "promotes innovation as the answer to pressing questions of reproductive labor and ecological precarity while simultaneously foreclosing crucial questions about the root causes of these issues."[14]

By offering a quick tech fix for a vast array of "problems"—from medical racism, to the health consequences of chronic stress and oppression, to a lack of sperm or eggs, to actual medical infertility—fertility bio-capitalism further obscures the root problems that create barriers to and anxieties around reproduction in times when the future itself is in question.[15] Presented as a palliative and an uncontested social good, biotech solutions further entrench the power of investors and financial capitalism, even when these "products," like Modern Fertility's tests, are medically dubious. Such biotech fixes also privatize responsibility for the next generation within the reproductive neoliberal citizen who can access tools like Modern Fertility's products to demonstrate responsibility and self-care.[16]

This is dangerous because it further economically stratifies reproduction, also mystifying the many intersecting structural issues that pose barriers to child-rearing and raise insecurities about the future, as *Queering Families* has discussed. The speculative logic of finance bio-capitalism literally crowds out the radical imaginations of other futures that we need to build. In times of genocide in Palestine and beyond, it also further excludes the lives and futures of entire nations and communities that are posed as a hindrance to unending extraction and racial capitalist accumulation.

The Modern Fertilities of the world—and all that they represent—are cogent examples of what gets lost within LGBTQ+ family discourses that become entirely disarticulated from the radical politics of justice that this book has called for. Fertility bio-capitalism exploits desires for queer reproduction and draws from neoliberalism's capacity to convert marginalized bodies into a site of resource extraction. *Queering Families* has traced the consequences of this disarticulation in times when US empire and racial capitalism exploit the desire for a future among queer parents-to-be.

Fertility capitalism fuels bionormative hierarchies of family and the renorming of family as "biological," based upon popular and overly facile understandings of DNA and biological heredity that have been shaped by a variety of players. These influences range from the fertility industry itself, to politically connected religious and secular children's rights lobbyists, to major neoconservative funders, all the way to hundreds of grassroots influencers, activists, and policy organizations that proliferate on social media, often with the sponsorship of commercial DNA-testing companies. The discourses that emerge sideline queer histories of family making beyond the private nuclear family and silence the social constructedness of the genetic code, erasing the ways in which, to quote Sandra Patton-Imani, "all kinship relations are fictive."[17] This, in turn, further marginalizes modes of kinship that are not rooted through the Eurocentric models of privatized nuclear kinship, leading to troubling legal consequences, such as the loss of custody among "nonbiological" lesbian mothers—including the Oklahoma mom that I discussed in chapter 3 who lost custody to her child's sperm donor.[18]

Bionormativity also leads to policy agendas to restrict—and in some cases ban—gamete donation, criminalizing a donor's failure to disclose their criminal record and history of mental health, as in recent proposed legislation in New York that requires fertility providers to verify detailed "medical, educational, and criminal felony conviction history information" of all sperm and egg donors.[19] Dubbed "Steven's Law," this proposal was galvanized by the case of Laura and David Gunner, whose son, Steven, died of an opioid overdose after battling schizophrenia.[20] When Laura Gunner was inseminated, she was unaware of her donor's full medical history. The Gunners believe that Steven's death could have been avoided had they known this information—and they would have chosen a different donor.[21]

Steven's Law accompanies a rising tide of legislation nationally that asserts the primacy of gametes in establishing personhood *before* conception, furthering the idea of gamete personhood. This posits that everything—from one's future career, to one's most important familial relations—lies dormant in genes. Here the gamete itself is humanized as the source of personhood, which can be ranked in terms of eugenic categories of desirability according to hierarchies of ability, health, race, class, and more.[22]

The bionormative valorization of gamete personhood has troubling implications for reproductive justice in a post-*Dobbs* world, in which the codification of life beginning *before* conception sets precedence for further restrictions on abortion, contraception, and reproductive care.[23] For example, anti-ARTs groups like the Heritage Foundation–backed Center for Bioethics and Culture and Them Before Us seek to attribute life not only to the fetus but to the embryo—a position that is especially alarming amid moves in multiple states to classify abortion as homicide.[24] Feminist anthropologist Risa Cromer tracks the ascendency of the Far Right's Personhood Movement, which argues not only that life begins before birth with the embryo and zygote but that it begins before conception itself with the gamete. Positing that "each individual human life has an unalienable right to life from its earliest biological origins," the Personhood Movement confers legal personhood on fetuses, embryos, zygotes, and—increasingly, and especially in the wake of the *Dobbs* decision—gametes, denouncing many forms of birth control and abortion, even after rape and incest.[25] Meanwhile, we bear witness to the accelerated killings of already-born children, from Palestine to criminalized communities within the United States.

Importantly, while proponents of Steven's Law may not explicitly align with this antichoice politics, the law does work to further stretch the category of what legal scholar Cynthia Soohoo calls "the zygote-embryo-fetus as a legal person."[26] Steven's Law takes this logic even further to posit that life inheres within the gamete itself. This further locates the essence of personhood before birth, subjecting parents-to-be to state and social regulation—and with disproportionate effects upon LGBTQ, single, and infertile people, posing imminent risks, in particular to Black, Indigenous, and poor communities of color that are already subject to heightened reproductive surveillance.

While fetal personhood makes the fetus subject to state regulation and protection, embryonic and gamete personhood both make it possible for the state to intervene into the prereproductive body in what is constructed to be the best interest of the child-to-be. This is, by definition, ableist because it is geared toward preventing the birth of disabled life. It also, in turn, feeds into the kinds of moral panics that always target queer families and communities, and especially those with the least institutional power.

Bionormative ideologies also advance neo-eugenic understandings of reproduction, health, and mental illness, seeking to restrict reproduction among certain people. The implications of geneticizing criminality are dangerous, especially without a detailed discussion of the ways in which racialized identities themselves are inherently criminalized. Instead, we must reckon with the ways that criminalization is itself a process that reinforces hierarchies of race, class, and more. The project of queering reproductive justice is antithetical to the racist and simplistic construction of criminality as an essentialist and heritable trait.

Furthermore, the geneticization of all health conditions sounds the alarm bell for disability justice movements wary of the eugenic underpinnings of "screening" for disabilities in order to restrict who can reproduce and be born, foreclosing critical questions about the underlying social conditions of our communities. For example, Steven Gunner's tragic death by opioid overdose must be contextualized. His death is no anomaly in his hometown of East Aurora, New York, which has been facing an opioid epidemic. Papered over by medically controversial claims about genetic heredity, this fact must be addressed on a structural level as we build movements to transform the underlying conditions that lead to the loss of life.

As this book has argued more broadly, we must pay attention to how biogenetic cultural understandings mask the ways that the sanctioning of reproduction serves racist, colonialist, heterocentric, capitalist, and ableist agendas. The geneticization of life does little to cocreate a better world with and for future generations. It gets us further and further away from the forms of relationship and kinship building that we need to survive.

Offering alternatives, *Queering Families* has raised questions about what kinds of worlds LGBTQ family-building practices engender. Reading beneath the surface is vital if we are to support the projects of queering reproductive justice. What ideologies and practices do our practices of building families and worlds together promote? Are they world-making or world-destroying? Which lives do they enable or disenable? Such questions underscore a key argument of this book: that our work to build queer families and worlds for future generations must come into alignment with abolition and decolonization as the fundamental justice struggles of our times.

EXTRACTIVE ECONOMIES AND THE FAMILY REGULATION SYSTEM

The discussion above points to the need to think deeply about the implications of fertility bio-capitalism. However, it does not stop here. As I first completed this epilogue, the majority-conservative Supreme Court delivered an unexpected victory in a landmark case regarding adoption law and the fate of Native American children. In *Haaland v. Brackeen* (2023), plaintiffs sought to undermine the Indian Child Welfare Act (ICWA), the 1978 law that intended to help Native American children remain within their families and communities of origin, arguing that ICWA discriminated against non-Native peoples.[27]

Created in a time when about one-third of Native children had been removed from their families, ICWA serves as a vital safeguard against the tradition of the state-sanctioned kidnapping of Native American children.[28] Brought forth by the Texas-based white Evangelical adoptive parents of a Diné child, the case to destroy it hinged legally upon a decision over whether Native people are a racial group or are classified as sovereign nations. Had Native Americans been reclassified as a race, ICWA could have been declared to be a form of racial discrimination, and therefore in violation of the Fourteenth Amendment's equal protection clause.

The case thus relied upon the noxious claim that white people can be victims of racial discrimination—a particular passion of members of the Brackeens' legal team, and one that the recent catastrophic dismantlement of affirmative action by the same Supreme Court has reified.[29] For example, in Justice Thomas's dissenting opinion, he failed to acknowledge Native Americans as sovereign nations, arguing that the decision offered unwarranted privileges to "Indians who were also citizens and who lived within the sole jurisdiction of States . . . merely because the children involved happen to be Indians."[30] Both Thomas's language and the plaintiffs' arguments thus fed into a larger neoconservative legal strategy that, as chapter 2 discussed, increasingly frames white heterosexual Christian families as victims of discrimination.

By working to dismantle one of the few safeguards to keeping Native children within their communities, the Brackeens' legal case threatened to erode ICWA as an instrument of reproductive justice that was crafted to combat four hundred years of reproductive injustice waged upon Native communities.[31] This historical context was noted in Justice Gorsuch's opinion, in which he positioned ICWA as "a direct response to the mass removal of Indian children from their families ... by state officials and private parties [and] a much older policy of removing Indian children from their families—one initially spearheaded by federal officials with the aid of their state counterparts nearly 150 years ago."[32] A victory for the Brackeens would have rendered many Native children more "adoptable" to white and other non-native settler families, further fueling a system of family regulation that routinely makes it impossible for marginalized families to stay together.

Despite this victory, the discussion was still plagued by the long-standing assumption that white settler nuclear families provide more stability and opportunity to children.[33] This savior complex ideology was perpetuated in Justice Alito's dissent, in which he gave platitudes to the "loving non-Indian couple(s)" offering "stable" homes to Native children, arguing that the decision forced courts to betray the "the best interests of children."[34] Alito's language propagates the deep-rooted colonial idea that settlers offer more stable and appropriate homes to Native children than their families and communities of origin, or other Native communities. By suggesting that ICWA deprives Native children of their "best interest," Alito promotes the weaponization of the rhetoric of children's "best interest" that *Queering Families* has critiqued.

This case also brings many of the structural tensions of the family regulation system to the fore. Chapter 2 discussed *Marouf v. Becerra*, a case that involved a lesbian couple who sued the state for the "right" to adopt unaccompanied migrant minors.

The Brackeen case brought up many issues similar to those of *Marouf v. Becerra*, highlighting the political dangers of a superficial proadoption stance that declares LGBTQ adoption a social justice issue, regardless of the conditions and context. As chapter 2 argued, extreme cases like these reveal the deeper problems of a family regulation system that rips children away from their rightful kin in both dramatic and insidious ways. Like *Marouf v. Becerra, Haaland v. Brackeen* carries with it important implications for the fight for queer family, even if the initial litigants in the case are Evangelicals who oppose LGBTQ adoption. As such, it brings into focus the pitfalls of an uncritical fight for LGBTQ adoption that does not attend to larger power imbalances that routinely lead to the state-sanctioned removal of children from marginalized communities.

As *Queering Families* has argued, queer reproductive justice struggles must align with movements to transform the conditions confronted by communities that have been repeatedly destabilized by generations of imperialism, colonialism, war, racism, prisons, ecocide, and poverty.[35] These conditions are continually exploited through the forced removal of children, which all justice movements must adamantly oppose. Cases such as these highlight the embedded violences within a family regulation system that is an extension of slavery, settler colonialism, and border imperialism.

However, with *Haaland v. Brackeen*, it was not only the fate of children that was at stake. By working to define Native people as a racial class rather than sovereign nations, the case held the potential to dismantle Native American sovereignty writ large. This would have meant that Native nations could have lost all treaty rights over their lands. As Cherokee journalist Rebecca Nagle argued prior to the ruling, this was the case that might "break Native American sovereignty" because if Native Americans were reclassified as a "race" rather than sovereign nations, the ruling could have cleared the legal grounds to dissolve all tribes' relationships to the federal government.[36] This might have "position[ed] ICWA as the first domino to fall, potentially leading to the erosion—or total erasure—of Native rights in the only homelands Indigenous North Americans have ever known," to cite the Lakota Law Project.[37]

The effort to undermine ICWA offers another example of child-as-proxy logic that this book has discussed, extending the state's civilizing mission under the aegis of helping children. Funded by oil and gas companies and conservative think tanks like the Bradley and Goldwater Foundations, the Brackeens were represented pro bono by Gibson Dunn—the same law firm that represented oil companies in the Dakota Access and Line 3 pipelines.[38] These supporters have no interest in adoption policy per se. The dismantlement of ICWA was a front for unending extraction and plunder, using the mythology of the white savior and children's best interest as a Trojan horse.

This case underscores the grave dangers of a myopic proadoption agenda that does not attend to important social issues, including the devastating removal of children from their rightful communities. The fight to dismantle ICWA thus stood as a direct assault upon the ways that "Indigenous people are trying to drag the people of this land into the twenty-first century by advocating for the protection of healthy water and land, the very elements necessary for all life, a true universal aspiration for a future on a livable planet that benefits everyone," as Nick Estes argues.[39] As Estes also reminds us, this victory came only through tireless organizing efforts of tribes and activists— efforts that must be continual.[40] Ongoing "actions must be taken to ensure the collective rights of tribes are guarded against the individual and corporate desires to lay claim to Native lands, identities and children."[41] Intervening into these dynamics on a sustained basis is imperative if we are to halt the ongoing ecocide that imperils us all.

REPRODUCTIVE DYSTOPIAS, REPRODUCTIVE UTOPIAS

The nightmarish scenarios of fertility bio-capitalism and the family regulation system analyzed above sound a somber warning to anyone who wishes to shepherd in future generations of all living creatures who need healthy ecosystems. This holds true whether the resources being looted are Native lands or one's health fertility data that becomes encoded through platforms. There are no market-based solutions under racial capitalism that will deliver generations-to-be into the just futures that they deserve. The LGBTQ family cannot be a vehicle for the state's relentless drive toward extraction and the carceral state's relentless locking down of anyone who is inconvenient to its dominant worldview. It cannot be a means for the state's violent imperial securing of borders through kidnapping. Nor will the worlds we need be delivered through the technology of a "$2 billion women's fertility industry [that operates] on the premise that women should track their fertility like they track their steps."[42] These are the nightmares that threaten to be propagated in the name of an uncritical politics of queer family that is not attentive to these larger political commitments.

And yet, just beyond the purview of these nightmares lie other possibilities that *Queering Families* has examined. Arguing for a queer politics of reproductive justice and family abolition, this book has reanimated some of the lost dreams and radical experiments toward the creation of family, kin, and love that move us beyond such impasses. Chapters 1 and 4 offered histories of abolitionist and decolonial modes of remaking queer family centered on an insistence upon abiding care for the most marginalized in times of abandonment. These chapters revitalize radical queer experiments to collectivize family and to abolish the private nuclear private family—from intimate projects that intend to subvert parent/child hierarchies within the family, to the creation of large-scale activist efforts of collective love, care, and support to uphold and cherish communities that have been abandoned and forgotten by the state. Reproductive dystopias require us to draw novel solidarities in complicated times, but reproductive utopias can be claimed as well.

I draw the term *reproductive utopias* from Dorothy Roberts's 2009 article "Race, Gender, and Genetic Technologies: A New Reproductive Dystopia?"[43] In the article, Roberts analyzes the encroachment of reproductive technologies into the everyday lives of a wide spectrum of people. She theorizes the policing of human life that targets the reproductive body through a system that reinforces uneven but entwined oppression across an array of positionalities. Both elite and poor women, Roberts argues, are oppressed, though in very different ways, by a reproductive dystopia in which a "neoliberal trend toward privatization and punitive governance" shifts the onus for the proper reproduction of society to the individual reproductive body.[44] Within this dystopia, all reproductive bodies are subject to a system that "shifts responsibility for promoting well-being from the government to the individual by making women responsible for ensuring the genetic fitness of their children."[45]

Roberts's formulation of this "reproductive dystopia" enables a structural analysis that binds different reproductive bodies together. As scholars of racial capitalism and the opioid epidemic argue, biotechnology is one major site of racial capitalist production that reveals the stakes of cross-racial and cross-class solidarities that are required to abolish Whiteness as a system. Under racial capitalism, biotechnological innovations first and foremost kill "Black and Brown people."[46] Yet as the overdose epidemic starkly illustrates, the system does not stop short of harming white people who stand in its way. Authors Helena Hansen, Jules Netherland, and David Herzberg theorize racial capitalism's extraordinary ability to use biotechnologies to extract wealth from differentially racialized bodies in uneven but interlinked ways. This analysis resonates with that of Roberts, which reveals hidden links between various positionalities within an entwined system of reproductive regulation that violates everyone whose reproduction is under biogenetic surveillance and control.

Roberts's analysis of reproductive dystopia enables us to see a potential for common cause among those struggling in very different ways, from consumers of Modern Fertility's products to tribes fighting the dismantlement of ICWA. These links challenge the false binary between reproductive justice and queering reproduction and in turn clear space for the kind of coalitional thinking that *Queering Families* has advocated.

To these ends, Roberts offers a vision of reproductive utopia, founded on solidarity and shared resistance. "I ... imagine," she writes, "a new utopia arising from feminists' radical resistance to enlisting women as genetic screeners in service of a neoliberal agenda, a resistance that is emboldened by new alliances—

joining reproductive justice with antiracist, disability rights, and economic justice movements that recognize their common interest in contesting a race-based repro-genetic future."[47] Roberts calls for bold new alliances to resist the ways that the reproductive body is a prime site of governance and control. As Natalie Fixmer-Oraiz and Shui-yin Sharon Yam argue, "A queer reproductive justice framework demands communities and advocates from different positionalities to collectively reimagine and expand family structures and formations while remaining in solidarity with LGBTQ+ families who continue to negotiate their precarity."[48] The framework of reproductive utopia prompts larger questions about how we work collectively toward a world that sustains life for future generations, aligning with core tenets of a queer reproductive justice politics that is inherently coalitional.

Unearthing these links, as *Queering Families* has contended, is essential for moving beyond a politics that pits possible and necessary allies and co-strugglers against one another. Roberts's analysis offers one concrete way to engage with the necessity of demanding nothing less than reproductive utopia in our times. This nuanced thinking grows ever more important in times when, as Alexis Pauline Gumbs notes, "many queer families face the reality that the state will track down sperm donors and treat them as fathers in order to avoid giving lesbian parents state assistance," whereas "there is also a precedent for affirming lesbian and gay custody of children when it serves the state's financial interest."[49] Gumbs describes a contradictory system of family regulation and reproductive injustice that targets and privileges different races, classes, and genders of queer families. This, as *Queering Families* has argued, is a flexible system that strategically builds up and tears down different queer families.

While neoconservatives ruthlessly attack LGBTQ families and children within a broader culture war, neoliberals offer tepid support when, and only when, it serves the austerity state under racial capitalism, settler colonialism, and border imperialism.

Within this context, it becomes imperative that we generate analyses that locate the contradictions and friction points within a system that relentlessly exploits the claim to reproductive justice—the right to have children, the right to not have children, and the right to raise our children in healthy and life-affirming environments—that all communities must make. Moreover, it allows us to further develop a praxis that demands the honoring of kinship relations that defy the austerity state's relentless projects of extraction.

ALL ABOARD THE FREEDOM EXPRESS AND THE INTERGENERATIONAL PREFIGURING OF NEW WORLDS

As *Queering Families* has argued, the modes of justice for which we must fight extend far beyond the domain of gestation and procreation, into the actual world-building work that we do with and for our children. This requires that we prefigure worlds that will ultimately build "a society that turns towards, rather than away from, its forgotten places," as Robyn Maynard and Leanne Simpson put it.[50] These questions were dredged up during the COVID-19 pandemic, providing a broader audience for movement communities to raise questions about the worlds we must deliberately build for collective survival. This section examines one particular project that seized these political openings to engage in deliberate intergenerational world building.

As Arundhati Roy famously wrote in 2020, at its best, the pandemic might serve as an opportunity, offering a "portal, a gateway between one world and the next," inviting us to "imagine"—and embody—the "world anew."[51] One powerful example of this work can be found in a children's coloring book, *All Aboard the Freedom Express*, that was cowritten by Diana Rosario, Karen Hurtado, Karina Hurtado-Ocampo, and Brittney Washington. This collective of self-identified "frontline, women-identified artists of color" grew up in the same apartment building in Jackson Heights, New York City, and came together to write the book during the height of the pandemic as they engaged in "the solidarity economy via mutual aid, cop watching, child and elder care and community fridges," as they write in their artist statement.[52]

Available for free online, the book offers an exercise in prefiguration for young people as they are taken into a speculative future that invites them to imagine a better world. Narrated by a gender-queer protagonist of color named Sol, the book invites the young reader into a world after a time called "the *big transition,*" which followed a time when "it was normal for families to go hungry, to be separated, live without homes, and the planet to be destroyed."[53] By naming the "normalcy" experienced by the current young reader, the authors critique the routine horrors that youth currently experience and present the possibility of a very different world that must be built.

Sol takes the reader through an experience that resists the injuries of development and compulsory socialization into a broken world. In the book, the building that used to be a Chevron station is now a care center.[54] The roads are opened up only to foot traffic with no cars allowed and with a sign that reads

"Ritual Road," where the reader is invited to breathe.[55] A communal "Food Forest" brings together hungry humans and bees and butterflies. A housing cooperative named after Sylvia Rivera and Marsha P. Johnson is powered by solar panels and wind turbines, which leads to a lesson about clean energy.[56] All of these images invite parents and children to discuss the limitless possibilities for transformation, engaging intergenerational imaginations and conversations.

A central theme of *All Aboard the Freedom Express* is the power of collective organizing and the necessity of working together to resolve any problem. After a discussion of the wind turbines that power the city, for example, the book explains that "it's not just the fancy technology that lets us live in harmony with the earth … [because] … making decisions together about the things that will impact us every day gives us life!"[57] Here it is not the lure of big-tech fixes but rather collective commitments to one another that enable intergenerational communities to flourish. The tour of the city also leads children to a freedom circle where community members practice transformative justice to talk through disagreements and make decisions.[58] Sol invites the reader to imagine a world in which there is always the chance to "talk with healers who can help when we have big disagreements with each other."[59] They remind the reader that "building the future can be hard work," but turtle island is always a place where anyone can return to find six important tools: roots, connections, commitments, breaths, joys, and safe spaces.[60] This, in turn brings to reality our capacity to self-govern in ways that turn conflicts into opportunities to heal and grow, with the carceral state far from view. *All Aboard the Freedom Express* therefore models an insistence upon collective community-generated solutions to our problems, thus taking up themes of abolition that were discussed in chapter 4.

A consistent question runs through the book: What drains you and what sustains you? Examples of radical and life-affirming sustainability that are embedded in the community gardens include the care center where someone can always receive a hug and the recurrent metaphor of mangrove trees whose "strong roots help us withstand big storms."[61] The book ends with a parting gift: a "life watch that will tell you when something in your world gives life or drains it" and an invitation to return to the book whenever a child is feeling drained.[62] This concept welcomes youth to become aware of their inner capacities and limitations, offering the radical suggestion that they have the autonomy to draw boundaries when they are being drained. This also suggests that energy and rejuvenation are abundant and there for the claiming. This lesson of abundance cuts against the harsh lessons of racial capitalism, isolation, and catastrophe. Instead, it affirms the child's welcome into the beautiful imaginative worlds that are spaces for refuge and for the regeneration of energy and care.

This is an embodied journey, and throughout the book, mini-lessons on self-care and community sustenance interlace the story. For example, on one page Sol picks a mango that brings so much joy that they dance and sing.[63] This scene invites children to reflect upon what brings them joy and how they express happiness. "Did you know that deep joy gives life to our brains?"[64] Creating a moment for reflection, feeling, and stillness, the book calls readers into the pleasures of imagination and remembrance of all that is rich and beautiful about life. This is accompanied by other similar moments, such as an invitation to drink water as life at the start of the book, and an invitation to breathe that allows young readers to develop meditation practice.

Selectively colored but with many blank spaces to fill in, *All Aboard the Freedom Express* offers an opportunity for the reader to draw her worlds, ideas, and dreams into the story. At the end of the text is a study and discussion guide that also fosters intergenerational discussion on these themes between children and caring adults. This offers guidance not only for children but for parents who are working to heal the ruptured relationships with one another, our communities, and our planet.

The alternative reality engendered through *All Aboard the Freedom Express* embodies the abolitionist principle of crowding out dysfunctional systems with those that sustain and affirm life. It concretizes this praxis in action, inviting everyone—children and adults alike—to color in the spaces. All of these larger principles are embodied in Creative Wildfire, a project that funds artists like Rosario, Hurtado, Hurtado-Ocampo, and Washington to conduct community-engaged art projects. Led by the Climate Justice Alliance, Movement Generation, and the New Economy Coalition, Creative Wildfire issued a document in 2021 called the "Creative Wildfire Manifesto" that mirrors many of these values.[65] As authors of the manifesto explain, in the face of many different wildfires current conditions are "changing life as we know it." The authors call upon all of us to enact a bold and revolutionary commitment to a generative economy and the building of new worlds. They write:

> As communities on the frontlines, we study and learn from the freedom dreams and actions of our elders and ancestors. The ones who sowed the seeds to restore community self-determination that we see sprouting up today. The ones who broke the rules to change the rules. We carry forward their labors of love and struggles for

dignity, inspiring us to prepare and plan for the ecological ruptures that they knew were coming. We carry the strength and wisdom of our lineages to create the worlds we need, again.[66]

The beautiful image features ancestors sowing seeds that come to fruition in modern places of work, however often we may stumble in the face of pain and catastrophe. The authors remind us that collective survival is always rooted in utopic vision and radical memory, drawing from "the strength and wisdom of our lineages to create the worlds we need, again."[67] Importantly, this work does not happen from scratch; rather, as *Queering Families* has argued, it is part of larger lineages and genealogies of struggle that we must rekindle and reclaim. As an explicitly intergenerational project, part of the work of building these worlds is an honoring of ancestors—those "who sowed the seeds to restore community self-determination that we see sprouting up today."[68] This project reaches forward to foster this work among youth whose imaginations and dreams already reside in these other worlds. It is these intergenerational connections that *Queering Families* has sought to support.

CODA: HOPE

What is at stake in the bearing of a child, biologically or not? In the cultivation of life? In the ushering in of life forms that overlap with ours, but that neither begin nor end with us? I rise to feed my newborn at 3 a.m. in summer 2020. Wildfire smoke wafts into the bedroom as I check my phone for news about protests erupting across the country in response to the murder of George Floyd, the father of five who was killed while calling for his mama the week that our second baby was born. I grasp for clarity. What is the unattainable price of life in these times? What does it mean to bring generations into this world?

The words of Grace Lee Boggs pierce through my haze. "We need a vision that recognizes that we are at one of the great turning points in human history," she reminds us.[69] Boggs's words reach through my deep malaise, sparking memory in a time when every place I have ever called home up and down the West Coast is on fire. She teaches us that nothing less than revolution is required amid a "Great Turning," which is a time "when the survival of our planet and the restoration of our humanity require a great sea change in our ecological, economic, political, and spiritual values."[70] This idea brings clarity, affirming for me that it is not only our young children who are being asked to enter into shifting realities. We, too are being called into—and to make—the world anew.

Written against this backdrop, *Queering Families* has theorized the deeper stakes of queer family making in these times of ever-heightening contradiction. Because queer family so often involves painstaking intentionality among those for whom intergenerational kinship is not a birthright, it frequently becomes a flashpoint for fraught questions about the reproduction of our world. Whose children will be brought into this world? How? Under whose authority? Which futures will the earth's children inhabit? And what does this mean in times of acute heart-shattering genocide? These questions only intensify amid the Great Turning, driving home the stakes of *Queering Families:* the sustenance and continuation of sacred life itself.

In the time that I have written this book, that newborn has turned into a lively, free-spirited preschooler. As I often catch myself thinking, her sheer will and determination alone might be powerful enough to make the world spin in new directions. The depth and wisdom with which our eldest child entered the world have been shaped by the novel pandemic that framed their transition from babyhood into childhood. This reality splits my heart wide open in pain. At the same time, this reality brings joy, reminding me that the pandemic has offered a refuge from her compulsory socialization into the ugly worlds that no child should occupy. In the frantic drive to reimpose "the normal," the powers that be have yet to resolve fundamental questions about which futures the earth's children will inhabit—and who those children will be—a fact that is made excruciating as we bear witness to the cold-blooded massacre of Palestinian children in the face of much global complicity. Simultaneously, we watch global movements rise to fight back. Boggs's declaration that we remain in the throes of a sea change and a massive push against the restabilizing status quo reminds me that the future remains open and our struggles remain necessary.

As Black Lives Matter activist and writer Mai'a Williams writes in her book *Revolutionary Mothering on the Front Lines:*

> I want us to love and thrive and recreate the world in the image of joy and laughter. I want our humanity to survive into the next century. On this planet. With these plants and these songs and these myths and dreams and hopes and stories and skills. I want us to be whole and intact, with our ancient traditions of healing and celebrating and mourning. And the only way we are going to be able to do this is to take care of each other.[71]

Williams writes of the ultimate dreams she holds for her child, thus modeling what it means to take up Boggs's radical call to coconstruct the new realities that projects like *All Aboard the*

Freedom Express also build. This echoes June Jordan's radical call to honor youth's dreams with our lives that chapter 4 discussed. Continuing in this Black feminist lineage, Williams offers a wish, a prayer, and a form of guidance that can anchor us in our collective work. She speaks of the practices of care that must imbue our approach to our children but also the entire world. We have no time or energy for anything less amid many storms and fires that rage and continue to await us.

Queering Families aspires to contribute to this vision and to traverse the vast gulfs between the awe and hope of our children and a dawning sense of dread over an increasingly uninhabitable world. I thus write with everything on the line, well aware that most parents throughout history have never had a guarantee about children's futures. This feels especially poignant as I humbly reflect upon the legacy of parents who have always brought children into worlds riddled by slavery, genocide, apocalypse, war: worlds ablaze. *Gaza we will never forget.*

Hope is an insistence upon prefiguring the futures our children deserve through a fierce engagement with the present that opens into endless possibility. Current organizers speak of hope as a discipline and collective practice. Hope for one's children, it occurs to me, entails an unflinching commitment to sharing the intimate and immediate present with our children. This requires a dedication to cohabitate their worlds, which have yet to be curtailed by the harsh stories of a future already foreclosed.

Love compels us toward a future, even as we wander through the wreckage. Children bring into our lives a reverence for and belief in the miraculous, offering a window into a transformed world befitting future generations that we must build if we want it to become manifest. "If we can keep this earth spinning and remain upon it long enough," Lorde writes, "the future belongs to us and our children because we are fashioning it with a vision rooted in human possibility and growth, a vision that does not shrivel before adversity."[72] This project is my attempt to do just that.

NOTES

INTRODUCTION

1. adrienne m. brown, *Emergent Strategy: Shaping Change, Changing Worlds* (Chico, CA: AK Press, 2017), 12.

2. June Jordan and Terri Bush, eds., *The Voice of the Children* (San Francisco: Holt, Rinehart, and Winston, 1968), 92–93.

3. Henry A. Giroux, *America's Education Deficit and the War on Youth: Reform beyond Electoral Politics* (New York: NYU Press, 2013); Arshad Imtiaz Ali and Tracy L. Buenavista, eds., *Education at War: The Fight for Students of Color in America's Public Schools* (New York: Fordham University Press, 2018).

4. Vic Barrett, "'This Is Our Time. This Is Our Future.' Voices from the Historic Youth Climate Strike in NYC," *Democracy Now!*, September 23, 2019, www.youtube.com/watch?v=Eb_vAYVgbeI; Greta Thunberg, "Transcript: Greta Thunberg's Speech at the U.N. Climate Action Summit," National Public Radio, September 23, 2019, www.npr.org/2019/09/23/763452863/transcript-greta-thunbergs-speech-at-the-u-n-climate-action-summit.

5. Palestinian Feminist Collective, "The Palestinian Feminist Collective Condemns Reproductive Genocide in Gaza," May 27, 2024,

https://palestinianfeministcollective.org/the-pfc-condemns-reproductive-genocide-in-gaza/.

6. Ruha Benjamin, "Black AfterLives Matter: Cultivating Kinfulness as Reproductive Justice," in *Making Kin Not Population: Reconceiving Generations*, ed. Adele E. Clarke and Donna Haraway (Chicago: Prickly Paradigm Press, 2018), 42–65.

7. Dorothy Roberts, *Shattered Bonds: The Color of Child Welfare* (New York: Basic Books/Civitas, 2001); Rickie Solinger, *Beggars and Choosers: How the Politics of Choice Shapes Adoption, Abortion, and Welfare in the United States* (New York: Macmillan, 2001).

8. Daniel Rivers, "'In the Best Interests of the Child': Lesbian and Gay Parenting Custody Cases, 1967–1985," *Journal of Social History* 43, no. 4 (2010): 917–43.

9. Rivers, "In the Best Interests of the Child."

10. Kate Shellnutt, "America's Largest Christian Adoption Agency Lets LGBT Couples Foster in 1 of 35 States," *Christianity Today*, April 25, 2019, www.christianitytoday.com/news/2019/april/bethany-christian-services-michigan-foster-lgbt-couples.html.

11. Hannah Dreier, "Searching for the Faces of Migrant Child Labor: Times Insider," *New York Times*, March 3, 2023, www.nytimes.com/2023/03/03/insider/searching-for-the-faces-of-child-migrant-labor.html.

12. Of course, many queer peoples engage in procreative sex, just as many who identify as heterosexual do not reproduce through coital reproduction. This book primarily engages with those for whom conception, pregnancy, childbirth, and child-rearing are not an outcome of procreative sex, and thus for whom parenthood is queered regardless of individual identity.

13. Tiffany Lethabo King, "Black 'Feminisms' and Pessimism: Abolishing Moynihan's Negro Family," *Theory and Event* 1, no. 1 (2018): 68–87; Sophie Lewis, *Full Surrogacy Now: Feminism against Family* (London: Verso, 2019); Zoe Belinsky, "Gender and Family Abolition as an Expansive and Not Reductive Process," Medium, September 11, 2019, https://medium.com/@malkekvmachashayfele/gender-and-family-abolition-as-an-expansive-and-not-reductive-process-d933f1f-

71da2; Tamara Lea Spira et al., "ACAB Means Abolishing the Cop in Our Heads, Hearts, and Homes: An Intergenerational Demand for Family Abolition," in *Abolition Feminisms: Feminist Ruptures against the Carceral State*, ed. Alisa Bierria, Jakeya Caruthers, and Brooke Lober (Chicago: Haymarket Books, 2022), 13–43.

14. Cherríe Moraga, *Waiting in the Wings: Portrait of a Queer Motherhood* (New York: Firebrand Books, 1997), 65.

15. Neoliberal amnesia, as I elaborate elsewhere, can be defined by the trading in of historical memory for the seductive lure of inclusion, however provisional, as well as what Henry Giroux adds are the "spectacles of consumerism, celebrity culture, hyped-up violence, and a market-driven obsession with the self." Henry A. Giroux, "Living in the Age of Imposed Amnesia: The Eclipse of Democratic Formative Culture," Truthout, November 16, 2010, https://truthout.org/articles/living-in-the-age-of-imposed-amnesia-the-eclipse-of-democratic-formative-culture/; Anna M. Agathangelou, Morgan Bassichis, and Tamara Lea Spira, "Intimate Investments: Homonormativity, Global Lockdown, and the Seductions of Empire," *Radical History Review*, no. 100 (2008): 120–43.

16. C. Moraga, *Waiting in the Wings*, 35.

17. For more on the cancer epidemic among Black and queer-of-color feminists of this time, see Aimee M. Cox, Aishah Shahidah Simmons, and Tamura A. Lomax, "Take Care: Notes on the Black (Academic) Women's Health Forum," *Feminist Wire*, November 12, 2012, https://thefeministwire.com/2012/11/take-care-notes-on-the-black-academic-womens-health-forum/; Grace Hong, "'The Future of Our Worlds': Black Feminism and the Politics of Knowledge in the University under Globalization," *Meridians* 8, no. 2 (2008): 95–115; Myisha Priest, "Salvation Is the Issue," *Meridians* 8, no. 2 (2008): 116–17.

18. C. Moraga, *Waiting in the Wings*, 22.

19. M. Jacqui Alexander, *Pedagogies of Crossing: Meditations on Feminism, Sexual Politics, Memory, and the Sacred* (Durham, NC: Duke University Press, 2006), 265.

20. Matthews alternately identified as a gay man, as a cross-dresser, and, later, across the gender binary. Greg Youmans defines Matthews's

public persona as an androgynous genderqueer man. For this reason, I will, provisionally, use "masculine" pronouns. Greg Youmans, *Word Is Out: A Queer Film Classic* (Vancouver, BC: Arsenal Pulp Press, 2011), 116.

21. C. Moraga, *Waiting in the Wings*, 68.

22. Queer temporalities "allow their participants to believe that their futures can be imagined according to logics that lie outside of those paradigmatic markers of life experience—namely, birth, marriage, reproduction, and death." Jack Halberstam, *In a Queer Time and Place: Transgender Bodies, Subcultural Lives* (New York: New York University Press, 2005), 2.

23. Halberstam, *In a Queer Time*, 62.

24. Benjamin, "Black AfterLives Matter," 50.

25. Benjamin, "Black AfterLives Matter," 65.

26. Benjamin, "Black AfterLives Matter," 48. Original italics.

27. Benjamin, "Black AfterLives Matter," 48.

28. Cherríe Moraga, "Foreword: From Inside the First World," in *This Bridge Called My Back: Writings by Radical Women of Color*, 3rd ed. (Berkeley, CA: Third Woman Press, 2001), xvi.

29. C. Moraga, "Foreword," xxii.

30. Christine Finley, "Ghostly Care: Boarding Schools, Prisons, and Debt in *Rhymes for Young Ghouls*," in *Abolition Feminisms*, vol. 1, *Organizing, Survival, and Transformative Practice*, ed. Alisa Bierria, Jakeya Caruthers, and Brooke Lober (Chicago: Haymarket Books, 2022), 260.

31. Finley, "Ghostly Care."

32. Alexander, *Pedagogies of Crossing*, 285.

33. Alexander, *Pedagogies of* Crossing, 285.

34. Tamara Lea Spira, *Movements of Feeling: Feminist Radical Imaginations in Neoliberal Times* (Seattle: University of Washington Press, forthcoming).

35. Agathangelou, Bassichis, and Spira, "Intimate Investments."

36. Jodi Melamed, *Represent and Destroy: Rationalizing Violence in the New Racial Capitalism* (Minneapolis: University of Minnesota Press, 2011), xxi.

37. Audre Lorde, "Turning the Beat Around: Lesbian Parenting 1986," in *Politics of the Heart: A Lesbian Parenting Anthology*, ed. Sandra Pollack and Jeanne Vaughn (Ithaca, NY: Firebrand Books, 1986), 313.

38. Tamara Lea Spira, "The Geopolitics of the Erotic: Audre Lorde's Mexico and the De-colonization of the Revolutionary Imagination," in *Audre Lorde's Transnational Legacies*, ed. Stella Bolaki and Sabine Broeck (Amherst: University of Massachusetts Press, 2015), 177–90.

39. Audre Lorde, "Oberlin College Commencement Address," in *I Am Your Sister: Collected and Unpublished Writings of Audre Lorde*, ed. Rudolph P. Byrd, Johnnetta Betsch Cole, and Beverly Guy-Sheftall (Oxford: Oxford University Press, 2009), 214.

40. Gloria Anzaldúa, "Refugees of a World on Fire," cited in Alexander, *Pedagogies of Crossing*, 281.

41. June Jordan, "A New Politics of Sexuality," in *Some of Us Did Not Die* (New York: Basic Books, 2003), 133.

42. In their 2017 watershed text, *Reproductive Justice: An Introduction*, Loretta Ross and Rickie Solinger offer the following critical definition of reproductive justice: "(1) the right not to have a child; (2) the right to have a child; and (3) the right to parent children in safe and healthy environments." Emerging out of Black feminist interventions, this framework asks that we consider key topics, such as racialized population control, eugenics, the forced sterilization of women of color, and the life conditions imposed upon racialized communities under racial capitalism. Loretta Ross and Rickie Solinger, *Reproductive Justice: An Introduction* (Berkeley: University of California Press, 2017), 9.

43. Hannah Dyer, "Queer Futurity and Childhood Innocence: Beyond the Injury of Development," *Global Studies of Childhood* 7, no. 3 (2017): 294.

44. Alexis Pauline Gumbs, "'We Can Learn to Mother Ourselves': A Dialogically Produced Audience and Black Feminist Publishing 1979 to the 'Present,'" *Gender Forum: An Internet Journal for Gender Studies* 22 (2008): 1–6, www.genderforum.org/issues/black-womens-writing-revisited/we-can-learn-to-mother-ourselves/.

45. Alexis Pauline Gumbs, "m/other ourselves," in *Revolutionary Mothering: Love on the Front Lines*, ed. Alexis Pauline Gumbs, China Martens, and Mai'a Williams (Oakland, CA: PM Press, 2016), 20–21.

46. Gumbs, "m/other ourselves," 20–21.

47. José Esteban Muñoz, *Cruising Utopia: The Then and There of Queer Futurity* (New York: NYU Press, 2009), 1.

48. Muñoz, *Cruising Utopia*, 1.

49. Tina Campt, *Listening to Images* (Durham, NC: Duke University Press, 2017), 17.

50. Campt, *Listening to Images*, 17.

51. Campt, *Listening to Images*, 17.

52. Campt, *Listening to Images*, 17.

53. Dean Spade, *Mutual Aid: Building Solidarity during This Crisis (and the Next)* (London: Verso Books, 2020), 38.

54. Spade, *Mutual Aid*.

55. Grace Lee Boggs, *The Next American Revolution: Sustainable Activism for the Twenty-First Century* (Berkeley: University of California Press, 2012), 29, 31.

56. Boggs, *Next American Revolution*, 198.

57. Grace Lee Boggs, "These Are Times That Grow Our Souls," transcript of speech delivered at Animating Democracy's National Exchange on Art and Civic Dialogue, Flint, MI, October 9, 2003, https://intranet.americansforthearts.org/sites/default/files/Grace_Lee _Boggs_Grow_Our_Souls.pdf.

58. Robyn Maynard and Leanne Betasamosake Simpson, *Rehearsals for Living* (Chicago: Haymarket Books, 2022), 44.

59. Kim TallBear, "A Sharpening of the Already Present: Apocalypse and Radical Hope," *Unsettle* substack, October 12, 2022, https://kimtallbear.substack.com/p/a-sharpening-of-the-already-present.

60. TallBear, "Sharpening of the Already Present."

61. Gayle S. Rubin, "Thinking Sex: Notes for a Radical Theory of the Politics of Sexuality," in *Culture, Society and Sexuality: A Reader*, ed. Richard Parker and Peter Aggleton (London: Routledge, 2002), 143.

62. Erica R. Meiners, *For the Children? Protecting Innocence in a Carceral State* (Minneapolis: University of Minnesota Press, 2016), 9.

63. Meiners, *For the Children?*, 9.

64. Rebekah Sheldon, *The Child to Come: Life after Human Catastrophe* (Minneapolis: University of Minnesota Press, 2016), 6.

65. Nicole Hunt, "The Mama Bear Movement Is Rising," *Daily Citizen*, November 4, 2021, https://dailycitizen.focusonthefamily.com

/the-mama-bear-movement-is-rising/. I am grateful to Alexandra Kimball for her work on this subject.

66. Parents Bill of Rights Act, H.R.5, 118th Congress (2023).

67. Robin Bernstein, *Racial Innocence: Performing American Childhood from Slavery to Civil Rights* (New York: NYU Press, 2011).

68. Julian Gill-Peterson, Rebekah Sheldon, and Kathryn Bond Stockton, "Introduction: What Is the Now, Even of Then," *GLQ* 22 no. 4 (October 1, 2016): 496.

69. This contradiction is embedded in the longer history of white Christian heterosexual mothers who have long garnered cultural capital as child saviors while promoting policies that harm children's health and the environment. See, for example, Anita Bryant, the infamous architect of the 1977 antigay "Save Our Children" campaign, or Sarah Palin, who helped to popularize the idea of the "Mama Bear" among conservative Christians. Lisa Miller, "What Does 'Mama Grizzly' Really Mean?" *Newsweek*, September 27, 2010, www.newsweek.com/what-does-mama-grizzly-really-mean-72001.

70. Michael Bronski, "Grooming and the Christian Politics of Innocence," *Boston Review*, May 3, 2022, www.bostonreview.net/articles/grooming-and-the-christian-politics-of-innocence/.

71. Melody Schreiber, "Why Is This Group of Doctors So Intent on Unmasking Kids?," *New Republic*, February 22, 2022, https://newrepublic.com/article/165413/mask-mandates-kids-back-to-normal.

72. Laura Briggs, *Somebody's Children: The Politics of Transracial and Transnational Adoption* (Durham, NC: Duke University Press, 2012), 242.

73. The language at the time was *reproductive technologies*; now the term is *ARTs*. I will use these terms interchangeably. Dorothy Roberts, *Killing the Black Body: Race, Reproduction and the Meaning of Liberty* (New York: Vintage, 2014), 248.

74. Roberts, *Killing the Black Body*, 214.

75. Davis argued that while "the new reproductive technologies [could not] … be constructed as inherently affirmative or violative of women's reproductive rights," they could not be abstracted from the racialized labor arrangements that could allow us to predict who would bear the brunt of them. Angela Y. Davis, "Surrogates and Outcast

Mothers: Racism and Reproductive Politics in the Nineties," in *The Angela Y. Davis Reader*, ed. Joy James (Malden, MA: Blackwell, 1998), 220.

76. See, for example, Kalindi Vora, *Life Support: Biocapital and the New History of Outsourced Labor* (Minneapolis: University of Minnesota Press, 2015), and France Winddance Twine, *Outsourcing the Womb: Race, Class, and Gestational Surrogacy in a Global Market* (New York: Routledge, 2015).

77. Teagan Bradway and Elizabeth Freeman, "Introduction: Kin-coherence/Kin-aesthetics/Kinematics," in *Queer Kinship: Race, Sex, Belonging, Form*, ed. Teagan Bradway and Elizabeth Freeman (Durham, NC: Duke University Press, 2022), 2.

78. Laura Mamo and Eli Alston-Stepnitz, "Queer Intimacies and Structural Inequalities: New Directions in Stratified Reproduction," *Journal of Family Issues* 36, no. 4 (2015): 521.

79. Laura Mamo, "Fertility Inc.: Consumption and Subjectification in U.S. Lesbian Reproductive Practices," in *Biomedicalization: Techno-science, Health, and Illness in the U.S.*, ed. A.E. Clarke et al. (Durham, NC: Duke University Press, 2010), 173–96. See also Kimberly M. Mutcherson, "Blood and Water in a Post-coital World," *Family Law Quarterly* 49, no. 1 (2015): 117–34.

80. Donna Haraway, *Simians, Cyborgs, and Women: The Reinvention of Nature* (London: Routledge, 1991); Lewis, *Full Surrogacy Now*.

81. Marcin Smietana and Charis Thompson, eds., "Making Families: Transnational Surrogacy, Queer Kinship, and Reproductive Justice," special issue, *Reproductive Biomedicine and Society Online* (2018).

82. Natalie Fixmer-Oraiz and Shui-yin Sharon Yam, "Queer(ing) Reproductive Justice," in *Oxford Encyclopedia of Queer Studies and Communication*, ed. Isaac N. West et al. (New York: Oxford University Press, 2021), 5–9.

83. Laura Mamo, "Queering Reproduction in Transnational Bio-Economies," *Reproductive Biomedicine and Society Online* 7 (November 2018): 30.

84. Melinda Cooper, *Family Values: Between Neoliberalism and the New Social Conservatism* (Cambridge, MA: MIT Press, 2017), 313.

85. Roberts, *Shattered Bonds*, 2001.

86. Donor Sibling Registry, "About DSR," accessed April 17, 2021, https://donorsiblingregistry.com/about-dsr.

CHAPTER ONE. THE LONG STORY

1. Elizabeth Freeman, "Queer Belongings: Kinship Theory and Queer Theory," in *A Companion to Lesbian, Gay, Bisexual, Transgender, and Queer Studies*, ed. George Haggerty and Molly McGarry (Oxford: Blackwell, 2007), 297.

2. Michael Bronski, "When Gays Wanted to Liberate Children," *Boston Review*, June 8, 2018, https://bostonreview.net/articles/michael-bronski-gay-family/.

3. Bronski, "When Gays Wanted to Liberate Children."

4. M. Cooper, *Family Values*, 313.

5. Rivers, "'In the Best Interests of the Child,'" 935.

6. Daniel Rivers, *Radical Relations: Lesbian Mothers, Gay Fathers, and Their Children in the United States since World War II* (Chapel Hill: University of North Carolina Press, 2013), 78.

7. Daniel Tsang, "Third World Gays and Lesbians Meet," in *Remaking Radicalism: A Grassroots Documentary Reader of the United States, 1973–2001* (Athens: University of Georgia Press, 2020), 44–46.

8. Audre Lorde, "When Will Ignorance End: Keynote Speech at National Conference of Third World Lesbians and Gay Men," *Off Our Backs*, November 1979, 8, quoted in Alexis Pauline Gumbs, "'We Can Learn to Mother Ourselves': The Queer Survival of Black Feminism" (PhD diss., Duke University, 2010), 255.

9. Audre Lorde, "When Will Ignorance End," in *I Am Your Sister: Collected and Unpublished Writings of Audre Lorde*, ed. Rudolph P. Byrd, Johnnetta Betsch Cole, and Beverly Guy-Sheftall (New York: Oxford University Press, 2009), 210.

10. Gumbs, "We Can Learn to Mother Ourselves" [2010], 255.

11. Michael Boucai, "Glorious Precedents: When Gay Marriage Was Radical," *Yale Journal of Law and the Humanities* 27, no. 1 (2015): 15.

12. Boucai, "Glorious Precedents," 15.

13. Michael Boucai, "Is Assisted Procreation an LGBT Right?," *Wisconsin Law Review*, no. 6 (2016): 1098–99.

14. Boucai, "Is Assisted Procreation an LGBT Right?," 1097.

15. Kate Millett, *Sexual Politics* (New York: Columbia University Press, 1970). Here it is important to note Millett's own exchanges with radical Indigenous and women-of-color feminists whose influence upon her has largely fallen out of the historical record, as well as her involvement in anti-imperialist struggles. For example, Millett hosted an autobiographical writing workshop at UC Berkeley where she met Menominee poet and activist Chrystos. See Kate Millett, *CATERPILLARS: Journal Entries by 11 Women* (n.p.: Epona Press, 1977).

16. Adrienne Rich, "Compulsory Heterosexuality and Lesbian Existence," *Signs: Journal of Women in Culture and Society*, 5, no. 4 (1980): 631–60. See also Adrienne Rich, introduction to *Legal Kidnapping: What Happens to a Family When the Father Kidnaps Two Children*, by Anna Demeter (Boston: Beacon Press, 1977), xi–xxi.

17. Andrew Lester, "'This Was My Utopia': Sexual Experimentation and Masculinity in the 1960s Bay Area Radical Left," *Journal of the History of Sexuality* 29, no. 3 (September 2020): 364–87.

18. Quoted in Lester, "'This Was My Utopia,'" 377.

19. Third World Gay Revolution, "Sixteen Point Platform and Program," *Pinko*, October 15, 2019, https://pinko.online/pinko-1/third-world-gay-revolution-archive.

20. Erin Blakemore, "How the Black Panthers' Breakfast Program Both Inspired and Threatened the Government," History Channel website, February 6, 2018, www.history.com/news/free-school-breakfast-black-panther-party.

21. Darrel Enck-Wanzer, *The Young Lords* (New York: New York University Press, 2010), 218–20.

22. Bronski, "When Gays Wanted to Liberate Children."

23. Mickey Ellinger, "We Made a Village for the Kids: Reflections on the Prairie Fire Organizing Committee," *Viewpoint Magazine*, January 26, 2017, https://viewpointmag.com/2017/01/26/we-made-a-village-for-the-kids-reflections-on-the-prairie-fire-organizing-committee/.

24. This included those identified as lesbians and gay men. I focus primarily upon those who identified as mothers in this chapter. See the Introduction for a note on language, gender, and history.

25. Rivers, "'In the Best Interest of the Child,'" 918–19.

26. For Anna Demeter's devastating memoir of this experience, see Demeter, *Legal Kidnapping*.

27. Rivers, *Radical Relations*, 82.

28. Minnie Bruce Pratt, "Declared Not Fit," in *Crime against Nature* (New York: A Midsummer Night's Press, 2013), 34–35.

29. Adrienne Rich, "Husband-Right and Father-Right" [1977], in *On Lies, Secrets, and Silence: Selected Prose, 1966–1978* (New York: W. W. Norton, 1995), 218.

30. Mom's Apple Pie, *Mom's Apple Pie: The Heart of the Lesbian Mother's Custody Movement*, directed by Shan Ottey, Shad Reinstein, and Jody Laine (San Francisco: Frameline, 2006), https://search.alexanderstreet.com/preview/work/bibliographic_entity%7Cvideo_work%7C1865517.

31. "Lesbian Women Say No to the Welfare Cuts, Yes to Wages for Housework" [flyer], 1976, in *Wages for Housework: New York Committee, 1972–1977: History, Theory Documents*, ed. Silvia Federici and Arlen Austen (Brooklyn, NY: Autonomedia, 2017), 125.

32. "Lesbian Women Say No," 125; Silvia Federici, "Introduction: Wages for Housework in Historical Perspective," in Federici and Austen, *Wages for Housework*, 12–28.

33. Federici, "Introduction," 21.

34. Rivers, *Radical Relations*, 100; Rivers, "'In the Best Interest of the Child,'" 918–19.

35. Rivers, *Radical Relations*, 99.

36. Rivers, *Radical Relations*, 101. For a great historical context to Wanrow's struggle, see Emily Thuma, "Lessons in Self-Defense: Gender Violence, Racial Criminalization, and Anticarceral Feminism," *Women's Studies Quarterly* 43, nos. 3/4 (2015): 52–71.

37. Rivers, *Radical Relations*, 101.

38. Audre Lorde, "Poetry Is Not a Luxury," "The Uses of the Erotic: The Erotic as Power," and "Grenada Revisited," in *Sister Outsider: Essays and Speeches* (Berkeley, CA: Crossing Press, 1984), 36–39, 53–59, and 176–89.

39. Minnie Bruce Pratt, "Justice, Come Down," in *The Dirt She Ate: New and Selected Poems* (Pittsburgh, PA: University of Pittsburgh Press, 2003).

40. Tamara Lea Spira, "Intimate Internationalisms: 1970s 'Third World' Queer Feminist Solidarity with Chile," *Feminist Theory* 15, no. 2 (August 2014): 121.

41. Deborah A. Miranda, "Beth Brant: May Her Memory Be a Blessing," *Bad NDNS*, September 11, 2015, https://badndns.blogspot.com/2015/09/may-her-memory-be-blessing.html.

42. Miranda identifies as Two Spirit in recent written work but uses she/her pronouns in public bios. Deborah A. Miranda, "Extermination of the *Joyas*: Gendercide in Spanish California," *GLQ: A Journal of Lesbian and Gay Studies* 16, nos. 1–2 (2010): 253–84.

43. Miranda, "Beth Brant."

44. Miranda, "Beth Brant."

45. Miranda, "Beth Brant."

46. "Annie" is in quotes because it is a name imposed by the colonizers, which Brant questions.

47. Beth Brant, "The Fifth Floor, 1967," in *Mohawk Trail* (Ithaca, NY: Firebrand Books, 1985), 69–76. In letters to an incarcerated Eastern Cherokee woman, Brant confesses to have herself been "in a mental institution ... unable to stop the drugs they shoved down my throat ... threatened with shock treatments." Beth Brant, "Letters between Raven and Beth," in *A Gathering of Spirit: A Collection of North American Indian Women*, ed. Beth Brant (Ithaca, NY: Firebrand Books, 1988), 207.

48. Beth Brant, "A Long Story," in Brant, *Gathering of Spirit*, 77.

49. Brant, "Long Story," 77.

50. Brant, "Long Story," 77.

51. Brant, "Long Story," 79.

52. Brant, "Long Story," 77.

53. Brant, "Long Story," 84.

54. Brant, "Long Story," 79.

55. Brant, "Long Story," 80.

56. Interestingly, the readers are able to access "Martha's" true name, She Sees Deer, and thus we are offered a quick glimmer of hope into the recovery of her more authentic self, despite her terrible circumstances.

57. Brant, "Long Story," 80.

58. Brant, "Long Story," 80.

59. Brant, "Long Story," 81.

60. Brant, "Long Story," 78.

61. Brant, "Long Story," 78.

62. Brant, "Long Story," 78.

63. Brant, "Long Story," 84.

64. Brant, "Long Story," 85.

65. Kim TallBear, "Making Love and Relations beyond Settler Sex and Family," in A. Clarke and Haraway, *Making Kin Not Population*, 147.

66. Beth Brant, "Giveaway: Native Lesbian Writers," *Signs: Journal of Women in Culture and Society* 18 (Summer 1993): 946–47.

67. Beth Brant, introduction to Brant, *Gathering of Spirit*, 7.

68. Brant, "Introduction," 82.

69. Arianne Burford, "'Her Mouth Is Medicine': Beth Brant and Paula Gunn Allen's Decolonizing Queer Erotics," *Journal of Lesbian Studies* 17, no.2 (2013): 175.

70. Brant, "Long Story," 79.

71. Brant, "Long Story," 82–83.

72. Qwo-Li Driskill and Lisa Tatonetti, "Introduction: Writing the Present," in *Sovereign Erotics: A Collection of Two-Spirit Literature*, ed. Qwo-Li Driskill et al. (Tucson: University of Arizona Press, 2011), 3. After this book was typeset, Dr. Driskill left their position at Oregon State University. The Tribal Alliance Against Fraud revealed that Driskill's claims to Indigenous identity were false, confirming concerns already raised by Cherokee scholars. This came after Driskill's graduate students demonstrated a clear pattern of abuse each time they were questioned. I thank Kyles Gemmell, one of Driskill's former students, for advising me on this matter.

73. Brant, "Long Story," 83.

74. Brant, "Long Story," 85.

75. Beth Brant, quoted in Qwo-Li Driskill, "Stolen from Our Bodies: First Nations Two-Spirits/Queers and the Journey to a Sovereign Erotic," *Studies in American Indian Literatures* 16, no. 2 (2004): 55.

76. Krista L. Benson, "Carrying Stories of Incarcerated Indigenous Women as Tools for Prison Abolition," *Frontiers: A Journal of Women Studies* 41, no. 2 (2020): 143–67.

77. Daniel Rivers, "Rally in Support of Jeanne Jullion," in *Radical Relations*, 86.

78. As Parker details in personal letters, Anastasia's young birth mother came to live with her, her partner Marty, and Parker's daughter from a previous relationship, Cassidy. This was arranged after Parker received a phone call from an adoption agency that was looking for a family to take in and care for a sixteen year-old pregnant Black woman in order to hide her away from her family and ultimately adopt her baby. However, while Parker hid her lesbianism from the young woman's mother, pretending to be roommates with her partner Marty, this strategy backfired, and Parker was forced to defend her right to mother Anastasia. Pat Parker, "Untitled Letter to Nancy K. Bereano," Schlesinger Archives, Harvard University, December 11, 1983; Pat Parker, "Untitled Letter to Whiteness," Schlesinger Archives, Harvard University, February 18, 1983.

79. Pat Parker, "Legacy," in *Jonestown and Other Madness* (Ithaca, NY: Firebrand Books, 1985), 67.

80. Parker, "Legacy," 74.

81. Parker, "Legacy," 67–68.

82. Parker, "Legacy," 68.

83. Parker, "Legacy," 74.

84. Parker, "Legacy," 69–70.

85. Parker, "Legacy," 69–71.

86. Parker, "Legacy," 70–72.

87. Parker, "Legacy," 74.

88. Parker, "Legacy," 74.

89. Cheryl Clarke, "Living the Texts *Out*: Lesbians and the Use of Black Women's Traditions," in *Theorizing Black Feminisms: The Visionary Pragmatism of Black Women*, ed. Stanlie Myrise James and Abena P. A. Busia (Oxford: Routledge, 1993), 225.

90. Mecca Jamilah Sullivan, introduction to *Sister Love: The Letters of Audre Lorde and Pat Parker, 1974–1979*, ed. Julie Enszer (Dover, FL: Sinister Wisdom, 2018), 24.

91. Angela Hume, *Deep Care: The Radical Activists Who Provided Abortions, Defied the Law, and Fought to Keep Clinics Open* (Chico, CA: AK Press, 2023), 99.

92. Pat Parker, "Gay Parenting: Or, Look Out, Anita," in Pollack and Vaughn, *Politics of the Heart*, 97.

93. Parker, "Gay Parenting," 99.

94. Parker, "Gay Parenting," 99.

95. Benjamin, "Black AfterLives Matter," 48.

96. Parker, "Legacy," 75.

97. Saidiya V. Hartman, *Wayward Lives, Beautiful Experiments: Intimate Histories of Social Upheaval* (New York: W. W. Norton, 2019).

98. Neferti Tadiar, *Things Fall Away: Philippine Historical Experience and the Makings of Globalization* (Durham, NC: Duke University Press, 2009).

99. Spira, *Movements of Feeling*.

100. Shabnam Grewal, preface to *Charting the Journey: Writings by Black and Third World Women*, ed. Shabnam Grewal (London: Sheba Feminist Publishers, 1988), 2–3.

101. Sonia E. Alvarez, "Advocating Feminisms: The Latin American NGO 'Boom,'" *International Feminist Journal of Politics* 1, no. 2 (November 1999): 181–209.

102. See Anna M. Agathangelou et al., "Sexual Divestments from Empire: Women's Studies, Institutional Feeling, and the 'Odious Machine,'" *Feminist Formations* 27, no. 3 (2015): 139–67; and Piya Chatterjee and Maira Sunaina, *The Imperial University: Academic Repression and Scholarly Dissent* (Minneapolis: University of Minnesota Press, 2014). See also Roderick Ferguson, *The Reorder of Things: The University and its Pedagogies of Minority Difference* (Minneapolis: University of Minnesota Press, 2012).

103. Chrystos, "Looking for a Blanket to Cover Myself Once the Horses Are Free," in *In Her, I Am* (Vancouver, BC: Press Gang, 1993), 81. I thank Heather Turcotte for this citation. Brant thanked Chrystos and Anzaldúa for inspiration in "A Long Story." Chrystos also briefly dated Parker, and the two wrote incredible letters for years after Chrystos left the Bay Area and moved to Washington State.

104. AnaLouise Keating, *The Gloria Anzaldúa Reader* (Durham, NC: Duke University Press, 2009), 113.

105. Keating, *Gloria Anzaldúa Reader*, 112.

106. Lorde, "Grenada Revisited," 184.

107. Lorde, "Grenada Revisited," 184.

108. June Jordan, *Directed by Desire: The Collected Poems of June Jordan*, ed. Jan Heller and Sara Miles (Port Townsend, WA: Copper Canyon Press, 2005).

109. Tamara Lea Spira, "For June," *Feminist Wire*, March 16, 2016, https://thefeministwire.com/2016/03/for-june/.

110. Spira, "For June."

111. Pat Parker, foreword to Parker, *Jonestown and Other Madness*, 5.

112. Spira, "Intimate Internationalisms," 135.

113. Julie R. Enszer, "What Remains: Remembering Michelle Cliff, Beth Brant, and Stephania Byrd," August 4, 2016, *Lambda Literary*, https://lambdaliterary.org/2016/08/what-remains-remembering-michelle-cliff-beth-brant-and-stephania-byrd/.

114. Enszer, "What Remains."

115. For reflections upon the loss of a generation, see Cox, Simmons, and Lomax, "Take Care"; Hong, "'The Future of Our Worlds'"; and Priest, "Salvation Is the Issue."

116. M. Cooper, *Family Values*, 173.

117. Laura Briggs, *How All Politics Became Reproductive Politics: From Welfare Reform to Foreclosure to Trump* (Oakland: University of California Press, 2017).

118. Dorothy Roberts, *Killing the Black Body: Race, Reproduction, and the Meaning of Liberty* (Toronto: Random House, 1998), 202–3.

119. Roberts, *Killing the Black Body*.

120. Liz Montegary, *Familiar Perversions: The Racial, Sexual, and Economic Politics of LGBT Families* (New Brunswick, NJ: Rutgers University Press, 2018), 23.

121. Dean Spade and Craig Willse, "Norms and Normalization," in *The Oxford Handbook of Feminist Theory*, ed. Lisa Disch and Mary Hawkesworth (Oxford: Oxford University Press, 2015), 8.

122. Agathangelou, Bassichis, and Spira, "Intimate Investments."

123. Minnie Bruce Pratt, "Shame," in *Crime against Nature* (Ithaca, NY: Firebrand Books, 1990), 60.

124. Pratt, "Shame," 58.

125. Minnie Bruce Pratt, email to author, February 7, 2022.

126. Minnie Bruce Pratt, email to author, February 7, 2022.

CHAPTER TWO. OPPOSING FIGURES

1. Lorelei Laird, "Same-Sex Couple Sues Federally Funded Refugee Adoption Agency for Discrimination," *ABA Journal*, February 23, 2018, www.abajournal.com/news/article/same_sex_couple_sues_federally_funded_refugee_adoption_agency_for_discrimin.

2. Masterpiece Cakeshop, Ltd. v. Colorado Civil Rights Commission, 584 U.S. 1 (2018); 303 Creative LLC v. Elenis, 600 U.S. 17 (2023).

3. A Colorado cake shop refused to bake a wedding cake for a gay couple, and their "right" to do so was upheld in court, though it is in legal limbo in a larger sense in that the details of the victory may not apply to other cases and therefore will not set a strong legal precedent. James Esseks, "In Masterpiece, the Bakery Wins the Battle but Loses the War," ACLU, June 14, 2018, www.aclu.org/news/lgbtq-rights/masterpiece-bakery-wins-battle-loses-war.

4. More than one hundred bills have been passed in 2020–21 to deny trans young people basic services. This includes HB 1570 in Arkansas, a bill passed in 2021 to ban gender-affirming healthcare for trans youth. See ACLU, "Special Report: Chase Strangio on the Legislative Assault on Trans Youth," ACLU, April 15, 2021, www.aclu.org/news/lgbtq-rights/special-report-chase-strangio-on-the-legislative-assault-on-trans-youth.

5. Elizabeth Boylan, "Dignity Denied: Religious Exemptions and LGBT Elder Services," Columbia Law School, December 15, 2017, https://lawrightsreligion.law.columbia.edu/news/dignity-denied-religious-exemptions-and-lgbt-elder-services.

6. Law, Rights, and Religion Project, "Unmarried and Unprotected: How Religious Liberty Bills Harm Pregnant People, Families, and Communities of Color," Columbia Law School, January 25, 2017, https://lawrightsreligion.law.columbia.edu/unmarriedandunprotected.

7. This was seen as a loss for LGBTQ advocates but a narrow one since, as Shannon Minter, legal director of the National Center for Lesbian Rights (NCLR) explained, "the Court ruled in favor of Catholic Social Services, but on the narrowest possible ground, based on language in the City of Philadelphia's contract that authorized individualized exemptions for any provider. The Court did not change the current constitutional framework, which permits governments to

enforce antidiscrimination laws that prohibit discrimination against LGBTQ people even when doing so may have a disparate burden on those who hold certain religious beliefs." Christopher Vasquez, "NCLR Relieved by Narrow SCOTUS Ruling in Fulton Allowing Governments to Prohibit Anti-LGBTQ Discrimination," National Center for Lesbian Rights, press release, June 17, 2021, www.nclrights.org/about-us/press-media/.

8. In this chapter, I refer to both foster care and adoption through the foster care system.

9. In addition to its broader social implications, children's "best interest" is the legal standard for determining custody, and it has historically been used to deny custody to LGBTQ parents.

10. M. Cooper, *Family Values*.

11. Briggs, *Somebody's Children*, 242.

12. Dana Nessel, "Attorney General Nessel's Statement on Dumont v Gordon Settlement Agreement," YouTube video, 00:01:02, March 22, 2019, www.youtube.com/watch?v=-iJwG59drCs.

13. ACLU, "ACLU, Same-Sex Couple Seek to Join Lawsuit to Keep a License to Discriminate Out of Michigan's Child Welfare System," ACLU, press release, May 22, 2019, www.aclu.org/press-releases/aclu-same-sex-couple-seek-join-lawsuit-keep-license-discriminate-out-michigans-child.

14. Nessel, "Attorney General Nessel's Statement," 2019.

15. Deborah Gould, *Moving Politics: Emotion and ACT Up's Fight against AIDS* (Chicago: University of Chicago Press, 2009), 89.

16. Cathy J. Cohen, "Punks, Bulldaggers, and Welfare Queens: The Radical Potential of Queer Politics?," *GLQ* 3, no. 3 (1997): 438.

17. Cohen, "Punks, Bulldaggers."

18. M. Cooper, *Family Values*, 68–69.

19. M. Cooper, *Family Values*, 69.

20. ACLU Michigan, "ACLU Challenges Discriminatory Practices in Michigan's Foster Care System," YouTube video, 00:03:29, September 20, 2017, www.youtube.com/watch?v=_M-1lf-y7cg.

21. Quoted in Dean Spade, "Trans Law and Politics on a Neoliberal Landscape," in *Normal Life: Administrative Violence, Critical Trans*

Politics, and the Limits of Law (Durham, NC: Duke University Press, 2015), 362.

22. Cyril Ghosh, "Marriage Equality and the Injunction to Assimilate: Romantic Love, Children, Monogamy, and Parenting in Obergefell v. Hodges," *Polity* 50, no. 2 (April 2018): 277.

23. Rivers, "'In the Best Interests of the Child,'" 921.

24. ACLU Michigan, "ACLU Challenges Discriminatory Practices."

25. Spade, "Trans Law and Politics," 362.

26. ACLU Michigan, "ACLU Challenges Discriminatory Practices."

27. Obergefell, 576 U.S. (2015).

28. Spade, "Trans Law and Politics," 362.

29. Spade, "Trans Law and Politics," 362.

30. Dorothy Roberts, *Torn Apart: How the Child Welfare System Destroys Black Families—and How Abolition Can Build a Safer World* (New York: Basic Books, 2023), 66.

31. Roberts, *Torn Apart*, 67.

32. Roberts, *Torn Apart*, 67.

33. Roberts, *Torn Apart*, 67.

34. Roberts, *Torn Apart*, 70–75.

35. Roberts, *Torn Apart*, 75–82.

36. Roberts, *Torn Apart*, 77–80.

37. Agathangelou, Bassichis, and Spira, "Intimate Investments."

38. Julie Moreau, "Lesbian Couple Sues Health and Human Services after Foster Care Application Rejected," NBC News, February 22, 2018, www.nbcnews.com/feature/nbc-out/lesbian-couple-sues-health-department-after-foster-care-application-rejected-n850371.

39. Lisa Cacho, *Social Death: Racialized Rightlessness and the Criminalization of the Unprotected* (New York: NYU Press, 2012).

40. Montegary, *Familiar Perversions*, 22.

41. Briggs, *Somebody's Children*, 246.

42. Briggs, *Somebody's Children*, 242.

43. Briggs, *Somebody's Children*.

44. Briggs, *Somebody's Children*, 263–64.

45. Dorothy Roberts, "I Have Studied Child Protective Services for Decades. It Needs to Be Abolished," *Mother Jones*, April 5, 2022, www.motherjones.com/criminal-justice/2022/04/abolish-child-protective-services-torn-apart-dorothy-roberts-book-excerpt/.

46. Dorothy Roberts and Lisa Sangoi, "Black Families Matter: How the Child Welfare System Punishes Poor Families of Color," *The Appeal*, March 26, 2018, https://theappeal.org/black-families-matter-how-the-child-welfare-system-punishes-poor-families-of-color-33ad20e2882e/.

47. Daniel Rivers, "Families," in *The Routledge History of Queer America*, ed. Don Romesburg (New York: Routledge, 2018), 276.

48. Jasbir Puar, *Terrorist Assemblages: Homonationalism in Queer Times* (Durham, NC: Duke University Press, 2007).

49. Agathangelou, Bassichis, and Spira, "Intimate Investments."

50. Agathangelou, Bassichis, and Spira, "Intimate Investments," 133–37.

51. Briggs, *Somebody's Children*, 242.

52. M. Cooper, *Family Values*, 164–65.

53. Tamara Metz, "Obergefell, Marriage, and the Neoliberal Politics of Care," in *Stating the Family: New Directions in the Study of American Politics*, ed. Carol Nackenoff (Lawrence: University Press of Kansas, 2020), 45.

54. Briggs, *Somebody's Children*, 263.

55. Laura Briggs, *Taking Children: A History of American Terror* (Berkeley: University of California Press, 2020), 10.

56. Briggs, *Somebody's Children*, 268.

57. Lambda Legal, "What Makes a 'Holy Family'?," YouTube video, 00:05:13, February 20, 2018, www.youtube.com/watch?time_continue=1&v=PygUqkfu-4Y&feature=emb_logo.

58. Bethany also stood out for its broader role as a well-resourced arm of the Evangelical antichoice movement, described by one journalist as "a well-connected powerhouse of the anti-choice movement." The agency also garnered the reputation for coercing pregnant unmarried women to relinquish their babies for adoption. Amy Littlefield and Tina Vasquez, "Bethany Christian Services Is Fostering

Migrant Kids. It Also Has a History of Coercive Adoptions," Rewire News Group, June 27, 2018, https://rewirenewsgroup.com/article/2018/06/27/christian-group-fostering-migrant-kids-history-coercive-adoptions/. See also Katherine Joyce, "Shotgun Adoption," *The Nation*, August 26, 2009, www.thenation.com/article/archive/shotgun-adoption/.

59. Dan MacGuill, "Christian Non-profit Faces Scrutiny over Government Foster Care Contract for Separated Children," Snopes, June 26, 2018, www.snopes.com/news/2018/06/26/bethany-christian-services-family-separation-betsy-devos/.

60. Erica Meiners, "The Trouble with the Child in the Carceral State," in *For the Children? Protecting Innocence in a Carceral State* (Minneapolis: University of Minnesota Press, 2017), 124.

61. Gayle Rubin, "Thinking Sex: Notes for a Radical Theory of the Politics of Sexuality," in *Pleasure and Danger: Exploring Female Sexuality*, ed. Carole S. Vance (London: Pandora, 1992), 143.

62. Rubin, "Thinking Sex," 147.

63. ACLU Michigan, "ACLU Challenges Discriminatory Practices."

64. Lambda Legal, "What Makes a 'Holy Family'?"

65. *Dumont*, 48 U.S. (2019).

66. Most cases involve Evangelical agencies, such as Miracle Hill Ministries and Bethany Christian Services, and Catholic agencies.

67. St. Vincent Catholic Charities, "Why We Resettle Refugees," video, 00:01:25, accessed December 15, 2021, https://stvcc.org/services/refugee-services/resettle-refugees/.

68. St. Vincent Catholic Charities, "St. Vincent Catholic Charities," accessed December 15, 2021, https://stvcc.org.

69. St. Vincent Catholic Charities, "Family Is Forever," accessed December 15, 2021, https://stvcc.org/family-is-forever/.

70. St. Vincent Catholic Charities, "Forever Family Christmas," accessed December 15, 2021, https://stvcc.org/forever-family-christmas.

71. St. Vincent Catholic Charities, "St. Vincent Catholic Charities."

72. Shamber Flore, "Column: My Adoption Agency Saved Me," *Detroit News*, March 7, 2018, www.detroitnews.com/story/opinion/2018/03/07/religious-adoption-agencies-aclu/32717127/.

73. St. Vincent Catholic Charities, "Refugee Services History," accessed December 15, 2021, https://stvcc.org/services/refugee-services/refugee-services-history/.

74. St. Vincent Catholic Charities, "St. Vincent Catholic Charities."

75. St. Vincent Catholic Charities, "St. Vincent Catholic Charities."

76. St. Vincent Catholic Charities, "Why We Resettle Refugees."

77. St. Vincent Catholic Charities, "St. Vincent Catholic Charities."

78. This includes general support for US imperialism, capitalism, and US militarism outlined above but also specific moves, such as the work of neoconservative agencies to ensure that white families face no barriers to adoption and fostering. Recent reporting highlights the active role of Far Right Christian wing philanthropist and policy organizations in the removal of children from their communities of origin, including the attempted elimination of the Indian Child Welfare Act that prioritizes the adoption of Native children back into their tribes. This comes in the wake of successful work to deprioritize the adoption of Black children into Black families, which Goldwater attorneys argued constituted "reverse discrimination." See Rebecca Nagle, "Trojan Horse," Episode 6 of *This Land* podcast, September 20, 2021, Crooked Media, https://crooked.com/podcast/6-trojan-horse/.

79. Katherine Joyce, *The Child Catchers: Rescue, Trafficking and New Gospel of Adoption* (New York: Public Affairs, 2018).

80. Daniel Denvir, "Today's Evangelicalism Was Forged in the Fight against Communism and Feminism," *Jacobin*, October 17, 2021, www.jacobinmag.com/2021/10/american-christian-evangelicalism-anti-communism-gender-feminism-race-maga-trump-culture-wars-du-mez-interview.

81. Denvir, "Today's Evangelicalism."

82. Joyce, "Trouble with the Christian Adoption Movement." Consistent with their work to erode the Indian Child Welfare Act and make more babies of color available for white families, the Heritage Foundation decried critiques of Barrett's adoption, arguing that it amounted to so-called reverse racism. See Charles Stimson, "How Low Can Far Left Go? Attacks on Barrett for Adopting Haitian Orphans Hit Rock Bottom," Heritage Foundation, October 1, 2020,

www.heritage.org/courts/commentary/how-low-can-far-left-go-attacks-barrett-adopting-haitian-orphans-hit-rock-bottom.

83. Garance Burke and Martha Mendoza, "Separated from Parents, Some Migrant Children Are Adopted by Americans," *Christian Science Monitor*, October 9, 2019, www.csmonitor.com/USA/2018/1009/Separated-from-parents-some-migrant-children-are-adopted-by-Americans.

84. Burke and Mendoza, "Separated from Parents."

85. Myah Ward, "At Least 3,900 Children Separated from Families under Trump 'Zero Tolerance' Policy, Task Force Finds," *Politico*, June 8, 2021, www.politico.com/news/2021/06/08/trump-zero-tolerance-policy-child-separations-492099.

86. MacGuill, "Christian Non-profit Faces Scrutiny."

87. Briggs, *Taking Children*, 76.

88. Michael Shear, Katie Benner, and Michael Schmidt, "We Need to Take Away Children,' No Matter How Young, Justice Dept. Officials Said," *New York Times*, October 28, 2021, www.nytimes.com/2020/10/06/us/politics/family-separation-border-immigration-jeff-sessions-rod-rosenstein.html.

89. MSNBC, "Trump Lost, So Why Are Trump Ideas Watering Down Police Reform Bill in 2021?," video, August 18, 2021, 00:05:16, www.msnbc.com/the-beat-with-ari/watch/trump-lost-so-why-are-trump-ideas-watering-down-police-reform-bill-in-2021-118996549509.

90. Justin Wise, "American Academy of Pediatrics President: Trump Family Separation Policy Is 'Child Abuse,'" The Hill, June 18, 2018, https://thehill.com/latino/392790-american-academy-of-pediatrics-president-trumps-family-separation-policy-is-child.

91. Bethany Children's Services, "Family Separation and Detention at the Border—Impacts on Children," accessed December 15, 2021, https://bethany.org/media/get-involved/serve/advocate/advocate-for-refugees/family-separation-and-detention-at-the-border.pdf.

92. Caitlin Dickerson, "What It Looks Like to Care for Separated Migrant Children," *New York Times*, June 18, 2019, www.nytimes.com/2019/06/18/reader-center/separated-migrant-children.html.

93. Briggs, *Taking Children*, 5.

94. See Briggs, *Taking Children,* chapter 1, for this discussion.

95. Soma De Bourbon, "White Property Interests in Native Women's Reproductive Freedom," in *Reproductive Justice and Sexual Rights* (New York: Routledge, 2019), 1–18.

96. Joseph Pierce, "Trace, Blood, and Native Identity," *Critical Ethnic Studies* 3, no. 2 (Fall 2017): 58. See also Laura Trace Hentz, *One Small Sacrifice: A Memoir: Lost Children of the Indian Adoption Projects* (Greenfield, MA: Blue Hand Books, 2017).

97. Roberts, *Shattered Bonds.*

98. Roberts, *Torn Apart,* 191–220.

99. E. K. Monahan et al., *Economic and Concrete Supports: An Evidence-Based Service for Child Welfare Prevention* (Chicago: Chapin Hall at the University of Chicago, 2023).

100. Erin Miles Cloud, "Toward the Abolition of the Foster System," *S&F Online,* 15, no. 3 (2019), http://sfonline.barnard.edu/unraveling-criminalizing-webs-building-police-free-futures/toward-theabolition-of-the-foster-system/.

101. Movement for Family Power, "Our Vision and Values," accessed December 15, 2021, www.movementforfamilypower.org/indexa.

102. Dorothy Roberts, "Abolishing Policing Also Means Abolishing Family Regulation," *The Imprint,* June 16, 2020, https://imprintnews.org/child-welfare-2/abolishing-policing-also-means-abolishing-family-regulation/44480.

103. Roberts, "Abolishing Policing."

104. Lambda Legal, "What Makes a 'Holy Family'?"

105. Lambda Legal, "What Makes a 'Holy Family'?"

106. Lambda Legal, "What Makes a 'Holy Family'?"

107. Lambda Legal, "What Makes a 'Holy Family'?"

108. Lambda Legal, "What Makes a 'Holy Family'?"

109. Melamed, *Represent and Destroy.*

110. Agathangelou, Bassichis, and Spira, "Intimate Investments," 123–24.

111. Lambda Legal, "What Makes a 'Holy Family'?"

112. Marouf v. Azar, 391 F. Supp. 3d 23 (D.D.C. 2019), 1, https://ecf.dcd.uscourts.gov/cgi-bin/show_public_doc?2018cv0378-48.

113. Marouf v. Azar, 22.

114. Marouf v. Azar, 17.

115. Briggs, *Somebody's Children*, 242.

116. Peg Hunter, "Month of Momentum: Looking Back at 30 Days of Actions to Close the Camps," IMMPrint: Freedom for Immigrants, September 21, 2021, https://imm-print.com/month-of-momentum-looking-back-at-30-days-of-actions-to-close-the-camps/?fbclid=IwARo Ml7eCZEiSq_LpUonpOPYjoWewisV5Co3Qo_zU47X338MkdpJbwq AvpD4.

117. Hunter, "Month of Momentum."

118. Hunter, "Month of Momentum."

119. Karma Chávez, "Border (In)securities: Normative and Differential Belonging in LGBTQ and Immigrant Rights Discourse," *Communication and Critical/Cultural Studies* 7, no. 2, (June 2010): 137.

120. Hunter, "Month of Momentum."

121. Verónica Vélez, "Madres en la Lucha: Forging Motherhood as a Political Movement across Borders," in *The Chicana M(other)work Anthology: Porque sin Madres No Hay Revolución* (Tucson: University of Arizona Press, 2019), 168.

122. Vélez, "Madres en la Lucha."

123. Vélez, "Madres en la Lucha."

124. Mai'a Williams, *This Is How We Survive: Revolutionary Mothering, War, and Exile in the 21st Century* (Oakland, CA: PM Press, 2019), 497.

125. Williams, *This Is How We Survive*, 510.

126. Williams, *This Is How We Survive*, 10–11.

127. Williams, *This Is How We Survive*, 497.

128. Gumbs, "m/other ourselves," 29.

129. King, "Black 'Feminisms' and Pessimism"; Saidiya V. Hartman, "The Belly of the World: A Note on Black Women's Labors," *Souls* 18, no. 1 (2016): 165–73; Aliyyah Abdur-Rahman, "The Strangest Freaks of Despotism: Queer Sexuality in Antebellum African American Slave Narratives," *Division on Black American Literature and Culture of the Modern Language Association* 40, no. 2 (2016): 223–37.

130. Ruha Benjamin, "Black AfterLives Matter," 65.

CHAPTER THREE. YOUR CHILDREN ARE NOT YOUR CHILDREN

1. Alice MacLachlan, "Conceiving Differently within the Ethics of Assisted Reproduction," *APA Newsletter*, Fall 2019, 16.

2. Mason Boycott-Owen, "British Lesbian Couple First to Carry Baby In Both Their Wombs," *The Telegraph*, December 2, 2019, www .telegraph.co.uk/news/2019/12/03/british-lesbian-couple-first-carry-baby-wombs/.

3. In this instance, both partners identified as female, but this technology can also be used with desiring parents of any gender identification with uteruses.

4. Boycott-Owen, "British Lesbian Couple."

5. Anecova, Anecova website, accessed July 17, 2023, www.apollo.io /companies/Anecova/54a1291c69702d9313907701?chart=count.

6. Derek M. Norman, "A Glittering Goodbye to Hector Xtravaganza," *New York Times*, March 11, 2019, www.nytimes.com/2019/03/11 /nyregion/hector-xtravaganza-memorial-death.html.

7. Rivers, *Radical Relations*.

8. Quoted in Hume, *Deep Care*, 125.

9. Quoted in Hume, *Deep Care*, 130.

10. For a discussion of a legal case in which Jennifer Cramblett, a white intending lesbian mother, sued because she was accidentally inseminated with sperm from an African American person, see Camille Gear Rich, "Contracting Our Way to Inequality: Race, Reproductive Freedom, and the Quest for the Perfect Child," *Minnesota Law Review* 104, no. 5 (May 2020): 2375–2470. See also Savannah Shange, "Black on Purpose: Race, Inheritance and Queer Reproduction," *Feminist Wire*, October 10, 2014, https://thefeministwire .com/2014/10/black-purpose-race-inheritance-queer-reproduction/; Nadine Ehlers, "Racial Futurity: Biolegality and the Question of Black Life," in *Personhood in the Age of Biolegality*, ed. Marc de Leeuw and Sonja Van Wichelen (London: Routledge, 2020); Suzanne Lenon and Danielle Peers, "Wrongful Inheritance: Race, Disability, and Sexuality in Cramblett v. Midwest Sperm Bank," *Feminist Legal Studies* 25 (2017): 141–63. This cuts both ways, and critiques have been made of

white intending parents' selection of sperm from donors of color. For a good piece critiquing white liberal attempts to circumvent racism through this, see Jaya Keaney, "Queer Multiracial Family: Figuring Race in Donor-Assisted Conception," in *The Reproduction Industry: Intimate Experiences and Global Processes*, ed. Vera Mackie (Lanham, MD: Rowan and Littlefield, 2019), 79–95. For a discussion of the transnational racial politics of white gay men who use surrogates, see Wei Wei, "Queering the Rise of China: Gay Parenthood, Transnational ARTs, and Dislocated Reproductive Rights," *Feminist Studies* 47, no. 2 (2021): 312–40, https://doi.org/10.1353/fem.2021.0018.

11. Michael Boucai, "Is Assisted Procreation and LGBT Right?," *Wisconsin Law Review*, no. 6 (2016): 1065–66.

12. Lia Eustachewich, "Lesbian Couple Welcomes 'Two-Womb' Baby," *New York Post*, December 4, 2019, https://nypost.com/2019/12/04/british-lesbian-couple-first-to-carry-baby-in-both-of-their-wombs/.

13. It should also be noted that this equates an embryo with a child in ways that raise other questions for a feminist politics of reproductive justice and autonomy.

14. Jenny Gunnarsson Payne, "Grammars of Kinship: Biological Motherhood and Assisted Reproduction in the Age of Epigenetics," *Signs: Journal of Women in Culture and Society* 41, no. 3 (2016): 483–506.

15. For more on the legal distinctions between the authenticity conferred upon genetic material compared to gestational labor, see Lewis, *Full Surrogacy Now*.

16. For a brief genealogy of the pull of LGBTQ communities into bionormative ideas of family, and specifically the discourse of DNA, see Alexandra Kimball and Tamara Lea Spira, "The Parent Trap: How DNA Testing Complicates Queer Family," *Real Life Magazine*, October 13, 2021, https://reallifemag.com/the-parent-trap/.

17. Tamara Lea Spira, "Life before Conception: Gamete Personhood in the Wake of Dobbs," *Nursing Clio*, December 13, 2023, https://nursingclio.org/2023/12/13/life-before-conception-gamete-personhood-in-the-wake-of-dobbs/.

18. Donor Sibling Registry, "About DSR."

19. Nikolas Rose, *The Politics of Life Itself* (Princeton, NJ: Princeton University Press, 2007), quoted in Adele E. Clarke et al., *Biomedicalization: Technoscience, Health, and Illness in the U.S.* (Durham, NC: Duke University Press, 2010), 4.

20. Siobhan Somerville, "Scientific Racism and the Emergence of the Homosexual Body," *Journal of the History of Sexuality* 5, no. 2 (1994): 266.

21. Somerville, "Scientific Racism," 266.

22. In 2019, a large European study concluded that, while there is no single "gay gene," homosexual behavior is linked to genetics. Zeke Stokes, chief programs officer for GLAAD, argued that this was a positive development because it proved how queerness is normal and unchangeable. See Lindsey Bever, "There's No One 'Gay Gene,' but Genetics Are Linked to Same-Sex Behavior, New Study Says," *Washington Post*, August 19, 2019, www.ncbi.nlm.nih.gov/search/research-news/4482/.

23. This includes cases in which white intending parents rely upon surrogates of color to birth "white" babies, and the infamous case of Jennifer Cramblett (see note 10 above). See Harrison, *Brown Bodies, White Babies: The Politics of Cross-racial Surrogacy* (New York: New York University Press, 2016), for an analysis of the ways that white intending parents make sense of the use of surrogates of color for their "white" babies and his note 6 for analysis of the Cramblett case. I thank Anna E. Ward for making this connection.

24. Amade M'Charek, "Beyond Fact or Fiction: On the Materiality of Race in Practice," *Cultural Anthropology* 28, no. 3 (2013): 436.

25. M'Charek, "Beyond Fact or Fiction," 435.

26. Daniela Cutas and Anna Smajdor, "Duped Fathers, Cuckoo Children, and the Problem of Basing Fatherhood on Biology: A Philosophical Analysis," in *Assistierte Reproduktion mit Hilfe Dritter*, ed. Katharina Beier et al. (New York: Springer, 2020), 171–82.

27. Cutas and Smajdor, "Duped Fathers," 181.

28. Over the last several decades, an important body of feminist scholarship has sought to account for these inequities embedded within the surrogacy industry in the context of flourishing economies of bodies and reproductive labor that hinge on the material exploitation of

racialized women (see Vora, *Life Support*). This includes work on global economies of eggs, sperm, embryos, and uteruses (Charis Thompson, *Making Parents: The Ontological Choreography of Reproductive Technologies* [Cambridge, MA: MIT Press, 2005]; Rene Almeling, *Sex Cells: The Medical Market for Eggs and Sperm* [Berkeley: University of California Press, 2011]; Catherine Waldby, *The Oocyte Economy: The Changing Meaning of Human Eggs* [Durham, NC: Duke University Press, 2019]), as well as the transnational commercialization of surrogacy, which has largely depended upon the racialized gestational labor of Black women and women of color in the United States (Harrison, *Brown Bodies, White Babies*; Alys Eve Weinbaum, *The Afterlife of Reproductive Slavery: Biocapitalism and Black Feminism's Philosophy of History* [Durham, NC: Duke University Press, 2019]) and women of color transnationally (Natalie Fixmer-Oraiz, "Speaking of Solidarity: Transnational Gestational Surrogacy and the Rhetorics of Reproductive (In)Justice," *Frontiers* 34, no. 3 [2013]: 141–61; Sharmila Rudrappa, *Discounted Life: The Price of Global Surrogacy in India* [New York: New York University Press, 2015]; Lewis, *Full Surrogacy Now*). For this discussion on the post-Soviet region, see Adriana Petryna, *When Experiments Travel: Clinical Trials and the Global Search for Human Subjects* (Princeton, NJ: Princeton University Press, 2009).

29. In 1986, the now-famous case of Baby M denied custody to a white contracted surrogate who wished to retain custody of the child she had carried and cared for until the age of four months. This was based upon the legal decision that, while surrogacy contracts were inherently flawed and against public policy, nonetheless a "best interest of the child" was to go to the intending parents. In *Johnson v. Calvert* (1990), an African American surrogate named Anna Johnson lost custody of the baby she had gestated to a white and Filipino couple. In this case, the court upheld the validity of surrogacy contracts. Thus, through different legal reasoning, both cases concluded that a surrogate would not have parental rights. For a good analysis of this case, see Harrison, *Brown Bodies, White Babies*.

30. This differs from cases of queer or infertile people with uteruses who have paid to gestate donor eggs, where legal contracts protect the gestating parent.

31. Weinbaum, *Afterlife of Reproductive Slavery.*

32. Payne, "Grammars of Kinship," 493.

33. Rose, *Politics of Life Itself,* quoted in A. Clarke et al., *Biomedicalization,* 4.

34. Payne, "Grammars of Kinship," 493.

35. Stephan Guttinger and John Dupré, "Genomics and Postgenomics," in *The Stanford Encyclopedia of Philosophy,* ed. Edward N. Zalta and Uri Nodelman, first published October 20, 2016, https://plato.stanford.edu/entries/genomics/#InteHapMProj.

36. Nathaniel Comfort, "The Genetic Self," *The Point Mag, Examined Life,* November 14, 2014, https://thepointmag.com/examined-life/genetic-self/.

37. Comfort, "Genetic Self."

38. Natali Valdez, "The Redistribution of Reproductive Responsibility: On the Epigenetics of 'Environment,'" *Medical Anthropology Quarterly* 32, no. 3 (2018): 427.

39. Valdez, "Redistribution of Reproductive Responsibility."

40. Valdez, "Redistribution of Reproductive Responsibility." See also Sarah S. Richardson's brilliant analysis of "the figure of the maternal body as an 'epigenetic vector'" that comes to reinscribe biological determinism and pathologize pregnant people's "choices" in "Maternal Bodies in the Postgenomic Order: Gender and the Explanatory Landscape of Epigenetics," in *Postgenomics: Perspectives on Biology after the Genome,* ed. S. Richardson and H. Stevens (Durham, NC: Duke University Press, 2015), 210–29.

41. Payne, "Grammars of Kinship," 502–3.

42. Stephanie Clare, quoting Victoria Pitts-Taylor, *The Brain's Body: Neuroscience and Corporeal Politics* (Durham, NC: Duke University Press, 2016), in "Reimagining Biological Relatedness: Epigenetics and Queer Kin," *Signs: Journal of Women in Culture and Society* 45, no. 1 (2019): 52.

43. Carl Zimmer, "Seven Big Misconceptions about Heredity," *Skeptical Inquirer* 43, no. 3 (May/June 2019), https://skepticalinquirer.org/2019/05/seven-big-misconceptions-about-heredity/.

44. Donna Jeanne Haraway, *Modest_Witness@Second_Millennium. FemaleMan_Meets_OncoMouse: Feminism and Technoscience* (London: Routledge, 2018), 142.

45. Kaushik Sunder Rajan, *Biocapital: The Constitution of Postgenomic Life* (Durham, NC: Duke University Press, 2006), 172.

46. Wendy Kramer, *Donor Family Matters: My Story of Raising a Profoundly Gifted Donor-Conceived Child, Redefining Family, and Building the Donor Sibling Registry* (Nederland, CO: Donor Sibling Registry, 2020); Wendy Kramer and Naomi Cahn, *Finding Our Families: A First-of-Its-Kind Book for Donor-Conceived People and Their Families* (New York: Random House, 2012); Sarah Franklin, *Biological Relatives: IVF, Stem Cells, and the Future of Kinship* (Durham, NC: Duke University Press, 2013).

47. This diagram is reproduced in Wendy Kramer, "Words Have Power in Sperm and Egg Donor Families," *Psychology Today*, April 19, 2022, www.psychologytoday.com/us/blog/donor-family-matters/202204/words-have-power-in-sperm-and-egg-donor-families.

48. MacLachlan, "Conceiving Differently," 16.

49. While Franklin is addressing IVF specifically, the same argument could be made for other methods, including intracervical conception (ICI) and intrauterine conception (IUI), though the complexity of the technology differs vastly.

50. Michael Foucault, *The Order of Things*, 2nd ed., Routledge Classics (London: Routledge, 2001).

51. Mutcherson, "Blood and Water," 127.

52. Emily A. Owens, "Reproducing Racial Fictions: Critical Meditations on (a) Lesbian Pregnancy," *Signs: Journal of Women in Culture and Society* 44, no. 4 (2019): 866.

53. Owens, "Reproducing Racial Fictions," 867.

54. Kramer, *Donor Family Matters*, 6.

55. Kramer, *Donor Family Matters*, 12, 17.

56. Kramer, *Donor Family Matters*, 5.

57. Kramer, *Donor Family Matters*.

58. Kramer, *Donor Family Matters*, 12.

59. Kramer, *Donor Family Matters*, 13–16.

60. Kramer, *Donor Family Matters*, 13.

61. Kramer, *Donor Family Matters*, 16.

62. Alondra Nelson, "The Social Life of DNA: Racial Reconciliation and Institutional Morality after the Genome," *British Journal of Sociology* 69, no. 3 (2018): 27.

63. A. Nelson, "Social Life of DNA," 27.

64. For a broader critique of this dynamic, see Ruha Benjamin, *Race after Technology: Abolitionist Tools for the New Jim Code* (Cambridge: Polity, 2019).

65. Kramer, *Donor Family Matters*, 84.

66. A. Nelson, "Social Life of DNA," 165.

67. Spira, "Life before Conception," and Kimball and Spira, "Parent Trap."

68. Importantly, the DSR has marketed specifically to queer families, placing ads for their organization in mainstream LGBT publications such as *Gay Parent Magazine* and *Philadelphia Pride*, and hosting webinars for the Family Equality Council.

69. Donor Sibling Registry, "Non-Biological Perspective," accessed December 2012, https://dsr-static-files.s3.us-west-2.amazon-aws.com/0e215cf71649252f.

70. Donor Sibling Registry, "Non-Biological Perspective."

71. Donor Sibling Registry, "Non-Biological Perspective."

72. Donor Sibling Registry, "Our LGBTQ Families," accessed April 17, 2021, www.donorsiblingregistry.com/lgbt#our_lgbtq_families.

73. Stephanie Fairyington, "A Lesson in Queer Parenting That's Good for Any Family," *Boston Globe*, December 20, 2020, www.bostonglobe.com/2020/12/20/opinion/lesson-queer-parenting-thats-good-any-family/?fbclid=IwAR2MPDYxVD6wUjSm6gRmQccibV8t46399mMSowUDUdKBf3yIZFPUpXNksyc.

74. Fairyington, "Lesson in Queer Parenting."

75. Gena Jaffe (@connectingrainbowsorg), "Lessons learned from donor conceived adults," *Instagram*, September 4, 2021, www.instagram.com/p/CTZsiPOLVMo/?igsh=MWtheTcyc2pyM2YodA%3D%3D.

76. Gena Jaffe (@connectingrainbowsorg), "A donor is not a parent period," *Instagram*, September 3, 2021, www.instagram.com/p/CTW3_m4LJgo/?igsh=MTBqcnkza2dtMmpvdA%3D%3D.

77. Gena Jaffe (@connectingrainbowsorg), "A donor is not a parent period," *Instagram*, September 3, 2021, www.instagram.com/p/CTW3_m4LJgo/?igsh=MTBqcnkza2dtMmpvdA%3D%3D.

78. Mary Kate (@sterlingmoms), "I'm finally coming out," *Instagram*, July 2, 2021, www.instagram.com/p/CQ1rSxph7wZ/?hl=en.

79. Mary Kate (@sterlingmoms), "I'm finally coming out," *Instagram*, July 2, 2021, www.instagram.com/p/CQ1rSxph7wZ/?hl=en.

80. Gena Jaffe (@connectingrainbowsorg), "Lessons learned from donor conceived adults," *Instagram*, September 4, 2021, www.instagram.com/p/CTZsiPOLVMo/?igsh=MWtheTcyc2pyM2YodA%3D%3D.

81. Kramer, *Donor Family Matters*, 16.

82. I thank Peggy Lee for asking me to draw out this argument. For a fuller overview of these debates, see Robyn Weigman, "Sex and Negativity; Or What Queer Theory Has for You," *Cultural Critique* 95 (Winter 2017): 219–43.

83. In *No Future: Queer Theory and the Death Drive* (Durham, NC: Duke University Press, 2004), Lee Edelman famously positioned queerness as an antithesis to a reproductive futurism. This was in dialogue with Leo Bersani's equally canonical rejection of a politics of redemption (or a queer politics at all). See Leo Bersani, "Is the Rectum a Grave?," *AIDS: Cultural Analysis/Cultural Activism* 43 (Winter 1987): 197–222, www.jstor.org/stable/3397574.

84. Muñoz, *Cruising Utopia*, 52.

85. See, for example, Eve Kosofsky Sedgwick and Adam Frank, eds., *Shame and Its Sisters: A Silvan Tomkins Reader* (Durham, NC: Duke University Press, 1995), and Eve Kosofsky Sedgwick, *Touching Feeling: Affect, Pedagogy, Performativity* (Durham, NC: Duke University Press, 2003). For a more contemporary uptake applied to the political sphere, see Eric Stanley, "The Affective Commons: Gay Shame, Queer Hate, and Other Collective Feelings," *GLQ* 24, no. 4 (2018): 489–508.

86. Gayatri Gopinath, *Impossible Desires* (Durham, NC: Duke University Press, 2005).

87. Heather Love, *Feeling Backward: Loss and the Politics of Queer History* (Cambridge, MA: Harvard University Press, 2009).

88. This was embodied, most notably, in José Esteban Muñoz's call for a utopic queer-of-color politics that lives in the failure to grasp a future that has yet to arrive. Muñoz, *Cruising Utopia*, 2009.

89. Jack Halberstam, *The Queer Art of Failure* (Durham, NC: Duke University Press, 2011), 187.

90. A. Rich, "Compulsory Heterosexuality"; Shannon Cole and L. C. Cate, "Compulsory Gender and Transgender Existence: Adrienne Rich's Queer Possibility," *WSQ: Women's Studies Quarterly* 36, nos. 3–4 (2008): 279–87.

91. Wendy Kramer quoting the counselor Olivia Montuschi in Kramer and Cahn, *Finding Our Families*, 95.

92. Laura Mamo, *Queering Reproduction: Achieving Pregnancy in the Age of Technoscience* (Durham, NC: Duke University Press, 2007).

93. Mamo uses the language of women and lesbians in her text to reflect the gender and sexual identifications of those with whom she spoke. Later work reflects a shifting vocabulary of gender and sexuality.

94. Charlotte Witt, "A Critique of the Bionormative Concept of Family," in *Family-Making: Contemporary Ethical* Challenges, ed. Françoise Baylis and Carolyn McLeod (Oxford: Oxford University Press, 2014), 2.

95. Kramer and Cahn, *Finding Our Families*, 94.

96. Abby Lippman, "Worrying—and Not Worrying about—the Geneticization of Reproduction and Health," in *Misconceptions: The Social Construction of Choice and the New Reproductive Technology*, ed. Gwynne Basen, Margrit Eichler, and Abby Lippman (Hull: Voyager, 1993), chap. 2.

97. Kath Weston, *Families We Choose: Lesbians, Gays, Kinship*, rev. ed. (New York: Columbia University Press, 1997).

98. Juana María Rodríguez, *Sexual Futures, Queer Gestures, and Other Latina Longings* (New York: New York University Press, 2014).

99. Mignon Moore, *Invisible Families: Gay Identities, Relationships and Motherhood among Black Women* (Berkeley: University of California Press, 2011), 114.

100. Benjamin, "Black AfterLives Matter," 48.

101. Sarah Franklin and Susan McKinnon, introduction to *Relative Values: Reconfiguring Kinship Studies*, ed. Sarah Franklin and Susan McKinnon (Durham, NC: Duke University Press, 2001), 21.

102. Franklin and Susan McKinnon, *Relative Values*, 21.

103. There is a long history of parents being advised to lie to children about both adoption and the usage of donor gametes in order to protect paternity legally and otherwise. One of the earliest medical texts on "artificial insemination" (AI) advised that sperm of the intending father was to be mixed with donor sperm (including sperm from doctors themselves). No one, and especially not the child or future medical providers, was to know that this had happened in order to protect the father's paternity. "To prevent the courts from establishing that a donor was the father of the child, some gynecologists mix the husband's semen with that of the donor. Many doctors refer their pregnant A.I. patients to an obstetrician who is not aware of the donor insemination … A well-known and respected author on infertility insists that the 'white lie' is a kindly, humane act." Dani Shapiro, *Inheritance: A Memoir of Genealogy, Paternity, and Love* (New York: Knopf, 2019), 223.

104. Kramer and Cahn, *Finding Our Families*, 248.

105. Kramer and Cahn, *Finding Our Families*, 249.

106. Them Before Us, "Them Before Us," accessed July 17, 2023, https://thembeforeus.com.

107. To be very clear, I completely support openness and the sharing of information transparently, an ethic that does not contradict the larger discussion of this chapter. As Laura Mamo and coauthors contend, secrecy has never been part of lesbian conception, particularly since "knowing the men who donated sperm for reproduction or who contributed sperm to co-create families has long been a part of achieving pregnancy for lesbians." Even with the later use of sperm banks, "secrecy of the use of a donor was never part of the narrative of conception." Laura Mamo et al., "Queer Intimacies and Structural Inequalities: New Directions in Stratified Reproduction," *Journal of Family Issues* 36, no. 4 (2015): 526. This is confirmed in research conducted with data from the DSR, which revealed that 80 percent of children from "lesbian" households report having always known of their origins, whereas "heterosexual families often kept the secret in order to preserve the interest of the nongenetic parent," with only 34 percent of donor-conceived children reporting that they had been told at a young age. See Naomi Cahn, *The New Kinship: Constructing Donor-Conceived*

Families (New York: New York University Press, 2013), 66. Additionally, it was OFWHC, the first and only lesbian-run clinic and eventual sperm bank, that was the first to encourage open disclosure of donors, ultimately creating an industry standard. See Hume, *Deep Care.*

108. Kimberley Leighton quoted in Margaret Homans, "Critical Adoption Studies: Conversation in Progress," *Adoption and Culture* 6, no. 1 (2018): 39.

109. Kimberley Leighton, "Analogies to Adoption in Arguments against Anonymous Gamete Donation: Geneticizing the Desire to Know," in *Family-Making: Contemporary Ethical Challenges*, ed. Francoise Baylis and Carolyn McLeod (Oxford: Oxford University Press, 2014), 241.

110. There is an argument that anonymous gamete donation is a human rights violation. It draws from the UN Convention on the Rights of the Child to assert that "the right to know and be cared for by one's parents" is violated in the case of gamete donation. However, as Samantha Besson points out, this is a very vague interpretation, as the UNCRC never defines parents as exclusively biogenetic. Besson quoted in Leighton, "Analogies to Adoption," 247.

111. Leighton, "Analogies to Adoption," 241.

112. Donor Sibling Registry, "The Donor-Conceived People's Bill of Rights," accessed January 27, 2021, https://donorsiblingregistry .com/blog/the-donor-conceived-bill-of-rights.

113. Among the organizations that call for an end to all sperm donation are Jennifer Lahl's Center for Bioethics and Culture. See Chris Lisee, "Conservatives Line Up against Sperm Donors, but Lack the Power to Ban Them," *Christian Century*, June 28, 2012, www.christiancentury.org/article/2012–06/conservatives-line-against-sperm-donorslack-power-ban-them. Recent legislation to ban anonymous sperm donation has passed in Colorado, where critics decry not only the lack of medical history of donors but also the lack of criminal history—which is therefore constructed as genetically relevant—as a reason to ban the practice. See Naomi Cahn and Sonia Suter, "Generations Later, the Rights of Donor-Conceived People Are Becoming Law," TheHill,April23,2022,https://thehill.com/opinion/healthcare/3460149-generations-later-the-rights-of-donor-conceived-people-are-becoming-

law/. While criminal history did not make it into the bill, it was proposed in New York State law as well, and is currently being debated.

114. United Nations, "Convention on the Rights of the Child," United Nations Human Rights, Office of the High Commissioner, November 20, 1989, www.ohchr.org/en/professionalinterest/pages /crc.aspx.

115. Rita Arditti, "Do You Know Who You Are? The Grandmothers of the Plaza De Mayo," *Women's Review of Books* 24 (September-October 2007): 12–15, www.jstor.org/stable/pdf/20476634.pdf?refreqid= excelsior%3Aacae288504f77ba0b6obda182462491f.

116. In a parallel but related history, what was once the movement to reunite stolen children with relatives (blood or not) and bring families the remains of their loved ones has turned into its own forensic endeavor, involving extensive DNA testing. For more on this, see Tamara Lea Spira, "Race, Sexuality and Indigeneity in Patricio Guzmán's Nostalgia for the Light: Toward a New Ontology and Archive of Revolution," *E-Misférica* 8, no. 3 (2012), http://hemisphericinstitute .org/hemi/en/e-misferica-91/spira. For a specific discussion of the complex relationship between DNA tests and the quest for social justice, see Lindsay Smith, *Subversive Genes: Making DNA and Human Rights in Argentina* (forthcoming).

117. Sarah Dingle, "Making Humans: International Principles for Donor Conception and Surrogacy," Change.org, accessed June 9, 2021, www.change.org/p/united-nations-making-humans-international-principles-for-donor-conception-and-surrogacy.

118. *Severance,* "About Severance," accessed June 8, 2021, https://severancemag.com/about-severance/.

119. *Severance,* "About Severance."

120. A list of groups that *Severance* offers as resources for donor-conceived individuals is given at *Severance,* "Donor Conception," accessed July 4, 2024, https://severancemag.com/donor-conception/.

121. While Leighton does not go into this, another major problem with the conflation of gamete donation and adoption is the different dynamics that mark gamete donation and the racial politics of

adoption, or what many would call the state-sanctioned kidnapping of Native American, Black, and other children of color. For an important history of this, see Briggs, *Somebody's Children.* For an important discussion of the specific links between slavery and the current foster system, see Cloud, "Toward the Abolition of the Foster System."

122. Moreover, one must note the odd figure of the (generally white) child randomly kidnapped by a stranger, a trope that itself carries histories used to bolster the expansion of prisons and the targeting of the very communities who are most likely to have their children taken from them.

123. Alex Haley, quoted in Kramer and Cahn, *Finding Our Families*, 1.

124. Alex Haley, quoted in Kramer and Cahn, *Finding Our Families*, 81.

125. A cultural hit, *Roots* followed the story of Kunta Kinte, a fictional character based on a person enslaved from Gambia to whom Haley claimed to be related. Itself the subject of much controversy, *Roots* raised thorny issues about bloodline, genealogy, and what it means to attempt to recover lost histories through a set of tools and metrics that are neither transhistorical nor transcultural—particularly with Henry Louis Gates's more recent uptake, in his contemporary television show *Finding Your Roots*, which uses DNA in attempt to chronicle the genealogies of celebrities. These controversies notwithstanding, Haley's *Roots* represented a pivotal cultural moment, forcing Americans to grapple with the traumas of slavery in an unprecedented way, as historian Matthew F. Delmont argues in *Making Roots: A Nation Captivated* (Berkeley: University of California Press, 2016).

126. Jared Sexton, "People-of-Color-Blindness: Notes on the Afterlife of Slavery," *Social Text* 28 (2010): 31–56; Saidiya V. Hartman, *Scenes of Subjection: Terror, Slavery, and Self-Making in Nineteenth-Century America* (Oxford: Oxford University Press, 1997).

127. James Lopez, "Gender Matters," Them Before Us, May 3, 2017, https://thembeforeus.com/gender-matters-2/.

128. Them Before Us, "Them Before Us," accessed July 17, 2023, https://thembeforeus.com.

129. Faust draws on studies of child abuse at the hands of mothers' male boyfriends and on child poverty rates among children raised by

stepmothers to argue that "unrelated adults are less protected, invested, and connected to children." See Katy Faust, "Biology Matters," Them Before Us, May 6, 2017, https://thembeforeus.com /biology-matters/.

130. For a good critical overview of these histories, see Meiners, *For the Children?* For an important discussion of the ways that queers have been constructed as a threat to children to be legislated, one only need look at the long-standing discourses of gay men as pedophiles or of lesbians as unfit parents. See, for example, Gillian Frank, "'The Civil Rights of Parents': Race and Conservative Politics in Anita Bryant's Campaign against Gay Rights in 1970s Florida," *Journal of the History of Sexuality* 22, no. 1 (January 2013): 126–60, and Rivers, "'In the Best Interests of the Child.'"

131. "Championing the Donor-Conceived Community," Center for Bioethics and Culture Network, March 16, 2021, www.cbc-network .org/2021/03/championing-the-donor-conceived-community/.

132. Kramer, *Donor Family Matters*, 29.

133. Kramer, *Donor Family Matters*, 29.

134. Kramer, *Donor Family Matters*, 29.

135. Joey L. Mogul, Andrea J. Ritchie, and Kay Whitlock, "Setting the Historical Stage: Colonial Legacies," in *Queer (In)justice: The Criminalization of LGBT People in the United States* (Boston: Beacon Press, 2011), 1. For a discussion of how binary gender was a critical part of this formulation, see Miranda, "Extermination of the *Joyas*," and Qwo-Li Driskill, "Double-Weaving Two Spirit Critiques: Building Alliances between Native and Queer Studies," *GLQ: A Journal of Lesbian and Gay Studies* 16, nos. 1–2 (2010): 69–92.

136. TallBear, "Making Love and Relations," 147.

137. Angela Y. Davis, "Rape, Racism and the Capitalist Setting," *Black Scholar* 12, no. 6 (1981): 39–45.

138. Abdur-Rahman, "Strangest Freaks of Despotism," 234.

139. Abdur-Rahman, "Strangest Freaks of Despotism," 226.

140. Abdur-Rahman, "Strangest Freaks of Despotism," 226.

141. Owens, "Reproducing Racial Fictions," 867.

142. Owens, "Reproducing Racial Fictions," 867.

143. Michelle Murphy, *The Economization of Life* (Durham, NC: Duke University Press, 2017), 6.

144. Kim TallBear, *Native American DNA: Tribal Belonging and the False Promise of Genetic Science* (Minneapolis: University of Minnesota Press, 2013), 6.

145. This is in the context of Benjamin's discussion of the usage of genetic research for the development of ethnic drug markets, but I would argue that it applies to the question of tracking identity and relationships for individuals through the commercial DNA test as well. See Ruha Benjamin, "A Lab of Their Own: Genomic Sovereignty as Postcolonial Science Policy," *Policy and Society* 28, no. 4 (2009): 341–55.

146. Efforts to study human genetic variation since the 1990s have been riddled with controversy and critique, particularly from Indigenous communities and communities of color who question the classification of racial and ethnic groups by outside scientific experts. For a good overview of these early debates, see Jenny Reardon, "Race without Salvation," in *Revisiting Race in a Genomic Age*, ed. Barbara Koenig, Sandra Soo-Jin, and Sarah S. Richardson (New Brunswick, NJ: Rutgers University Press, 2008), 304–19.

147. Rajan, *Biocapital*, 170.

148. Simone Browne, *Dark Matters: On the Surveillance of Blackness* (Durham, NC: Duke University Press, 2015), 110; see also Ruha Benjamin, "Catching Our Breath: Critical Race STS and the Carceral Imagination," *Engaging Science, Technology, and Society* 2 (2016): 152.

149. Browne, *Dark Matters*, 109.

150. Abigail Hauslohner, "U.S. Immigration Authorities Will Collect DNA from Detained Migrants," *Washington Post*, March 6, 2020, www.washingtonpost.com/immigration/us-immigration-authorities-will-collect-dna-from-detained-migrants/2020/03/06/63376696-5fc7-11ea-9055-5fa1298ibbbf_story.html.

151. Benjamin, "Catching Our Breath," 153.

152. A. Nelson, "Social Life of DNA."

153. Yves Moreau, "Crack Down on Genomic Surveillance," Nature.com, December 3, 2019, www.nature.com/articles/d41586-0190-3687-x?sf225143202=1.

154. M'charek, "Beyond Fact or Fiction."

155. TallBear, *Native American DNA*, 5.

156. Browne, *Dark Matters*, 109–10.

157. Paige St. John, "DNA Genealogical Databases Are a Gold Mine for Police, but with Few Rules and Little Transparency," *Los Angeles Times*, November 24, 2019, www.latimes.com/california/story/2019-11-24/law-enforcement-dna-crime-cases-privacy.

158. 23andMe, "About," accessed April 17, 2021, www.23andme.com/.

159. D. Shapiro, *Inheritance*, 9.

160. Dani Shapiro's memoir is one in a cottage industry of memoirs, podcasts, and blogs of donor-conceived children who learned of this fact late in life, and whose stories activist networks such as the US Donor Conceived Council (USDCC) use to advocate for policies to regulate gamete donation.

161. D. Shapiro, *Inheritance*, 14.

162. D. Shapiro, *Inheritance*, 9.

163. Families reproduced through coital reproduction with trans and/or nonbinary parents still stray from bionormative even though they may technically be biogenetic.

164. TallBear, *Native American DNA*, 6.

165. Severance, "Conceiving People: Q&A with Daniel Groll," *Severance Magazine*, accessed July 5, 2023, https://severancemag.com/tag/books/.

166. *Severance,* "Conceiving People."

167. *Severance,* "Conceiving People."

168. Donor Sibling Registry, "Our LGBTQ Families."

169. This adds a bizarre twist to fantasies such as the one played out in the 2010 hit film *The Kids Are All Right*, in which a queer mom and her sperm donor begin an affair after her children find him.

170. Donor Sibling Registry, "Our LGBTQ Families."

171. Donor Sibling Registry, "One LGBT Parent's Story," Donor Sibling Registry, December 2012, https://dsr-static-files.s3.us-west-2.amazonaws.com/3e1b54b1e975cd90.

172. Laura Mamo, "Queering the Fertility Clinic," *Journal of Medical Humanities* 34, no. 2 (2013): 237.

173. Mamo, "Queering the Fertility Clinic."

174. Nick Macklon, "Everything You Need to Know about Shared Motherhood," Female First, November 23, 2017, www.femalefirst .co.uk/parenting/shared-motherhood-1108987.html.

175. Macklon, "Everything You Need to Know."

176. Rebekah Wilson-Williams, "Time to Be Brave," Metro Family, accessed July 17, 2023, www.metrofamilymagazine.com/time-to-be-brave/.

177. Wilson v. Williams, Volume #FD-2021-3681 (2023), District Court, Seventh Judicial District, State of Oklahoma, Letter Ruling, www.documentcloud.org/documents/23649403-1053622896-20230214-105340-1?responsive=1&title=1.

178. Austin Breasette, Ali Meyer and Raache Hicham, "Birth Certificate Battle: Sperm Donor Petitions for Court Custody of Baby Boy," Oklahoma's News 4, June 1, 2022, https://kfor.com/news/local /birth-certificate-battle-sperm-donor-petitions-court-for-custody-of-baby-boy/.

179. Spira, "Life before Conception."

180. Petra Nordqvist, "Feminist Heterosexual Imaginaries of Reproduction: Lesbian Conception in Feminist Studies of Reproductive Technologies," Feminist Theory 9, no. 3 (2008): 273–92.

181. Shulamith Firestone, The Dialectic of Sex: The Case for Feminist Revolution (New York: Farrar, Straus, and Giroux, 1970). 19. See also Sarah Franklin, "Revisiting Reprotech: Firestone and the Question of Equality," in Further Adventures of the Dialectic of Sex: Critical Essays on Shulamith Firestone, ed. Mandy Merck and Stella Sandford (New York: Palgrave Macmillan, 2010), 29–60.

182. Third World Gay Revolution, "What We Want, What We Believe," in Out of the Closets: Voices of Gay Liberation, ed. Karla Jay and Allen Young (New York: Douglas Book Corporation, 1972); Out History, "Gay Liberation in New York City," accessed June 21, 2020, http://outhistory.org/exhibits/show/gay-liberation-in-new-york-cit/3rd-world/pg-1. I thank Madi Stapleton for finding these archives and articulating this connection.

183. Pat Parker, "Revolution: It's Not Neat or Pretty or Quick," in This Bridge Called My Back: Writings by Radical Women of Color, 4th ed., ed.

Cherríe Moraga and Gloria Anzaldúa (New York: University of New York Press, 2015), 242.

184. John D'Emilio, "Capitalism and Gay Identity," in *Powers of Desire: The Politics of Sexuality*, New Feminist Library Series (New York: Monthly Review Press, 1983), 111.

185. Jin Haritaworn, "Murderous Inclusions," *International Feminist Journal of Politics* 15, no. 4 (2013): 445–52.

CHAPTER FOUR. QUEERING FAMILY ABOLITION

1. Angela Y. Davis et al., *Abolition. Feminism. Now.* (Chicago: Haymarket Books, 2022), 131.

2. Davis et al., *Abolition. Feminism. Now.*, 164.

3. Davis et al., *Abolition. Feminism. Now.*, 164.

4. Davis et al., *Abolition. Feminism. Now.*, 8, 164.

5. Davis et al., *Abolition. Feminism. Now.*, 161.

6. I owe this lesson to Angela Y. Davis and my work organizing with Critical Resistance and Justice Now in the early 2000s. Ruth Wilson Gilmore has a recent book that elaborates upon this idea beautifully. See *Change Everything: Racial Capitalism and the Case for Abolition* (Chicago: Haymarket Books, 2021).

7. Belinsky, "Gender and Family Abolition."

8. Ann Cvetkovich, *An Archive of Feelings: Trauma, Sexuality, and Lesbian Public Cultures* (Durham, NC: Duke University Press, 2003), 241.

9. Hartman, *Wayward Lives, Beautiful Experiments*, xv.

10. Hartman, *Wayward Lives, Beautiful Experiments*, xvi–xvii.

11. June Jordan, "The Creative Spirit: Children's Literature," in Gumbs et al., *Revolutionary Mothering*, 11–18. I am thankful to Alexis Pauline Gumbs for bringing this previously unpublished essay into publication.

12. Douglas Crimp, "How to Have Promiscuity in an Epidemic," *AIDS: Cultural Analysis/Cultural Activism* 43 (Winter 1987): 237–71, www.jstor.org/stable/pdf/3397576.pdf.

13. Alisa Bierria, Jakeya Caruthers, and Brooke Lober, introduction to Bierria, Caruthers, and Lober, *Abolition Feminisms*, 1:3.

14. For a more complete genealogy of family abolition, see Spira et al., "ACAB Means Abolishing the Cops," 13–42. For other readings, see also Kathi Weeks, "Abolition of the Family: The Most Infamous Feminist Proposal," *Feminist Theory* 24, no. 3 (2021), https://doi.org /10.1177/14647001211015841, and Sophie Lewis, *Abolish the Family: A Manifesto for Care and Liberation* (London: Verso, 2022).

15. Weeks, "Abolition of the Family," 6 (original italics).

16. Spira et al., "ACAB Means Abolishing the Cops."

17. These debates are extensive and rich. For a great gloss on them, see Kalindi Vora, "After the Housewife: Surrogacy, Labour and Human Reproduction," *Radical Philosophy* 2 no. 4 (Spring 2019): 42–46, www .radicalphilosophy.com/article/after-the-housewife/.

18. Andreas Chatzidakis et al., *The Care Manifesto: The Politics of Interdependence* (London: Verso Books, 2020), 17–18.

19. This requires a centering of the "conflicting and diverse bonds between labor, emotions and corporeality that do not line up neatly in terms of gender binaries and normative familial arrangements," as Martin F. Manalansan IV reminds us in "Queering the Chain of Care Paradigm," *Scholar and Feminist Online* 6, no. 3 (Summer 2008), http:// sfonline.barnard.edu/immigration/print_manalansan.htm.

20. D'Emilio, "Capitalism and Gay Identity," 475.

21. D'Emilio, "Capitalism and Gay Identity."

22. Quoted in Gumbs, "m/other ourselves," 27.

23. Baba Cooper, "The Radical Potential in Lesbian Mothering of Daughters," in Pollack and Vaughn, *Politics of the Heart*, 239. There were long-standing debates in lesbian separatist communities over what to do with sons. See Audre Lorde, "Man Child: A Black Feminist's Response," in Lorde, *Sister Outsider*, 72–80.

24. Kay Lindsey, "The Black Woman as Woman," in *The Black Woman: An Anthology*, ed. Toni Cade Bambara (New York: Mentor Books, 1970), 86.

25. Lindsey, "Black Woman as Woman," 87.

26. For example, as Aliyyah Abdur-Rahman argues, under slavery "whiteness [was the foundation for] … heteronormative qualification [and] … claims to familial, spousal and hereditary bonds." Abdur-

Rahman, "'Strangest Freaks of Despotism,'" 226, 223. See also Kim TallBear, "Making Love and Relations," 146–47. See chapter 3 for further analysis.

27. As Tiffany Lethabo King elegantly puts it, Lindsey understood the family to be "an amalgamation of land, slaves, property, conquest and the state" that would always position Black women outside the "coordinates of the human." King, "Black Feminisms' and Pessimism."

28. Bronski, "When Gays Wanted to Liberate Children."

29. Rafael Moraga, "Afterword: 100 Nights," in *Waiting in the Wings: A Portrait of Queer Motherhood*, by Cherríe Moraga, 25th anniversary ed. (Chicago: Haymarket Books, 2023), 237, 249. Note, this is the new reprint, whereas in the Introduction I am working from the original text.

30. R. Moraga, "Afterword," 251.

31. R. Moraga, "Afterword," 251–52.

32. R. Moraga, "Afterword," 208.

33. R. Moraga, "Afterword," 207.

34. R. Moraga, "Afterword," 207.

35. R. Moraga, "Afterword," 207.

36. Cherríe Moraga and Gloria Anzaldúa, a section introduction in *This Bridge Called My Back: Writings by Radical Women of Color* (Watertown, MA: Persephone Press, 1981), 19.

37. R. Moraga, "Afterword," 238.

38. C. Moraga, *Waiting in the Wings*, 53.

39. R. Moraga, "Afterword," 238.

40. L. Ben-Moshe, N. Erevelles, and E. R. Meiners, "Abolishing Innocence: Disrupting the Racist/Ableist Pathologies of Childhood," in *Building Abolition: Decarceration and Social Justice*, ed. K. Montford and C. Taylor (London: Routledge, 2021), 58–67.

41. Dyer, "Queer Futurity."

42. Hannah Dyer, "The Contested Design of Children's Sexual Education: Queer Growth and Epistemic Uncertainty," *Gender and Education* 31, no. 6 (2019): 743–44.

43. Kathryn Bond Stockton, *The Queer Child, or Growing Up Sideways in the Twentieth Century* (Durham, NC: Duke University Press, 2009), 5, 7.

44. C. Moraga, *Waiting in the Wings*, 106.

45. C. Moraga, *Waiting in the Wings*.

46. C. Moraga, *Waiting in the Wings*.

47. Sheldon, *Child to Come*, 4.

48. C. Moraga, *Waiting in the Wings*, 20.

49. Jordan, "Creative Spirit," 14.

50. Jordan, "Creative Spirit," 14.

51. Jordan, "Creative Spirit," 14.

52. Jordan, "Creative Spirit," 13. Today, of course, we would say "their own freedom" to express an expansion of the notion of children's freedom beyond the binary categories of 'his or her.'"

53. Jordan, "Creative Spirit," 11.

54. Jordan, "Creative Spirit," 12.

55. Jordan, "Creative Spirit," 12.

56. Jordan, "Creative Spirit," 13.

57. Jordan, "Creative Spirit," 18.

58. Lewis, *Abolish the Family*, 61–66.

59. Lewis, *Abolish the Family*, 9.

60. Jordan, "Creative Spirit," 13.

61. Amber J. Musser, "Re-membering Audre," in *No Tea, No Shade: New Writings in Black Queer Studies* (Durham, NC: Duke University Press, 2016), 354.

62. Lorde, "Uses of the Erotic," 53.

63. Lorde, "Uses of the Erotic."

64. For a discussion of nonmonogamy and family abolition among queers engaged in eros as a political practice, see Michelle E. O'Brien, "To Abolish the Family: The Working-Class Family and Gender Liberation in Capitalist Development," *Endnotes* 5 (2020): 390–97.

65. Alexis De Veaux, *Warrior Poet: A Biography of Audre Lorde* (Chico, CA: AK Press, 2006), 57.

66. Lorde, "Uses of the Erotic," 57.

67. Lorde, "Uses of the Erotic," 57.

68. Neferti X. M. Tadiar, "If Not Mere Metaphor... Sexual Economies Reconsidered," *S&F Online* 7, no. 3 (Summer 2009), https://sfonline.barnard.edu/sexecon/tadiar_05.htm. Tadiar is quoting Marx

here. See Karl Marx, *Grundrisse: Foundations of the Critique of Political Economy*, trans. Martin Nicolaus (New York: Penguin, 1973), 272. The italics are hers.

69. Tadiar, "If Not Mere Metaphor."

70. Lorde, "Uses of the Erotic," 55.

71. Lorde, "Uses of the Erotic."

72. Lorde, "Oberlin College Commencement Address," 218.

73. Audre Lorde, "When Will Ignorance End: Keynote Speech at the National Third World Gay and Lesbian Conference," in *I Am Your Sister: Collected and Unpublished Writings of Audre* Lorde, ed. Rudolph Byrd, Johnetta Cole, and Beverly Guy-Sheftall (New York: Oxford University Press, 2009), 221. See chapter 1 for a further discussion of Lorde's ideas of collective parenting.

74. Lorde, "Turning the Beat Around," 75.

75. Lorde, "Turning the Beat Around," 75.

76. Lorde, "Turning the Beat Around," 75.

77. Lorde, "Turning the Beat Around," 77.

78. Lorde, "Man Child," 77.

79. Gabrielle Owen, *A Queer History of Adolescence: Developmental Pasts, Relational Futures* (Athens: University of Georgia Press, 2020), 6.

80. Lorde, "Man Child," 77.

81. Lorde, "Turning the Beat Around," 77.

82. Lorde, "Turning the Beat Around," 76.

83. Lorde, "Turning the Beat Around," 79.

84. Lorde, "Turning the Beat Around," 79, 80.

85. Lewis, *Abolish the Family*, 28. See also O'Brien, "To Abolish the Family," 402.

86. Lorde, "Uses of the Erotic," 55.

87. Angela Y. Davis, "Reflections on the Black Woman's Role in the Community of Slaves," in *The Angela Y. Davis Reader* (Boston: Blackwell, 1998), 115–16.

88. Hartman, "Belly of the World," 171.

89. Hartman, "Belly of the World," 171.

90. Tadiar, "If Not Mere Metaphor," quoting Marx, *Grundrisse*, 272.

91. Lorde, "Turning the Beat Around," 80.

92. Jordan, "Creative Spirit," 18.

93. Lorde, "Turning the Beat Around," 80.

94. Elizabeth Lorde-Rollins, "Second November," *Motherhood Literature and Art*, June 13, 2017, https://momeggreview.com/2017/06/13/poetry-by-elizabeth-lorde-rollins/.

95. Lorde-Rollins, "Second November."

96. Lorde-Rollins, "Second November."

97. Lorde-Rollins, "Second November."

98. Lorde-Rollins, "Second November."

99. Lorde-Rollins, "Second November."

100. Stockton, *Queer Child*.

101. Rivers, *Radical Relations*, 193.

102. Crimp, "How to Have Promiscuity."

103. Crimp, "How to Have Promiscuity," 253.

104. Chatzidakis et al., *Care Manifesto*, 17–18.

105. Hil Malatino, "Theorizing Trans Care," chap. 3 in *Trans Care* (Minneapolis: University of Minnesota Press, 2020), https://manifold.umn.edu/read/trans-care/section/cd2afc3e-2f71-49aa-b249-cda1edad9951.

106. Spade, *Mutual Aid*, 8.

107. Cohen, "Punks, Bulldaggers," 438.

108. Nancy E. Stoller, *Lessons from the Damned: Queers, Whores and Junkies Respond to AIDS* (New York: Routledge, 1998), 155.

109. Stoller, *Lessons from the Damned*.

110. C. Moraga, *Waiting in the Wings*, 22.

111. C. Moraga, *Waiting in the Wings*, 54, 59, 117.

112. C. Moraga, *Waiting in the Wings*, 93, 106. See chapter 1 for a fuller discussion of Matthews.

113. Audre Lorde, *A Burst of Light: And Other Essays* (Chico, CA: AK Press, 2017), 130.

114. Lorde, *Burst of Light*, 130.

115. Lorde, *Burst of Light*, 130.

116. Audre Lorde and Pat Parker, *Sister Love: The Letters of Audre Lorde and Pat Parker, 1974–1989*, ed. Julie Enszer (Dover, FL: Sinister Wisdom, 2018), 89.

117. Susan Shapiro, founder of the Women's Community Cancer Project, directly credited Lorde for inspiration, and Jackie Winnow,

cofounder of the Women's Cancer Resource Center, stated that her cancer activism blended "some of what [she] learned in AIDS work" with "much of what [she] … learned from feminist organizing and Women's Liberation," which Lorde indelibly shaped. See Jackie Winnow, "Lesbians Evolving Health Care: Cancer and AIDS," *Feminist Review* 41 (Summer 1992): 71. See also Susan Shapiro, "Cancer as a Feminist Issue," *Sojourner Magazine*, 15, no. 1 (1989): 18–19. For an overview, see Barbara E Ley, *From Pink to Green: Disease Prevention and the Environmental Breast Cancer Movement* (New Brunswick, NJ: Rutgers University Press, 2009), 26. Additionally, Sarah Schulman traces how feminists and lesbians who emerged from the women's health movement brought already-politicized notions of care into ACT UP. See *Let the Record Show: A Political History of ACT UP New York, 1987–1993* (New York: Farrar, Straus and Giroux, 2021).

118. Opal Palmer Adisa, "Audre Lorde's Cancer Journals; Harbinger of Public Breast Cancer Conversation," in *The Wind Is Spirit: The Life, Love, and Legacy of Audre Lorde*, ed. Gloria Joseph (New York: Villarosa Media, 2016), 308–11.

119. Stephen Vider, *The Queerness of Home: Gender, Sexuality, and the Politics of Domesticity after World War II* (Chicago: University of Chicago Press, 2022), 185.

120. See the chapters "'Picture a Coalition': Community Caregiving and the Politics of AIDS/HIV at Home," and "'Some Hearts go Hungering': Homelessness and the First Wave of LGBTQ Shelter Activism," in Vider, *Queerness of Home*, 177–213, 143–78.

121. Vider, *Queerness of Home*, 227.

122. D'Emilio, "Capitalism and the Gay Identity," 475.

123. Ann Cvetkovich, "Legacies of Trauma, Legacies of Activism: ACT UP's Lesbians," in *Loss: The Politics of Mourning*, ed. David Eng and David Kazanjian (Berkeley: University of California Press, 2003), 427–57.

124. Gould, *Moving Politics*.

125. Cited in Christina B. Hanhardt, "Dead Addicts Don't Recover: ACT UP's Needle Exchange and the Subjects of Queer Activist History," *GLQ* 24, no. 4 (2018): 436.

126. Lorde, "Turning the Beat Around," 75.

127. Elizabeth Lorde-Rollins, "117: How My Mother's Book Shaped My Journey with Dr. Elizabeth Lorde-Rollins," *Rise Together Podcast*, https://podcasts.apple.com/us/podcast/117-how-my-mothers-book-shaped-my-journey-with-dr/id1407481308?i=1000495630387.

128. Malatino, "Theorizing Trans Care."

129. Malatino, "Theorizing Trans Care."

130. Andrea Ritchie, *Practicing New Worlds: Abolition and Emergent Strategies* (Chico, CA: AK Press, 2023).

131. A. Ritchie, *Practicing New Worlds*, 6.

132. A. Ritchie, *Practicing New Worlds*, 7.

133. Brooke Lober and Jane Segal, "Notes for a Special Issue," in "Out of Control," ed. Brooke Lober and Jane Segal, special issue, *Sinister Wisdom* 126 (Fall 2022): 27–28.

134. Susan Rosenberg, *An American Radical: A Political Prisoner in My Own Country* (New York: Citadel Press, 2011).

135. Agathangelou, Bassichis, and Spira, "Intimate Investments," 100.

136. Emily Hobson, "Fighting HIV/AIDS in Prison," in "Out of Control," ed. Brooke Lober and Jane Segal, special issue, *Sinister Wisdom* 126 (Fall 2022): 156–63.

137. While I was finalizing this manuscript, Dr. Shakur passed away, adding to the list of ancestors who crossed to the other side while I was writing this, and whose tireless work for justice has enabled this book.

138. Shira Hassan, "Liberatory Harm Reduction Saved My Life," in *Saving Our Own Lives: A Liberatory Practice of Harm Reduction* (Chicago: Haymarket Books, 2022), 13.

139. Jina B. Kim and Sami Schalk, "Reclaiming the Radical Politics of Self-Care: A Crip-of-Color Critique," *South Atlantic Quarterly* 120, no. 2 (2021): 327; Leah Lakshmi Piepzna-Samarasinha, *The Future Is Disabled: Prophecies, Love Notes and Mourning Songs* (Vancouver, BC: Arsenal Pulp Press, 2022). See also Mia Mingus, "I Am Continuing the Work," in *The Wind Is Spirit: The Life, Love, and Legacy of Audre Lorde*, ed. Gloria Joseph (New York, Villarosa Media, 2016), 253–55.

140. Angela Y. Davis, *Are Prisons Obsolete?* (New York: Seven Stories Press, 2011), 16.

141. Hassan, "Liberatory Harm Reduction," 13.

142. For an important ethnography of queer Ballroom culture in Detroit, see M. Bailey's *Butch Queens Up in Pumps*, a text that gives shape to the queer-of-color ethics of care produced in Houses; Marion M. Bailey, *Butch Queens Up in Pumps: Gender, Performance, and Ballroom Culture in Detroit* (Ann Arbor: University of Michigan Press, 2013). For a good ethnography of queer families developed on the street, see Joseph Plaster's ethnography, *Kids on the Street*, which examines how queer runaways in the Tenderloin generated complex modes of mutual aid through practices like collective housing and the pooling of resources. As Plaster argues, in particular, the ethos of "having one's back" emerged as a way for those abandoned by capitalism and the private heteronormative family to form elaborate economies of survival, insisting "on the value of sociality and sexuality untethered from the nuclear family, reproduction, and the gender binary," especially on the part of those marginalized from these mainstream institutions. Joseph Plaster, *Kids on the Street: Queer Kinship and Religion in San Francisco's Tenderloin* (Durham, NC: Duke University Press, 2023), 7.

143. M. Cooper, *Family Values*, 313, 214. See also Rosenberg, *American Radical*, 153–63 and 266–85.

144. Hanhardt, "Dead Addicts Don't Recover," 426, citing Lower East Side Harm Reduction Center, https://alliance.nyc/leshrc.

145. Davis et al., *Abolition. Feminism. Now.*, 2:131.

146. Robin D. G. Kelley, "Afterwor(l)d," in *Rehearsals for Living*, by Robin Maynard and Leanne Betasamosake Simpson (Chicago: Haymarket Books, 2022), 274.

147. Maynard and Simpson, *Rehearsals for Living*, 130–31.

148. Leanne Betasamosake Simpson, *As We Have Always Done: Indigenous Freedom through Radical Resistance*, cited in Maynard and Simpson, *Rehearsals for Living*, 184.

149. See, especially, "A Summer of Protest," in Maynard and Simpson, *Rehearsals for Living*, 101–48.

150. Maynard and Simpson, *Rehearsals for Living*, 113.

151. Jin Haritaworn, "#NoGoingBack: Queering Racial Capitalism on the Conjuncture of Protest and Pandemic," in *Sex and Pandemics*, ed. Ricky Varghese (Toronto: University of Toronto Press, forthcoming).

152. Haritaworn, "#NoGoingBack."

153. Maynard and Simpson, *Rehearsals for Living*, 72.

154. Kelley, "Afterwor(l)d," 274.

155. Kelley, "Afterwor(l)d," 267.

156. Maynard and Simpson, *Rehearsals for Living*, 177.

EPILOGUE

1. Kaitlin Menza, "How Afton Vechery Sold Modern Fertility for $225 Million, Just Four Years after Launch," *The Helm*, September 14, 2021, https://thehelm.co/afton-vechery-modern-fertility-interview/.

2. Tiffany Onyejiaka, "Why Black Patients Treated by Black Doctors Fare Better," *Ro* (blog), July 21, 2020, https://modernfertility.com/blog/racial-bias-disparities-black-womens-health/.

3. Health Guide Team, "IVF Egg Retrieval: Process, Recovery, Cost, Results," *Ro* (blog), December 6, 2021, https://modernfertility.com/blog/conceiving-when-lgbtq-iui-ivf-costs/.

4. Ro, "Modern Fertility," accessed July 17, 2023, https://ro.co/modern-fertility/?ro_ch=cpc&ro_p=google&ro_c=14494630967&ro_g=131133256946&ro_con=101&ro_a=649786582010&ro_t=kwd-1803625546008&ro_n=g&ro_d=c&gad=1&gclid=CjwKCAjwg-GjBhBnEiwAMUvNW6H5X-ZDZyYWBCRmrv5JS6vgliJWf8eGLXI-lqViJ5e4FgcFwEOHcRoC3B4QAvD_BwE.

5. Menza, "How Afton Vechery Sold."

6. Anna Allendale, "The Problem with Trusting a Startup to Monitor Your Fertility," HuffPost, August 14, 2018, www.huffpost.com/entry/at-home-fertility-tests_n_5b7335abe4b025e3596ba0fe.

7. Connie Loizos, "Modern Fertility Raises $15 Million to Sell Its Hormone Tests—and Gather More Fertility Data from Its Users," TechCrunch, June 11, 2019, https://social.techcrunch.com/2019/06/11/modern-fertility-raises-15-million-to-sell-its-hormone-tests-and-gather-more-fertility-data-from-its-users/.

8. Heather Landi, "Ro Will Acquire Women's Health Startup Modern Fertility in $225M Deal," Fierce Healthcare, May 19, 2021, www.fiercehealthcare.com/digital-health/ro-will-acquire-women-s-health-startup-modern-fertility-225m-deal.

9. Ro homepage, accessed June 14, 2023, https://ro.co/.

10. Michael Martin, "How to Make Your Penis Bigger: 10 Penis Enlargement Methods," Ro website, accessed March 14, 2023, https://ro.co/health-guide/how-to-make-your-penis-bigger/.

11. *FemTech* is a term that is meant to "encompass a range of technology-enabled, consumer-centric products and solutions" to issues in "women's healthcare." This includes devices "to improve healthcare for women across a number of female-specific conditions, including maternal health, menstrual health, pelvic and sexual health, fertility, menopause, and contraception, as well as a number of general health conditions that affect women disproportionately or differently." See McKinsey & Company, "The Dawn of the FemTech Revolution," February 15, 2022, www.mckinsey.com/industries/healthcare/our-insights/the-dawn-of-the-femtech-revolution.

12. *The Economist*, "'The Fertility Sector Has Always Played on Hope; Now It Also Plays on Fear'—The Modern Fertility Business," *The Economist* podcast, August 13, 2019, www.economist.com/podcasts/2019/08/13/the-fertility-sector-has-always-played-on-hope-now-it-also-plays-on-fear-the-modern-fertility-business.

13. Afton Vechery, "The Business of Fertility and Why It Took So Long," interview by *Fortune Magazine*, December 11, 2019, YouTube video, www.youtube.com/watch?v=5Z1I5CBzuvI.

14. See Jennifer Denbow, *In the Name of Innovation: Neoliberalism, Biotechnology, and Reproductive Labor* (Durham, NC: Duke University Press, forthcoming).

15. Jennifer Denbow and Tamara Lea Spira, "Shared Futures or Financialized Futures: Polygenic Screening, Reproductive Justice, and the Radical Charge of Collective Care," *Signs: Journal of Women in Culture and Society* 46, no. 2 (2023).

16. Denbow and Spira, "Shared Futures."

17. Sandra Patton-Imani, *Queering Family Trees: Race, Reproductive Justice, and Lesbian Motherhood* (New York: New York University Press, 2020), 81.

18. Ali Meyer, "Oklahoma Mom Fights to Keep Name on Birth Certificate," Oklahoma's News 4, April 8, 2022, https://kfor.com

/news/local/oklahoma-mother-to-be-removed-from-babys-birth-certificate-because-shes-not-the-gestational-parent/.

19. Donor Conceived Person Protection Act, Senate Bill S7602A, 2021, https://www.nysenate.gov/legislation/bills/2021/s7602.

20. Amy Dockster Marcus, "A Son's Death Raises Questions about Sperm Donor's Medical History," *Wall Street Journal*, January 19, 2022, www.wsj.com/story/a-sons-death-raises-questions-about-sperm-donors-medical-history-52053a3c.

21. The irony of this particular case is that it is unclear how genetically determined Steven's mental health issues were. Furthermore, Steven's donor was not diagnosed with any mental health conditions at the time of donation, so the law would not have prevented his donation. Amy Dockser Marcus, "A Grieving Family Wonders: What if They Had Known the Medical History of Sperm Donor 1558?," *Wall Street Journal*, January 2, 2022, www.wsj.com/articles/a-grieving-family-wonders-what-if-they-had-known-the-medical-history-of-sperm-donor-1558-11641119405.

22. Spira, "Life before Conception."

23. Courtney Joslin, "Gamete Regulation and Family Protection in a Post-Dobbs World," *Bill of Health* (blog), May 17, 2023, https://blog.petrieflom.law.harvard.edu/2023/05/17/gamete-regulation-and-family-protection-in-a-post-dobbs-world/.

24. Katie Breckenridge, "IVF and Abortion Trigger Bans: The Reality That Not All Prenatal Life Is Protected," Them Before Us, December 14, 2022, https://thembeforeus.com/ivf-abortion-trigger-bans-the-reality-that-not-all-prenatal-life-is-protected/; Gerard Letterie and Dov Fox, "Legal Personhood and Frozen Embryos: Implications for Fertility Patients and Providers in Post-Roe America," PubMed Central, May 19, 2023, www.ncbi.nlm.nih.gov/pmc/articles/PMC10200124/#fn31.

25. Daniel Becker, *Personhood: A Pragmatic Guide to Prolife Victory in the 21st Century and the Return to First Principles in Politics* (Alpharetta, GA: TKS Publications, 2011), 23–24, quoted in Risa Cromer, "Racial Politics of Frozen Embryo Personhood in the US Antiabortion Movement," *Transforming Anthropology* 27, no. 1 (2019): 22–36; Spira, "Life before Conception."

26. Cynthia Soohoo, "An Embryo Is Not a Person: Rejecting Prenatal Personhood for a More Complex View of Prenatal Life," *Constitutional Law Now* 81 (2023): 81–115; Cynthia Soohoo, "After Dobbs, Are Rights for Zygotes, Embryos, and Fetuses Next?," *CUNY Law Review Blog*, November 10, 2022, https://papers.ssrn.com/sol3/papers.cfm?abstract_id=4273309.

27. On June 15, 2023, as I was about to send in this manuscript, the Supreme Court delivered the surprising but wonderful decision to keep ICWA intact. Many were shocked over this rare victory, especially given the court composition. Nonetheless, the main issues that this case raises remain germane to my analysis and the kinds of political commitments that I call upon LGBTQ communities to take.

28. Association on American Indian Affairs, "Indian Child Welfare Act," accessed July 17, 2023, www.indian-affairs.org/icwa.html.

29. As the conservative Cato Institute puts it, ICWA harms children by standing in the way of their adoption into a "potentially better situation with black, white, Asian, or Hispanic parents." Ilya Shapiro, "Stop Treating Adopted Kids Differently Based on Race," *Cato at Liberty* (blog), January 13, 2020. This argument within the Brackeens' legal case is not coincidental, given the fact that one of the lawyers on the legal team is Clint Bolick, who previously fought the legal basis for the placement of African American children within African American adoptive families through a similar argument that considering a child's cultural origin when determining an adoptive family was harmful to that child.

30. Haaland v. Brackeen, 599 U.S. (2023), www.supremecourt.gov/opinions/22pdf/21-376_7l48.pdf, 31.

31. Neoshia Roemer, "The Indian Child Welfare Act as Reproductive Justice," *Boston University Law Review* 103, no. 55 (2023): 55–116, www.bu.edu/bulawreview/files/2023/04/ROEMER.pdf; Krista L. Benson, "Erosions of Settler State Recognition of Sovereignty and Reproductive Justice," *Adoption and Culture* 10, no. 2 (2022): 224–30, https://muse.jhu.edu/article/881463.

32. Haaland v. Brackeen 599 U.S. (2023), www.supremecourt.gov/opinions/22pdf/21-376_7l48.pdf, 2.

33. Julia Lurie, "Why Are Right-Wing Groups Targeting a Law Aimed at Protecting Native Families?," *Mother Jones*, November 7,

2022, www.motherjones.com/politics/2022/11/supreme-court-indian-child-welfare-act-native-sovereignty-icwa-tribes/.

34. Haaland v. Brackeen, 599 U.S. (2023), 2–3.

35. Roberts, "Abolishing Policing."

36. Rebecca Nagle, "The Supreme Court Case That Could Break Native American Sovereignty," *The Atlantic*, November 8, 2022, www.theatlantic.com/ideas/archive/2022/11/scotus-native-american-sovereignty-brackeen-v-haaland/672038/.

37. Sarah Rose Harper and Jesse Phelps, "Texas, Big Oil Lawyers Target Native Children in a Bid to End Tribal Sovereignty," Lakota People's Law Project, September 17, 2021, https://lakotalaw.org/news/2021-09-17/icwa-sovereignty.

38. Harper and Phelps, "Texas, Big Oil Lawyers"; Lurie, "Why Are Right-Wing Groups."

39. Nick Estes, "Why Is the US Right Suddenly Interested in Native American Adoption Law?" *The Guardian*, August 23, 2021, www.theguardian.com/commentisfree/2021/aug/23/why-is-the-right-suddenly-interested-in-native-american-adoption-law.

40. Nick Estes, "The Supreme Court Made a Surprising Ruling for Native American Rights," *The Guardian*, June 18, 2023, www.theguardian.com/commentisfree/2023/jun/18/supreme-court-icwa-ruling.

41. Estes, "Supreme Court."

42. Kaitlin Menza, "How Afton Vechery Sold."

43. Dorothy Roberts, "Race, Gender, and Genetic Technologies: A New Reproductive Dystopia?," *Signs* 34, no. 4 (2009): 783–804.

44. Roberts, "Race, Gender, and Genetic Technologies," 744.

45. Roberts, "Race, Gender, and Genetic Technologies," 744.

46. Helena Hansen, Jules Netherland, and David Herzberg, *Whiteout: How Racial Capitalism Changed the Color of Opioids in America* (Oakland: University of California Press, 2023), 26.

47. Roberts, "Race, Gender, and Genetic Technologies," 800.

48. Natalie Fixmer-Oraiz and Shui-yin Sharon Yam, "Queer(ing) Reproductive Justice," in *Oxford Encyclopedia of Queer Studies and Communication*, ed. Isaac N. West et al. (New York: Oxford University Press, 2021), 13.

49. Gumbs, "m/other ourselves," 27–28.

50. Maynard and Simpson, *Rehearsals for Living*, 72.

51. Arundhati Roy, "The Pandemic Is a Portal," Rethinking Schools, 2020, https://rethinkingschools.org/articles/the-pandemic-is-a-portal/.

52. "2021–2022 Creative Wildfire Artists," Creative Wildfire, accessed July 17, 2023, https://creativewildfire.org/artists/.

53. Diana Rosario et al., *All Aboard the Freedom Express*, coloring book (Macorina Films, 2021), 4, https://creativewildfire.org/wp-content/uploads/2022/01/all_aboard_the_freedom_express-small.pdf.

54. Rosario et al., *All Aboard the Freedom Express*, 9.

55. Rosario et al., *All Aboard the Freedom Express*, 11–12.

56. Rosario et al., *All Aboard the Freedom Express*, 13–14.

57. Rosario et al., *All Aboard the Freedom Express*, 15.

58. Rosario et al., *All Aboard the Freedom Express*.

59. Rosario et al., *All Aboard the Freedom Express*, 20.

60. Rosario et al., *All Aboard the Freedom Express*, 25.

61. Rosario et al., *All Aboard the Freedom Express*, 8.

62. Rosario et al., *All Aboard the Freedom Express*, 24.

63. Rosario et al., *All Aboard the Freedom Express*, 19.

64. Rosario et al., *All Aboard the Freedom Express*, 19.

65. Creative Wildfire, "Manifesto," June 2021, https://creativewildfire.org/#manifesto.

66. Creative Wildfire, "Manifesto."

67. Creative Wildfire, "Manifesto."

68. Creative Wildfire, "Manifesto."

69. Grace Lee Boggs, *Living for Change* (Minneapolis: University of Minnesota Press, 1998), 254.

70. As she explains further in her essay "These Are Times to Grow Our Souls," Boggs derives the idea of "The Great Turning" from Buddhist ecologist Joana Macy. Boggs, "These Are Times."

71. Williams, *This Is How We Survive*, 7.

72. Lorde, "Turning the Beat Around."

BIBLIOGRAPHY

Abdur-Rahman, Aliyyah. *Against the Closet: Black Political Longing and the Erotics of Race*. Durham, NC: Duke University Press, 2012.

———. "The Strangest Freaks of Despotism: Queer Sexuality in Antebellum African American Slave Narratives." *Division on Black American Literature and Culture of the Modern Language Association* 40, no. 2 (2016): 223–37.

ACLU. "ACLU, Same-Sex Couple Seek to Join Lawsuit to Keep a License to Discriminate Out of Michigan's Child Welfare System." ACLU, press release, May 22, 2019. www.aclu.org/press-releases /aclu-same-sex-couple-seek-join-lawsuit-keep-license-discriminate-out-michigans-child.

———. "Special Report: Chase Strangio on the Legislative Assault on Trans Youth." ACLU, April 15, 2021. www.aclu.org/news/lgbtq-rights/special-report-chase-strangio-on-the-legislative-assault-on-trans-youth/.

ACLU Michigan. "ACLU Challenges Discriminatory Practices in Michigan's Foster Care System." YouTube video, 00:03:29, September 20, 2017. www.youtube.com/watch?v=_M-1lf-y7cg.

Adisa, Opal Palmer. "Audre Lorde's Cancer Journals; Harbinger of Public Breast Cancer Conversation." In *The Wind Is Spirit: The Life,*

Love, and Legacy of Audre Lorde, edited by Gloria Joseph, 308–11. New York: Villarosa Media, 2016.

Agathangelou, Anna M. *The Global Political Economy of Sex: Desire, Violence, and Insecurity in Mediterranean Nation States*. New York: Palgrave Macmillan, 2004.

Agathangelou, Anna M., Morgan Bassichis, and Tamara Lea Spira. "Intimate Investments: Homonormativity, Global Lockdown, and the Seductions of Empire." *Radical History Review* 1, no. 100 (Winter 2008): 120–43.

Agathangelou, Anna M., Dana M. Olwan, Tamara Lea Spira, and Heather M. Turcotte. "Sexual Divestments from Empire: Women's Studies, Institutional Feeling, and the 'Odious Machine.'" *Feminist Formations* 27, no. 3 (2015): 139–67.

Alexander, M. Jacqui. *Pedagogies of Crossing: Meditations on Feminism, Sexual Politics, Memory, and the Sacred*. Durham, NC: Duke University Press, 2006.

Allen, Anita. "The Black Surrogate Mother." *Harvard Blackletter*, no. 8 (Spring 1991): 17–31.

Allendale, Anna. "The Problem with Trusting a Startup to Monitor Your Fertility." HuffPost, August 14, 2018. www.huffpost.com/entry/at-home-fertility-tests_n_5b7335abe4b025e3596baofe.

Almeling, Rene. *Sex Cells: The Medical Market for Eggs and Sperm*. Berkeley: University of California Press, 2011.

Alvarez, Sonia E. "Advocating Feminisms: The Latin American NGO 'Boom.'" *International Feminist Journal of Politics* 1, no. 2 (November 1999): 181–209.

Amar, Paul. "The Street, the Sponge, and the Ultra: Queer Logics of Children's Rebellion and Political Infantilization." *GLQ: Gay, Lesbian, Queer* 22, no. 4 (2016): 569–604.

Apfel, Alana. *Birth Work as Care Work: Stories from Activist Birth Communities*. Oakland, CA: PM Press, 2016.

Arditti, Rita. "Do You Know Who You Are? The Grandmothers of the Plaza De Mayo." *Women's Review of Books* 24 (September-October 2007): 12–15. www.jstor.org/stable/pdf/20476634.pdf?refreqid=excelsior%3Aacae288504f77baob6obda182462491f.

Association on American Indian Affairs. "Indian Child Welfare Act." Accessed July 17, 2023. www.indian-affairs.org/icwa.html.

Atanasoski, Neda, and Kalindi Vora. *Surrogate Humanity: Race, Robots, and the Politics of Technological Futures.* Durham, NC: Duke University Press, 2019.

Bailey, Marion M. *Butch Queens Up in Pumps: Gender, Performance, and Ballroom Culture in Detroit.* Ann Arbor: University of Michigan Press, 2013.

Ball, Kirstie, Kevin Haggerty, and David Lyon, eds. *Routledge Handbook of Surveillance Studies.* Routledge International Handbooks. Florence: Routledge, 2012.

Barrett, Vic. "'This Is Our Time. This Is Our Future.' Voices from the Historic Youth Climate Strike in NYC." *Democracy Now!*, September 23, 2019. www.youtube.com/watch?v=Eb_vAYVgbeI.

Batza, Katie. *Before AIDS: Gay Health Politics in the 1970s.* Philadelphia: University of Pennsylvania Press, 2018.

Beam, Myrl. *Gay, Inc.: The Nonprofitization of Queer Politics.* Minneapolis: University of Minnesota Press, 2018.

Belinsky, Zoe. "Gender and Family Abolition as an Expansive and Not Reductive Process." Medium, September 11, 2019. https://medium.com/@malkekvmachashayfele/gender-and-family-abolition-as-an-expansive-and-not-reductive-process-d933f1f71da2.

Benjamin, Ruha. "Black AfterLives Matter: Cultivating Kinfulness as Reproductive Justice." In *Making Kin Not Population: Reconceiving Generations*, edited by Adele E. Clarke and Donna Haraway, 41–66. Chicago: Prickly Paradigm Press, 2018.

———. "Catching Our Breath: Critical Race STS and the Carceral Imagination." *Engaging Science, Technology, and Society* 2 (2016): 145–56.

———. "A Lab of Their Own: Genomic Sovereignty as Postcolonial Science Policy." *Policy and Society* 28, no. 4 (2009): 341–55.

———. *Race after Technology: Abolitionist Tools for the New Jim Code.* Cambridge: Polity, 2019.

Ben-Moshe, L., N. Erevelles, and E. R. Meiners. "Abolishing Innocence: Disrupting the Racist/Ableist Pathologies of Childhood." In *Building Abolition: Decarceration and Social Justice*, edited by K. Montford and C. Taylor, 58–67. New York: Routledge, 2021.

Benson, Krista L. "Carrying Stories of Incarcerated Indigenous Women as Tools for Prison Abolition." *Frontiers: A Journal of Women Studies* 41, no. 2 (2020): 143–67.

———. "Erosions of Settler State Recognition of Sovereignty and Reproductive Justice." *Adoption and Culture* 10, no. 2 (2022): 224–30. https://muse.jhu.edu/article/881463.

Bernstein, Robin. *Racial Innocence: Performing American Childhood from Slavery to Civil Rights.* New York: NYU Press, 2011.

Bersani, Leo. "Is the Rectum a Grave?" *AIDS: Cultural Analysis/Cultural Activism* 43 (Winter 1987): 197–222. www.jstor.org/stable/3397574.

Bethany Children's Services. "Family Separation and Detention at the Border—Impacts on Children." December 15, 2021. https://bethany.org/media/get-involved/serve/advocate/advocate-for-refugees/family-separation-and-detention-at-the-border.pdf.

Bever, Lindsey. "There's No One 'Gay Gene,' but Genetics Are Linked to Same-Sex Behavior, New Study Says." *Washington Post*, August 29, 2019. www.washingtonpost.com/health/2019/08/29/theres-no-gay-gene-genetics-are-linked-same-sex-behavior-new-study-says/.

Bierria, Alisa, Jakeya Caruthers, and Brooke Lober, eds. *Abolition Feminisms.* Vol. 1, *Organizing, Survival, and Transformative Practice.* Chicago: Haymarket Books, 2022.

———, eds. *Abolition Feminisms.* Vol. 2, *Feminist Ruptures against the Carceral State.* Chicago: Haymarket Books, 2022.

———. Introduction to *Abolition Feminisms*, vol. 1, *Organizing, Survival, and Transformative Practice*, edited by Alisa Bierria, Jakeya Caruthers, and Brooke Lober. Chicago: Haymarket Books, 2022.

Blakemore, Erin. "How the Black Panthers' Breakfast Program Both Inspired and Threatened the Government." History Channel website, February 6, 2018. www.history.com/news/free-school-breakfast-black-panther-party.

Boggs, Grace Lee. *Living for Change.* Minneapolis: University of Minnesota Press, 1998.

———. *The Next American Revolution: Sustainable Activism for the Twenty-First Century.* Berkeley: University of California Press, 2012.

———. "These Are Times That Grow Our Souls." Transcript of speech delivered at Animating Democracy's National Exchange on

Art and Civic Dialogue, Flint, MI, October 9, 2003. Americans for the Arts. https://intranet.americansforthearts.org/sites/default /files/Grace_Lee_Boggs_Grow_Our_Souls.pdf.

Boggs, Grace Lee, and Scott Kurashige. *The Next American Revolution.* Berkeley: University of California Press, 2011.

Boucai, Michael. "Glorious Precedents: When Gay Marriage Was Radical." *Yale Journal of Law and the Humanities* 27, no. 1 (2015): 1–82.

———. "Is Assisted Procreation an LGBT Right?" *Wisconsin Law Review*, no. 6 (2016): 1065–1126.

Bowles, Nellie. "The Sperm Kings Have a Problem: Too Much Demand." *New York Times*, January 8, 2021.

Boycott-Owen, Mason. "British Lesbian Couple First to Carry Baby in Both Their Wombs." *The Telegraph*, December 3, 2019. www .telegraph.co.uk/news/2019/12/03/british-lesbian-couple-first-carry-baby-wombs/.

Boylan, Elizabeth. "Dignity Denied: Religious Exemptions and LGBT Elder Services." Columbia Law School, December 15, 2017. https:// lawrightsreligion.law.columbia.edu/news/dignity-denied-religious-exemptions-and-lgbt-elder-services.

Bradway, Tyler, and Elizabeth Freeman. "Introduction: Kincoherence/ Kin-aesthetics/Kinematics." In *Queer Kinship: Race, Sex, Belonging, Form*, edited by Tyler Bradway and Elizabeth Freeman, 1–24. Durham, NC: Duke University Press, 2022.

Brant, Beth. "The Fifth Floor, 1967." In *Mohawk Trail*, 69–76. Ithaca, NY: Firebrand Books, 1985.

———, ed. *A Gathering of Spirit: A Collection of North American Indian Women.* Ithaca, NY: Firebrand Books, 1988.

———. "Giveaway: Native Lesbian Writers." *Signs: Journal of Women in Culture and Society* 18 (Summer 1993): 944–47.

———. Introduction to "A Gathering of Spirit: North American Women's Issue," edited by Beth Brant, special issue, *Sinister Wisdom* 22/23 (1983): 5–9.

———. "Letters between Raven and Beth." In *A Gathering of Spirit: A Collection of North American Indian Women*, edited by Beth Brant (Ithaca, NY: Firebrand Books, 1983), 204–9.

————. "A Long Story." In *Mohawk Trail*, 145–50. Ithaca, NY: Firebrand Books, 1985.

Brantzel, Amy. *Against Citizenship: The Violence of the Normative.* Chicago: University of Illinois Press, 2016.

Breckenridge, Katie. "IVF and Abortion Trigger Bans: The Reality That Not All Prenatal Life Is Protected." Them Before Us website, December 14, 2022. https://thembeforeus.com/ivf-abortion-trigger-bans-the-reality-that-not-all-prenatal-life-is-protected/.

Bridges, Khiara M. "Windsor, Surrogacy, and Race." *Washington Law Review* 89 (2014): 1125–53.

Briggs, Laura. "Biopolitics of Adoption." *The Scholar and Feminist Online* 11, no. 3 (2013). https://sfonline.barnard.edu/biopolitics-of-adoption/.

————. *How All Politics Became Reproductive Politics: From Welfare Reform to Foreclosure to Trump.* Reproductive Justice 2. Oakland: University of California Press, 2017.

————. *Somebody's Children: The Politics of Transracial and Transnational Adoption.* Durham, NC: Duke University Press, 2012.

————. *Taking Children: A History of American Terror.* Oakland: University of California Press, 2020.

Briggs, Laura, Faye D. Ginsburg, Elena R. Gutierrez, Rosalind P. Petchesky, Rayna R. Reiter, Andrea Smith, and Chikako Takeshita. "Roundtable: Reproductive Technologies and Reproductive Justice." *Frontiers: A Journal of Women Studies* 34, no. 3 (2013): 102–25.

Bronski, Michael. "Grooming and the Christian Politics of Innocence." *Boston Review,* May 3, 2022. www.bostonreview.net/articles/grooming-and-the-christian-politics-of-innocence/.

————. "When Gays Wanted to Liberate Children." *Boston Review,* June 8, 2018. https://bostonreview.net/articles/michael-bronski-gay-family/.

brown, adrienne m. *Emergent Strategy: Shaping Change, Changing Worlds.* Chico, CA: AK Press, 2017.

Browne, Simone. *Dark Matters: On the Surveillance of Blackness.* Durham, NC: Duke University Press, 2015.

————. "Race and Surveillance." In *Routledge Handbook of Surveillance Studies,* edited by Kirstie Ball, Kevin Haggerty, and David Lyon, 72–79. London: Routledge, 2012.

Burford, Arianne. "'Her Mouth Is Medicine': Beth Brant and Paula Gunn Allen's Decolonizing Queer Erotics." *Journal of Lesbian Studies* 17, no. 2 (2013): 167–79.

Burke, Garance, and Martha Mendoza. "Separated from Parents, Some Migrant Children Are Adopted by Americans." *Christian Science Monitor,* October 9, 2018. www.csmonitor.com/USA/2018/1009 /Separated-from-parents-some-migrant-children-are-adopted-by-Americans.

Caballero, Cecilia, ed. *The Chicana M(other)work Anthology: Porque sin Madres No Hay Revolución.* Tucson: University of Arizona Press, 2019.

Cacho, Lisa. *Social Death: Racialized Rightlessness and the Criminalization of the Unprotected.* New York: NYU Press, 2012.

Cahn, Naomi. *The New Kinship: Constructing Donor-Conceived Families.* New York: NYU Press, 2013.

Cahn, Naomi, and Sonia Suter. "Generations Later, the Rights of Donor-Conceived People Are Becoming Law." The Hill, April 23, 2022. https://thehill.com/opinion/healthcare/3460149-generations-later-the-rights-of-donor-conceived-people-are-becoming-law/.

Cameron, Angela, Vanessa Gruben, and Fiona Kelly. "De-anonymising Sperm Donors in Canada: Some Doubts and Directions." *Canadian Journal of Family Law* 26 (2010): 95–148.

Campt, Tina. *Listening to Images.* Durham, NC: Duke University Press, 2017.

Card, Claudia. "Against Marriage and Motherhood." *Hypatia* 11, no. 3 (1996): 1–23.

Cárdenas, Micha. "Pregnancy: Reproductive Futures in Trans of Color Feminism." *TSQ: Transgender Studies Quarterly* 3, nos. 1–2 (2016): 48–57.

Center for Bioethics and Culture Network. "Championing the Donor-Conceived Community." March 16, 2021. www.cbc-network.org /2021/03/championing-the-donor-conceived-community/.

Center for Genetics and Society. "LGBTQI." www.geneticsandsociety .org/topics/lgbtqi.

Chatterjee, Piya, and Maira Sunaina, eds. *The Imperial University: Academic Repression and Scholarly Dissent.* Minneapolis: University of Minnesota Press, 2014.

Chatzidakis, Andreas, Jamie Hakim, Jo Litter, and Catherine Rottenberg. *The Care Manifesto: The Politics of Interdependence.* London: Verso, 2020.

Chávez, Karma. "Border (In)securities: Normative and Differential Belonging in LGBTQ and Immigrant Rights Discourse." *Communication and Critical/Cultural Studies* 7, no. 2 (June 2010): 136–55.

Child, Brenda J. *Boarding School Seasons: American Indian Families, 1900–1940.* Lincoln: University of Nebraska Press, 1999.

Cholodenko, Lisa, and Stuart Blumberg. *The Kids Are All Right.* Focus Features, film, July 30, 2010. https://en.wikipedia.org/wiki/The_Kids_Are_All_Right_(film).

Chrystos. "Looking for a Blanket to Cover Myself Once the Horses Are Free." In *In Her, I Am,* 79–82. Vancouver, BC: Press Gang, 1993.

Clare, Stephanie. "Reimagining Biological Relatedness: Epigenetics and Queer Kin." *Signs: Journal of Women in Culture and Society* 45, no. 1 (2019): 51–73.

Clarke, Adele E., and Donna Haraway, eds. *Making Kin Not Population: Reconceiving Generations.* Chicago: Prickly Pear Press, 2018.

Clarke, Adele E., Laura Mamo, Jennifer Ruth Fosket, Jennifer R. Fishman, and Janet K. Shim. *Biomedicalization: Technoscience, Health, and Illness in the U.S.* Durham, NC: Duke University Press, 2010.

Clarke, Cheryl. "Living the Texts *Out*: Lesbians and the Use of Black Women's Traditions." In *Theorizing Black Feminisms: The Visionary Pragmatism of Black Women,* edited by Stanlie Myrise James and Abena P. A. Busia, 214–27. Oxford: Routledge, 1993.

Cloud, Erin Miles. "Toward the Abolition of the Foster System." *S&F Online* 15, no. 3 (2019). http://sfonline.barnard.edu/unraveling-criminalizing-webs-building-police-free-futures/toward-theabolition-of-the-foster-system/.

Cohen, Cathy J. "Punks, Bulldaggers, and Welfare Queens: The Radical Potential of Queer Politics?" *GLQ* 3, no. 3 (1997): 437–65. https://985queer.queergeektheory.org/wp-content/uploads/2013/04/Cohen-Punks-Bulldaggers-and-Welfare-Queens.pdf.

Cole, Shannon, and L. C. Cate. "Compulsory Gender and Transgender Existence: Adrienne Rich's Queer Possibility." *WSQ: Women's Studies Quarterly* 36, nos. 3–4 (2008): 279–87.

Comfort, Nathaniel. "The Genetic Self." *The Point Mag, Examined Life*, November 14, 2014. https://thepointmag.com/examined-life/genetic-self/.

Cooper, Baba. "The Radical Potential in Lesbian Mothering of Daughters." In *Politics of the Heart: A Lesbian Parenting Anthology*, edited by Sandra Pollack and Jeanne Vaughn, 233–40. Ithaca, NY: Firebrand Books, 1987.

Cooper, Melinda. *Family Values: Between Neoliberalism and the New Social Conservatism*. Cambridge, MA: MIT Press, 2017.

Cooper, Melinda, and Catherine Waldby. *Clinical Labour: Tissue Donors and Research Subjects in the Global Bioeconomy*. Durham, NC: Duke University Press, 2014.

Cox, Aimee Meredith, Aishah Shahidah Simmons, and Tamura A. Lomax. "Take Care: Notes on the Black (Academic) Women's Health Forum." *Feminist Wire*, November 12, 2012. https://thefeministwire.com/2012/11/take-care-notes-on-the-black-academic-womens-health-forum/.

Craven, Christa. *Reproductive Losses: Challenges to LGBTQ Family-Making*. London: Routledge, 2019.

Creative Wildfire. "Manifesto." June 2021. https://creativewildfire.org/#manifesto.

———. "2021–2022 Creative Wildfire Artists." Accessed July 17, 2023. https://creativewildfire.org/artists/.

Crimp, Douglas. "How to Have Promiscuity in an Epidemic." *AIDS: Cultural Analysis/Cultural Activism* 43 (Winter 1987): 237–71. www.jstor.org/stable/pdf/3397576.pdf.

Cromer, Risa. "Racial Politics of Frozen Embryo Personhood in the US Antiabortion Movement." *Transforming Anthropology* 27, no. 1 (2019): 22–36.

Cutas, Daniela, and Anna Smajdor. "Duped Fathers, Cuckoo Children, and the Problem of Basing Fatherhood on Biology: A Philosophical Analysis." In *Assistierte Reproduktion mit Hilfe Dritter*, edited by Katharina Beier, Claudia Brügge, Petra Thorn, and Claudia Wiesemann, 171–82. New York: Springer, 2020. https://doi.org/10.1007/978-3-662-60298-0_11.

Cvetkovich, Ann. *An Archive of Feelings: Trauma, Sexuality, and Lesbian Public Cultures.* Durham, NC: Duke University Press, 2003.

———. "Legacies of Trauma, Legacies of Activism: ACT UP's Lesbians." In *Loss: The Politics of Mourning*, edited by David Eng and David Kazanjian, 427–57. Berkeley: University of California Press, 2003.

Dalla Costa, Mariarosa, and Selma James. *The Power of Women and the Subversion of the Community.* 3rd ed. Bristol: Falling Wall Press, 1975.

Danna, Daniela. *Contract Children: Questioning Surrogacy.* Stuttgart: Ibidem Press, 2015.

Darby, Luke. "The Trump Administration Is Making Immigrant Parents Pay $800 for DNA Tests to Get Their Kids Back." *GQ*, July 11, 2019. www.gq.com/story/immigration-dna-tests.

Davis, Angela Y. *Are Prisons Obsolete?* New York: Seven Stories Press, 2011.

———. "Rape, Racism and the Capitalist Setting." *Black Scholar* 12, no. 6 (1981): 39–45.

———. "Reflections on the Black Woman's Role in the Community of Slaves." In *The Angela Y. Davis Reader*, edited by Joy James, 111–29. Boston: Blackwell, 1998.

———. "Surrogates and Outcast Mothers: Racism and Reproductive Politics in the Nineties." In *The Angela Y. Davis Reader*, edited by Joy James, 210–21. Malden, MA: Blackwell, 1998.

Davis, Angela Y., Gina Dent, Erica R. Meiners, and Beth E. Richie. *Abolition. Feminism. Now.* Vol. 2. Chicago: Haymarket Books, 2022.

De Bourbon, Soma L. "Indigenous Genocidal Tracings: Slavery, Transracial Adoption, and the Indian Child Welfare Act." PhD diss., University of California Santa Cruz, 2013.

———. "White Property Interests in Native Women's Reproductive Freedom." In *Reproductive Justice and Sexual Rights*, 1–18. New York: Routledge, 2019. www.taylorfrancis.com/chapters/edit/10.4324/9781315099408-2/white-property-interests-native-women-reproductive-freedom-soma-de-bourbon.

Degroot, Jeff. "COLAGE Donor Insemination Guide." 2009. www.colage.org/resources/donor-insemination-guide/.

Delmont, Matthew F. *Making Roots: A Nation Captivated.* Oakland: University of California Press, 2016.

Demeter, Anna. *Legal Kidnapping: A Mother's Account of What Happens to a Family When the Father Kidnaps the Children.* Boston: Beacon Press, 1977.

D'Emilio, John. "Capitalism and Gay Identity." In *Powers of Desire: The Politics of Sexuality,* 100–113. New Feminist Library Series. New York: Monthly Review Press, 1983.

Denbow, Jennifer. *In the Name of Innovation: Neoliberalism, Biotechnology, and Reproductive Labor.* Durham, NC: Duke University Press, forthcoming.

Denbow, Jennifer, and Tamara Lea Spira. "Shared Futures or Financialized Futures: Polygenic Screening, Reproductive Justice, and the Radical Charge of Collective Care." *Signs: Journal of Women in Culture and Society* 46, no. 2 (2023).

Denvir, Daniel. "Today's Evangelicalism Was Forged in the Fight against Communism and Feminism." *Jacobin,* October 17, 2021. www.jacobinmag.com/2021/10/american-christian-evangelicalism-anti-communism-gender-feminism-race-maga-trump-culture-wars-du-mez-interview.

De Veaux, Alexis. *Warrior Poet: A Biography of Audre Lorde.* Chico, CA: AK Press, 2006.

Dickerson, Caitlin. "What It Looks Like to Care for Separated Migrant Children." *New York Times,* June 18, 2019. www.nytimes.com/2019/06/18/reader-center/separated-migrant-children.html.

Dingle, Sarah. "Making Humans: International Principles for Donor Conception and Surrogacy." Change.org. Accessed June 9, 2021. www.change.org/p/united-nations-making-humans-international-principles-for-donor-conception-and-surrogacy.

DiQuinzio, Patrice. *The Impossibility of Motherhood: Feminism, Individualism, and the Problem of Mothering.* New York: Routledge, 1999.

Dominus, Susan. "Sperm Donors Can't Stay Secret Anymore. Here's What That Means." *New York Times,* June 26, 2019. www.nytimes.com/2019/06/26/magazine/sperm-donor-questions.html.

Donor Conceived Person Protection Act. Senate Bill S7602A, 2021. www.nysenate.gov/legislation/bills/2021/s7602.

Donor Sibling Registry. "About DSR." Accessed April 17, 2021. www
.donorsiblingregistry.com/about-dsr.

———. "The Donor-Conceived People's Bill of Rights." Accessed
January 27, 2021. https://donorsiblingregistry.com/blog/the-donor-
conceived-bill-of-rights.

———. "Non-biological Perspective." Accessed December 2012.
https://dsr-static-files.s3.us-west-2.amazonaws.com/0e215cf71649252f.

———. "One LGBT Parent's Story." Accessed December 2012. https://
dsr-static-files.s3.us-west-2.amazonaws.com/3e1b54b1e975cd90.

———. "Our LGBTQ Families." Accessed April 17, 2021. www
.donorsiblingregistry.com/lgbt#our_lgbtq_families.

Dorow, Sara K. 2006. *Transnational Adoption: A Cultural Economy of Race,
Gender, and Kinship.* New York: New York University Press.

Dreier, Hannah. "Searching for the Faces of Migrant Child Labor:
Times Insider." *New York Times,* March 3, 2023. www.nytimes
.com/2023/03/03/insider/searching-for-the-faces-of-child-migrant-
labor.html.

Driskill, Qwo-Li. "Double-Weaving Two Spirit Critiques: Building
Alliances between Native and Queer Studies," *GLQ: A Journal of
Lesbian and Gay Studies* 16, nos. 1–2 (2010): 69–92.

———. "Stolen from Our Bodies: First Nations Two-Spirits/Queers
and the Journey to a Sovereign Erotic." *Studies in American Indian Literatures* 16, no. 2 (2004): 50–64. https://doi.org/10.1353/ail.2004.0020.

Driskill, Qwo-Li, and Lisa Tatonetti. "Introduction: Writing the
Present." In *Sovereign Erotics: A Collection of Two-Spirit Literature,* edited
by Qwo-Li Driskill, Daniel Heath Justice, Deborah Miranda, and
Lisa Tatonetti, 1–20. Tucson: University of Arizona Press, 2011.

Duggan, Lisa. "Equality, Inc." In *The Twilight of Equality? Neoliberalism,
Cultural Politics, and the Attack on Democracy,* 43–66. Boston: Beacon
Press, 2003.

Dyer, Hannah. "The Contested Design of Children's Sexual Education: Queer Growth and Epistemic Uncertainty." *Gender and Education* 31, no. 6 (2019): 742–55.

———. *The Queer Aesthetics of Childhood: Asymmetries of Innocence and the
Cultural Politics of Child Development.* New Brunswick, NJ: Rutgers
University Press, 2019.

————. "Queer Futurity and Childhood Innocence: Beyond the Injury of Development." *Global Studies of Childhood* 7, no. 3 (2017): 290–302.

The Economist. "The Fertility Sector Has Always Played on Hope; Now It Also Plays on Fear"—The Modern Fertility Business." *The Economist* podcast, August 13, 2019. www.economist.com/podcasts/2019/08/13/the-fertility-sector-has-always-played-on-hope-now-it-also-plays-on-fear-the-modern-fertility-business.

Edelman, Lee. *No Future: Queer Theory and the Death Drive.* Durham, NC: Duke University Press, 2004.

Ehlers, Nadine. "Racial Futurity: Biolegality and the Question of Black Life." In *Personhood in the Age of Biolegality,* edited by Marc de Leeuw and Sonja Van Wichelen, 109–24. London: Routledge, 2020.

Ehrensaft, D. "Just Molly and Me, and Donor Makes Three." *Journal of Lesbian Studies* 12 (2008): 161–78.

Ellinger, Mickey. "We Made a Village for the Kids: Reflections on the Prairie Fire Organizing Committee." *Viewpoint Magazine,* January 26, 2017. https://viewpointmag.com/2017/01/26/we-made-a-village-for-the-kids-reflections-on-the-prairie-fire-organizing-committee/.

Enck-Wanzer, Darrel. *The Young Lords.* New York: New York University Press, 2010.

Enszer, Julie R. "What Remains: Remembering Michelle Cliff, Beth Brant, and Stephania Byrd." *Lambda Literary,* August 4, 2016, https://lambdaliterary.org/2016/08/what-remains-remembering-michelle-cliff-beth-brant-and-stephania-byrd/.

————. "'The Whole Naked Truth of Our Lives:' Lesbian-Feminist Print Culture in the United States from 1969–1989." PhD diss., University of Maryland, 2013.

Esseks, James. "In Masterpiece, the Bakery Wins the Battle but Loses the War." ACLU, June 4, 2018. www.aclu.org/blog/lgbtq-rights/lgbtq-nondiscrimination-protections/masterpiece-bakery-wins-battle-loses-war.

Estes, Nick. "The Supreme Court Made a Surprising Ruling for Native American Rights." *The Guardian,* June 18, 2023. www.theguardian.com/commentisfree/2023/jun/18/supreme-court-icwa-ruling.

———. "Why Is the US Right Suddenly Interested in Native American Adoption Law?" *The Guardian*, August 23, 2021. www .theguardian.com/commentisfree/2021/aug/23/why-is-the-right-suddenly-interested-in-native-american-adoption-law.

Eustachewich, Lia. "Lesbian Couple Welcomes 'Two-Womb' Baby." *New York Post*, December 4, 2019. https://nypost.com/2019/12/04/british-lesbian-couple-first-to-carry-baby-in-both-of-their-wombs/.

Fairyington, Stephanie. "A Lesson in Queer Parenting That's Good for Any Family." *Boston Globe*, December 20, 2020. www.bostonglobe.com/2020/12/20/opinion/lesson-queer-parenting-thats-good-any-family/?fbclid=IwAR2MPDYxVD6wUjSm6gRmQccibV8t463 99mMSowUDUdKBf3yIZFPUpXNksyc.

Farr, Rachel H., and Charlotte J. Patterson. "Transracial Adoption by Lesbian, Gay, and Heterosexual Couples: Who Completes Transracial Adoptions and with What Results?" *Adoption Quarterly* 12 (2009): 187–204.

Farzan, Antonia N. "'We Stuck Together Like Neighbors Are Supposed To': A Community Thwarts Father's ICE Arrest," *Washington Post*, July 23, 2019. www.washingtonpost.com/nation/2019/07/23/we-stuck-together-like-neighbors-are-supposed-do-community-thwarts-fathers-ice-arrest/?fbclid=IwAR1Z__SgikQ83iB1wL9GaYC6bjohow NmmAp99C7tDYYcd_VTBZVv4Jftkso&noredirect=on.

Faust, Katy. "Biology Matters." Them Before Us, May 6, 2017. https:// thembeforeus.com/biology-matters/.

Federici, Sylvia. *Caliban and the Witch: Women, the Body and Primitive Accumulation*. Brooklyn, NY: Autonomedia, 2004.

———. "Introduction: Wages for Housework in Historical Perspective." In *Wages for Housework: New York Committee, 1972–1977: History, Theory Documents*, edited by Sylvia Federici and Arlen Austen, 12–28. Brooklyn, NY: Autonomedia, 2017.

———. *Re-enchanting the World: Feminism and the Politics of the Commons*. Kairos: PM Press, 2018. https://scholar.google.com/scholar?hl=en&as_ sdt=0%2C48&q=feminist+epigenetics&btnG=#d=gs_qabs&u=% 23p%3D3ZBVUmY-EP4J.

Federici, Sylvia, and Arlen Austen, eds. *Wages for Housework: New York Committee, 1972–1977: History, Theory Documents.* Brooklyn, NY: Autonomedia, 2017.

Ferguson, Roderick. *The Reorder of Things: The University and Its Pedagogies of Minority Difference.* Minneapolis: University of Minnesota Press, 2012.

Finley, Christine. "Ghostly Care: Boarding Schools, Prisons, and Debt in *Rhymes for Young Ghouls.*" In *Abolition Feminisms*, vol. 1, *Organizing, Survival, and Transformative Practice*, edited by Alisa Bierria, Jakeya Caruthers, and Brooke Lober, 251–61. Chicago: Haymarket Books, 2022.

Firestone, Shulamith. *The Dialectic of Sex: The Case for Feminist Revolution.* New York: Farrar, Straus, and Giroux, 1970.

Fixmer-Oraiz, Natalie. "Speaking of Solidarity: Transnational Gestational Surrogacy and the Rhetorics of Reproductive (In)Justice." *Frontiers* 34, no. 3 (2013): 141–61.

Fixmer-Oraiz, Natalie, and Shui-yin Sharon Yam. "Queer(ing) Reproductive Justice." In *Oxford Encyclopedia of Queer Studies and Communication*, edited by Isaac N. West, E. Cram, Frederik Dhaenens, Pamela Lannutti, and Gust Yep, 1–21. New York: Oxford University Press, 2021.

Flore, Shamber. "Column: My Adoption Agency Saved Me." *Detroit News*, March 7, 2018. www.detroitnews.com/story/opinion/2018/03/07/religious-adoption-agencies-aclu/32717127/.

Fortunati, Leopoldina. *The Arcane of Reproduction: Housework, Prostitution, Labor and Capital.* New York: Autonomedia, 1995.

Foucault, Michel. *The Order of Things.* 2nd ed. Routledge Classics. London: Routledge, 2001.

Frank, Gillian. "'The Civil Rights of Parents': Race and Conservative Politics in Anita Bryant's Campaign against Gay Rights in 1970s Florida." *Journal of the History of Sexuality* 22, no. 1 (January 2013): 126–60.

Franklin, Sarah. *Biological Relatives: IVF, Stem Cells, and the Future of Kinship.* Experimental Futures. Durham, NC: Duke University Press, 2013.

———. "Revisiting Reprotech: Firestone and the Question of Equality." In *Further Adventures of the Dialectic of Sex: Critical Essays on*

Shulamith Firestone, edited by Mandy Merck and Stella Sandford, 29–60. New York: Palgrave Macmillan, 2010.

Franklin, Sarah, and Susan McKinnon, eds. Introduction to *Relative Values: Reconfiguring Kinship Studies*, edited by Sarah Franklin and Susan McKinnon, 1–28. Durham, NC: Duke University Press, 2001.

Freeman, Elizabeth. "Queer Belongings: Queer Theory and Kinship Theory." In *A Companion to Lesbian, Gay, Bisexual, Transgender and Queer Studies*, edited by George Haggerty and Molly McGarry, 295–314. Oxford: Blackwell, 2007.

Gamson, Joshua. *Modern Families: Stories of Extraordinary Journeys to Kinship*. New York: New York University Press, 2015.

Gates, Gary J., and M.V. Lee Badgett. *Adoption and Foster Care by Gay and Lesbian Parents in the United States*. Los Angeles: Williams Institute, 2007.

Ghosh, Cyril. "Marriage Equality and the Injunction to Assimilate: Romantic Love, Children, Monogamy, and Parenting in Obergefell v. Hodges." *Polity* 50, no. 2 (April 2018): 275–99.

Gill-Peterson, Julian, Rebekah Sheldon, and Kathryn Bond Stockton. "Introduction: What Is the Now, Even of Then." *GLQ* 22, no. 4 (October 1, 2016): 496.

Gilmore, Ruth Wilson. *Change Everything: Racial Capitalism and the Case for Abolition*. Chicago: Haymarket Books, 2021.

Giroux, Henry A. *America's Education Deficit and the War on Youth: Reform beyond Electoral Politics*. New York: NYU Press, 2013.

———. "Living in the Age of Imposed Amnesia: The Eclipse of Democratic Formative Culture." Truthout, November 16, 2010. https://truthout.org/articles/ living-in-the-age-of-imposed-amnesia-the-eclipse-of-demo-cratic-formative-culture/.

Glick, Megan H. "The Infant as Biopolitical Absence: Materiality, Viability, Mortality." *American Quarterly* 71, no. 3 (2019): 881–88.

Goldberg, Abbie E, and Joanna E. Scheib. "Female-Partnered Women Conceiving Kinship: Does Sharing a Sperm Donor Mean We Are Family?" *Journal of Lesbian Studies* 20, nos. 3–4 (2016): 427–41.

Goldman, Emma. "Marriage and Love." In *Anarchism and Other Essays*. New York: Dover, 1969.

Goldstein, Alyosha. "Possessive Investment: Indian Removals and the Affective Entitlements of Whiteness." *American Quarterly* 66, no. 4 (2014): 1077–84.

Gopinath, Gayatri. *Impossible Desires*. Durham, NC: Duke University Press, 2005.

Gould, Deborah. *Moving Politics: Emotion and ACT UP's Fight against AIDS*. Chicago: Chicago University of Chicago Press, 2009.

Grayson, Debora. "Mediating Intimacy: Black Surrogate Mothers and the Law." *Critical Inquiry* 24, no. 2 (1998): 525–46.

Grewal, Shabnam. Preface to *Charting the Journey: Writings by Black and Third World Women*, edited by Shabnam Grewal. London: Sheba Feminist Publishers, 1988.

Griffiths, Kate, and Jules Gleeson. *Kinderkommunismus: A Feminist Analysis of the 21st Century Family and a Communist Proposal for Its Abolition*. Washington, DC: Subversion Press, 2015. https://subversionpress.wordpress.com/2015/06/30/kinderkommunismus/.

Gumbs, Alexis Pauline. "m/other ourselves." In *Revolutionary Mothering: Love on the Front Lines*, edited by Alexis Pauline Gumbs, China Martens, and Mai'a Williams, 19–31. Oakland, CA: PM Press, 2016.

———. "'We Can Learn to Mother Ourselves': A Dialogically Produced Audience and Black Feminist Publishing 1979 to the 'Present.'" *Gender Forum: An Internet Journal for Gender Studies* 22 (2008): 39–54.

———. "'We Can Learn to Mother Ourselves': The Queer Survival of Black Feminism." PhD diss., Duke University, 2010.

Gumbs, Alexis Pauline, China Martens, and Mai'a Williams, eds. *Revolutionary Mothering: Love on the Front Lines*. Oakland, CA: PM Press, 2016.

Guttinger, Stephan, and John Dupré. "Genomics and Postgenomics." In *The Stanford Encyclopedia of Philosophy*, edited by Edward N. Zalta and Uri Nodelman. First published October 20, 2016. https://plato.stanford.edu/entries/genomics/#InteHapMProj.

Haaland v. Brackeen, 599 U.S. (2023). www.supremecourt.gov/opinions/22pdf/21-376_7l48.pdf.

Halberstam, Jack. *The Queer Art of Failure*. Durham, NC: Duke University Press, 2011.

————. *In a Queer Time and Place: Transgender Bodies, Subcultural Lives.* New York: New York University Press, 2005.

Hanhardt, Christina B. "Dead Addicts Don't Recover: ACT UP's Needle Exchange and the Subjects of Queer Activist History." *GLQ* 24, no. 4 (2018): 421–44.

Hansen, Helena, Jules Netherland, and Herzberg, David. *Whiteout: How Racial Capitalism Changed the Color of Opioids in America.* Oakland: University of California Press, 2023.

Haraway, Donna Jeanne. *Modest_Witness_Second_Millennium.Female-Man_Meets_OncoMouse: Feminism and Technoscience.* New York: Routledge, 2018.

————. *Simians, Cyborgs, and Women: The Reinvention of Nature.* London: Routledge, 1991.

Haritaworn, Jin. "Murderous Inclusions." *International Feminist Journal of Politics* 15, no. 4 (2013): 445–52. www.tandfonline.com/doi/full/10.1 080/14616742.2013.841568.

————. "#NoGoingBack: Queering Racial Capitalism on the Conjuncture of Protest and Pandemic." In *Sex and Pandemics*, edited by Ricky Varghese. Toronto: University of Toronto Press, forthcoming.

Harper, Sarah Rose, and Jesse Phelps. "Texas, Big Oil Lawyers Target Native Children in a Bid to End Tribal Sovereignty." Lakota People's Law Project, September 17, 2021. https://lakotalaw.org /news/2021-09-17/icwa-sovereignty.

Harrison, Laura. *Brown Bodies, White Babies: The Politics of Cross-racial Surrogacy.* New York: New York University Press, 2016.

Hartman, Saidiya V. "The Belly of the World: A Note on Black Women's Labors." *Souls* 18, no. 1 (2016): 165–73.

————. *Scenes of Subjection: Terror, Slavery, and Self-Making in Nineteenth-Century America.* Oxford: Oxford University Press, 1997.

————. *Wayward Lives, Beautiful Experiments: Intimate Histories of Social Upheaval.* New York: W. W. Norton, 2019.

Hartouni, Valerie. *Cultural Conceptions: On Reproductive Technologies and the Remaking of Life,* Minneapolis: University of Minnesota Press, 1997.

Hassan, Shira. "Liberatory Harm Reduction Saved My Life." In *Saving Our Own Lives: A Liberatory Practice of Harm Reduction,* 10–41. Chicago: Haymarket Books, 2022.

Hauslohner, Abigail. "U.S. Immigration Authorities Will Collect DNA from Detained Migrants." *Washington Post*, March 6, 2020. www.washingtonpost.com/immigration/us-immigration-authorities-will-collect-dna-from-detained-migrants/2020/03/06/63376696-5fc7-11ea-9055-5fa12981bbbf_story.html.

Health Guide Team. "IVF Egg Retrieval: Process, Recovery, Cost, Results." *RO* (blog), December 6, 2021. https://modernfertility.com/blog/conceiving-when-lgbtq-iui-ivf-costs/.

Hentz, Trace Laura. *One Small Sacrifice: A Memoir: Lost Children of the Indian Adoption Projects.* Greenfield, MA: Blue Hand Books, 2017.

Hertz, Rosanna, and Margaret Nelson. *Random Families: Genetic Strangers, Sperm Donor Siblings, and the Creation of New Kin.* London: Oxford University Press, 2019.

Hobson, Emily K. "Fighting HIV/AIDS in Prison." In "Out of Control," edited by Brooke Lober and Jane Segal, special issue, *Sinister Wisdom* 126 (Fall 2022): 156–63.

———. *Lavender and Red: Liberation and Solidarity in the Gay and Lesbian Left.* American Crossroads 44. Oakland: University of California Press, 2016.

Hogan, Andrew J. "Expanding Perspectives on Heredity." *Historical Studies in the Natural Sciences* 49, no. 1 (2019): 104–15.

Homans, Margaret. "Critical Adoption Studies: Conversation in Progress." *Adoption and Culture* 6, no. 1 (2018): 1–49.

Hong, Grace. "'The Future of Our Worlds': Black Feminism and the Politics of Knowledge in the University under Globalization." *Meridians* 8, no. 2 (2008): 95–115.

Hume, Angela. *Deep Care: The Radical Activists Who Provided Abortions, Defied the Law, and Fought to Keep Clinics Open.* Chico, CA: AK Press, 2023.

Hunt, Nicole. "The Mama Bear Movement Is Rising." *Daily Citizen*, November 4, 2021. https://dailycitizen.focusonthefamily.com/the-mama-bear-movement-is-rising/.

Hunter, Peg. "Month of Momentum: Looking Back at 30 Days of Actions to Close the Camps." IMMPrint: Freedom for Immigrants, September 21, 2021. https://imm-print.com/month-of-momentum-looking-back-at-30-days-of-actions-to-close-the-camps/?fbclid=

IwARoMl7eCZEiSq_LpUonpOPYjoWewisV5Co3Qo_zU47X338M-kdpJbwqAvpD4.

Hurley, Natasha. "Reproduction/Non-reproduction." *Jeunesse: Young People, Texts, Cultures* 7, no. 2 (2015): 148–61.

Imtiaz Ali, Arshad, and Tracy L. Buenavista, eds. *Education at War: The Fight for Students of Color in America's Public Schools*. New York: Fordham University Press, 2018.

Jimenez, Karleen Pendleton. *How to Get a Girl Pregnant*. Toronto: Tightrope Books, 2011.

Jones, Stacey H. "(M)othering Loss: Telling Adoption Stories, Telling Performativity." *Text and Performance Quarterly* 25, no. 2 (2005): 113–35.

Jordan, June. "The Creative Spirit: Children's Literature." In *Revolutionary Mothering: Love On the Front Lines*, edited by Alexis Pauline Gumbs, China Martens, and Mai'a Williams, 11–18. Oakland, CA: PM Press, 2016.

———. *Directed by Desire: The Collected Poems of June Jordan*. Edited by Jan Heller and Sara Miles. Port Townsend, WA: Copper Canyon Press, 2005.

———. "A New Politics of Sexuality." In *Some of Us Did Not Die*, 131–36. New York: Basic Books, 2003.

Jordan, June, and Terri Bush, eds. *The Voice of the Children*. San Francisco: Holt, Rinehart, and Winston, 1968.

Joslin, Courtney. "Gamete Regulation and Family Protection in a Post-Dobbs World." *Bill of Health* (blog), Harvard Law School, May 17, 2023. https://blog.petrieflom.law.harvard.edu/2023/05/17/gamete-regulation-and-family-protection-in-a-post-dobbs-world/.

Joyce, Katherine. *The Child Catchers: Rescue, Trafficking and New Gospel of Adoption*. New York: PublicAffairs, 2018.

———. "Shotgun Adoption," *The Nation*, August 26, 2009. www.thenation.com/article/archive/shotgun-adoption/.

———. "The Trouble with the Christian Adoption Movement." *New Republic*, January 11, 2016. https://newrepublic.com/article/127311/trouble-christian-adoption-movement.

Jullion, Jeanne. *Long Way Home: The Odyssey of a Lesbian Mother and Her Children*. San Francisco: Cleis Press, 1985.

Kawash, Samira. "New Directions in Motherhood Studies." *Signs* 36, no. 4 (2011): 969–1003.

Keaney, Jaya. "Queer Multiracial Family: Figuring Race in Donor-Assisted Conception." In *The Reproduction Industry: Intimate Experiences and Global Processes*, edited by Vera Mackie, 79–95. Lanham, MD: Rowan and Littlefield, 2019.

Keating, AnaLouise. *The Gloria Anzaldúa Reader.* Durham, NC: Duke University Press, 2009.

Kelley, Robin D. G. "An Afterwor(l)d." In *Rehearsals for Living*, by Robin Maynard and Leanne Betasamosake Simpson, 265–74. Chicago: Haymarket Books, 2022.

Kim, Jina B., and Sami Schalk. "Reclaiming the Radical Politics of Self-Care: A Crip-of-Color Critique." *South Atlantic Quarterly* 120, no. 2 (2021): 325–42.

Kimball, Alexandra, and Tamara Lea Spira. "The Parent Trap: How DNA Testing Complicates Queer Family." *Real Life Magazine*, October 13, 2021. https://reallifemag.com/the-parent-trap/.

King, Tiffany Lethabo. "Black 'Feminisms' and Pessimism: Abolishing Moynihan's Negro Family." *Theory and Event* 21, no. 1 (2018): 68–87.

Kosofsky Sedgwick, Eve. *Touching Feeling: Affect, Pedagogy, Performativity.* Durham, NC: Duke University Press, 2003.

Kosofsky Sedgwick, Eve, and Adam Frank, eds. *Shame and Its Sisters: A Silvan Tomkins Reader.* Durham, NC: Duke University Press, 1995.

Kramer, Wendy. *Donor Family Matters: My Story of Raising a Profoundly Gifted Donor-Conceived Child, Redefining Family, and Building the Donor Sibling Registry.* Nederland, CO: Donor Sibling Registry, 2020.

Kramer, Wendy, and Naomi Cahn. *Finding Our Families: A First-of-Its-Kind Book for Donor-Conceived People and Their Families.* New York: Random House, 2012.

Laird, Lorelei. "Same-Sex Couple Sues Federally Funded Refugee Adoption Agency for Discrimination." *ABA Journal*, February 23, 2018. www.abajournal.com/news/article/same_sex_couple_sues_federally_funded_refugee_adoption_agency_for_discrimin.

Lambda Legal. "What Makes a 'Holy Family'?" YouTube video, 5:13. February 20, 2018. www.youtube.com/watch?time_continue=1&v= PygUqkfu-4Y&feature=emb_logo.

Landi, Heather. "Ro Will Acquire Women's Health Startup Modern Fertility in $225M Deal." Fierce Healthcare, May 19, 2021. www .fiercehealthcare.com/digital-health/ro-will-acquire-women-s-health-startup-modern-fertility-225m-deal.

Law, Rights, and Religion Project. "Unmarried and Unprotected: How Religious Liberty Bills Harm Pregnant People, Families, and Communities of Color." Columbia Law School. January 25, 2017. https:// lawrightsreligion.law.columbia.edu/unmarriedandunprotected.

Law, Vikki, and China Martens. *Don't Leave Your Friends Behind: Concrete Ways to Support Families in Social Justice Movements and Communities.* Oakland, CA: PM Press, 2012.

Lehr, Valerie. *Queer Family Values: Debunking the Myth of the Nuclear Family.* Philadelphia: Temple University Press, 1999.

Leighton, Kimberley. "Analogies to Adoption in Arguments against Anonymous Gamete Donation: Geneticizing the Desire to Know." In *Family-Making: Contemporary Ethical Challenges,* edited by Francoise Baylis and Carolyn McLeod, 239–64. Oxford: Oxford University Press, 2014.

Lenon, Suzanne, and Danielle Peers. "'Wrongful' Inheritance: Race, Disability and Sexuality in Cramblett v. Midwest Sperm Bank." *Feminist Legal Studies* 25 (2017): 141–63.

Lester, Andrew. "'This Was My Utopia': Sexual Experimentation and Masculinity in the 1960s Bay Area Radical Left." *Journal of the History of Sexuality* 29, no. 3 (September 2020): 364–87.

"Lesbian Couple First to Carry Baby in Both Their Wombs Using In Vivo Natural." CBS New York, December 4, 2019. https://newyork. cbslocal.com/2019/12/04/lesbian-couple-first-in-world-to-carry-baby-both-theirwombs/?utm_campaign=true_anthem&utm_medium= facebook&utm_source=social&fbclid=IwAR013DgVs1Yf0jtJLanz7x J7vGySAb9SrG3I4xTqbIi7tt1FK1DwXl3UIFQ.

Letterie, Gerard, and Dov Fox. "Legal Personhood and Frozen Embryos: Implications for Fertility Patients and Providers in Post-

Roe America." PubMed Central, May 19, 2023. www.ncbi.nlm.nih
.gov/pmc/articles/PMC10200124/#fn31

Lewis, Sophie. *Abolish the Family: A Manifesto for Care and Liberation.* London: Verso, 2022.

————. *Full Surrogacy Now: Feminism against Family.* London: Verso, 2019.

————. "International Solidarity in Reproductive Justice: Surrogacy and Gender-Inclusive Polymaternalism." *Gender, Place and Culture: A Journal of Feminist Geography* 25, no. 2 (2019): 207–27. https://doi.org/10.1080/0966369X.2018.1425286.

Ley, Barbara. *From Pink to Green: Disease Prevention and the Environmental Breast Cancer Movement.* New Brunswick, NJ: Rutgers University Press, 2009.

Lindsey, Kay. "The Black Woman as Woman." In *The Black Woman: An Anthology,* edited by Toni Cade Bambara, 85–89. New York: Mentor Books, 1970.

Lippman, A. "Worrying—and Worrying about—the Geneticization of Reproduction and Health." In *Misconceptions: The Social Construction of Choice and the New Reproductive Technology,* edited by Gwynne Basen, Margrit Eichler, and Abby Lippman, chap. 2. Hull: Voyager, 1993.

Lisee, Chris. "Conservatives Line Up against Sperm Donors but Lack the Power to Ban Them." *Christian Century,* June 28, 2012. www.christiancentury.org/article/2012-06/conservatives-line-against-sperm-donors-lack-power-ban-them.

Liss, Sarah. "Mommy Queerest." *The Hairpin,* May 6, 2015. www.the-hairpin.com/2015/05/mommy-queerest/#.5tlfbwk5x.

Littlefield, Amy, and Tina Vasquez. "Bethany Christian Services Is Fostering Migrant Kids. It Also Has a History of Coercive Adoptions," Rewire News Group, June 27, 2018. https://rewirenewsgroup.com/article/2018/06/27/christian-group-fostering-migrant-kids-history-coercive-adoptions/.

Llopis, María. *Maternidades subversisas.* Tafalla, Navarra, Spain: Editorial Txalaparta, 2015.

Lober, Brooke, and Jane Segal. "Notes for a Special Issue." In "Out of Control," edited by Brooke Lober and Jane Segal, special issue, *Sinister Wisdom* 126 (Fall 2022): 21–30.

Loizos, Connie. "Modern Fertility Raises $15 Million to Sell Its Hormone Tests—and Gather More Fertility Data from Its Users." TechCrunch, June 11, 2019. https://social.techcrunch.com/2019/06/11/modern-fertility-raises-15-million-to-sell-its-hormone-tests-and-gather-more-fertility-data-from-its-users/.

Lomawaima, K. Tsianina. "Domesticity in the Federal Indian Schools: The Power of Authority over Mind and Body." *American Ethnologist* 20, no. 2 (May 1993): 227–40.

Lopez, James. "Gender Matters." Them Before Us, May 3, 2017. https://thembeforeus.com/gender-matters-2/.

Lorde, Audre. *A Burst of Light: And Other Essays*. Chico, CA: AK Press, 2017.

———. "Grenada Revisited." In *Sister Outsider: Essays and Speeches*, 176–89. Berkeley, CA: Crossing Press, 1984.

———. "Man Child: A Black Feminist's Response." In *Sister Outsider: Essays and Speeches*, 72–80. Berkeley, CA: Crossing Press, 1984.

———. "Oberlin College Commencement Address." In *I Am Your Sister: Collected and Unpublished Writings of Audre* Lorde, edited by Rudolph Byrd, Johnetta Cole, and Beverly Guy-Sheftal, 213–18. New York: Oxford University Press, 2009.

———. "Poetry Is Not a Luxury." In *Sister Outsider: Essays and Speeches*, 36–39. Berkeley, CA: Crossing Press, 1984.

———. *Sister Outsider: Essays and Speeches*. Berkeley, CA: Crossing Press, 1984.

———. "Turning the Beat Around: Lesbian Parenting 1986." In *Politics of the Heart: A Lesbian Parenting Anthology*, edited by Sandra Pollack and Jeanne Vaughn. Ithaca, NY: Firebrand Books, 1987.

———. "The Uses of the Erotic: The Erotic as Power." In *Sister Outsider: Essays and Speeches*, 53–59. Berkeley, CA: Crossing Press, 1984.

———. "When Will Ignorance End: Keynote Speech at the National Third World Gay and Lesbian Conference." In *I Am Your Sister: Collected and Unpublished Writings of Audre Lorde*, edited by Rudolph P. Byrd, Johnnetta Betsch Cole, and Beverly Guy-Sheftall, 207–11. New York: Oxford University Press, 2009.

Lorde, Audre, and Pat Parker. *Sister Love: The Letters of Audre Lorde and Pat Parker, 1974–1989.* Edited by Julie Enszer. Dover, FL: Sinister Wisdom, 2018.

Lorde-Rollins, Elizabeth. "117: How My Mother's Book Shaped My Journey with Dr. Elizabeth Lorde-Rollins." *Rise Together Podcast,* October 22, 2020. https://podcasts.apple.com/us/podcast/117-how-my-mothers-book-shaped-my-journey-with-dr/id1407481308?i=1000495630387.

———. "Second November." *Motherhood Literature and Art,* June 13, 2017. https://momeggreview.com/2017/06/13/poetry-by-elizabeth-lorde-rollins/.

Love, Heather. *Feeling Backward: Loss and the Politics of Queer History.* Cambridge, MA: Harvard University Press, 2009.

Lowthorp, Leah. "3-Person IVF and Lesbian Motherhood: A Flawed Argument for Reproductive Equality." *Biopolitical Times,* April 9, 2018.

Lurie, Julia. "Why Are Right-Wing Groups Targeting a Law Aimed at Protecting Native Families?" *Mother Jones,* November 7, 2022. www.motherjones.com/politics/2022/11/supreme-court-indian-child-welfare-act-native-sovereignty-icwa-tribes/.

MacGuill, Dan. "Christian Non-profit Faces Scrutiny over Government Foster Care Contract for Separated Children." Snopes, June 26, 2018. www.snopes.com/news/2018/06/26/bethany-christian-services-family-separation-betsy-devos/.

Macklon, Nick. "Everything You Need to Know about Shared Motherhood." Female First, November 23, 2017. www.femalefirst.co.uk/parenting/shared-motherhood-1108987.html.

MacLachlan, Alice. "Conceiving Differently within the Ethics of Assisted Reproduction." *APA Newsletter* 19, no. 1 (Fall 2019).

Malatino, Hil. "Theorizing Trans Care." Chap. 3 in *Trans Care.* Minneapolis: University of Minnesota Press, 2020. https://manifold.umn.edu/read/trans-care/section/cd2afc3e-2f71-49aa-b249-cda1edad9951.

Mamo, Laura. "Biomedicalizing Kinship: Sperm Banks and the Creation of Affinity-Ties." *Science as Culture* 14, no. 3 (2005): 237–64.

———. "Fertility Inc.: Consumption and Subjectification in U.S. Lesbian Reproductive Practices." In *Biomedicalization: Technoscience,*

Health, and Illness in the U.S, edited by A.E. Clarke, L. Mamo, J.R. Fosket, J.R. Fishman, and J.K. Shim, 173–96. Durham, NC: Duke University Press, 2010.

———. *Queering Reproduction: Achieving Pregnancy in the Age of Technoscience*. Durham, NC: Duke University Press, 2007.

———. "Queering Reproduction in Transnational Bio-Economies." *Reproductive Biomedicine and Society Online* 7 (November 2018).

———. "Queering the Fertility Clinic." *Journal of Medical Humanities* 34, no. 2 (2013): 227–39.

Mamo, Laura, Eli Alston-Stepnitz, Rosanna Hertz, and Margaret K. Nelson. "Queer Intimacies and Structural Inequalities: New Directions in Stratified Reproduction." *Journal of Family Issues* 36, no. 4 (2015): 519–40.

Manalansan, Martin F., IV. "Queering the Chain of Care Paradigm." *Scholar and Feminist Online* 6, no. 3 (Summer 2008). http://sfonline.barnard.edu/immigration/print_manalansan.htm.

Marcus, Amy Dockser. "A Grieving Family Wonders: What if They Had Known the Medical History of Sperm Donor 1558?" *Wall Street Journal*, January 2, 2022. www.wsj.com/articles/a-grieving-family-wonders-what-if-they-had-known-the-medical-history-of-sperm-donor-1558-11641119405.

———. "A Son's Death Raises Questions about Sperm Donor's Medical History." *Wall Street Journal*, January 19, 2022. www.wsj.com/story/a-sons-death-raises-questions-about-sperm-donors-medical-history-52053a3c.

Maron, Dina Fine. "How a Transgender Woman Could Get Pregnant." *Scientific American*, June 15, 2016. www.scientificamerican.com/article/how-a-transgender-woman-could-get-pregnant/.

Martin, Michael. "How to Make Your Penis Bigger: 10 Penis Enlargement Methods." Ro website. Accessed March 14, 2023. https://ro.co/health-guide/how-to-make-your-penis-bigger/.

Marx, Karl. *Grundrisse: Foundations of the Critique of Political Economy*. Translated by Martin Nicolaus. New York: Penguin, 1973.

Maynard, Robyn, and Leanne Betasamosake Simpson. *Rehearsals for Living*. Chicago: Haymarket Books, 2022.

McClain, Dani. *We Live for the We: The Political Power of Black Mother-hood*. New York: Bold Type Books, 2019.

M'charek, Amade. "Beyond Fact or Fiction: On the Materiality of Race in Practice." *Cultural Anthropology* 28, no. 3 (2013): 420–42.

McKinnon, Susan, Rosanna Hertz, and Margaret K. Nelson. "Produc-tive Paradoxes of the Assisted Reproductive Technologies in the Context of the New Kinship Studies." *Journal of Family Issues* 36, no. 4 (2015): 461–79.

McKinsey & Company. "The Dawn of the FemTech Revolution." Feb-ruary 15, 2022. www.mckinsey.com/industries/healthcare/our-insights/the-dawn-of-the-femtech-revolution.

Meiners, Erica. *For the Children? Protecting Innocence in a Carceral State*. Minneapolis: University of Minnesota Press, 2017.

———. "The Trouble with the Child in the Carceral State." In *For the Children? Protecting Innocence in a Carceral State*. Minneapolis: Univer-sity of Minnesota Press, 2017.

Melamed, Jodi. *Represent and Destroy: Rationalizing Violence in the New Racial Capitalism*. Minneapolis: University of Minnesota Press, 2011.

Menza, Kaitlin. "How Afton Vechery Sold Modern Fertility for $225 Million, Just Four Years after Launch." The Helm, September 14, 2021. https://thehelm.co/afton-vechery-modern-fertility-interview/.

Metz, Tamara. "Obergefell, Marriage, and the Neoliberal Politics of Care." In *Stating the Family: New Directions in the Study of American Pol-itics*, edited by Carol Nackenoff, 45–71. Lawrence: University Press of Kansas, 2020.

Meyer, Ali. "Oklahoma Mom Fights to Keep Name on Birth Certificate." Oklahoma's News 4, April 8, 2022. https://kfor.com/news/local/oklahoma-mother-to-be-removed-from-babys-birth-certificate-because-shes-not-the-gestational-parent/.

Meyer, Ali, Austin Breasette, and Raache Hicham. "Birth Certificate Battle: Sperm Donor Petitions for Court Custody of Baby Boy." Okla-homa's News 4, June 1, 2022. https://kfor.com/news/local/birth-certificate-battle-sperm-donor-petitions-court-for-custody-of-baby-boy/.

Mies, Maria. *Patriarchy and Accumulation on a World Scale*. London: Third World Books, 1986.

Miller, Amie Klempnauer. *She Looks Just Like You: A Memoir of (Nonbiological Lesbian) Motherhood*. Boston: Beacon Press, 2010.

Miller, Lisa. "What Does 'Mama Grizzly' Really Mean?" *Newsweek*, September 27, 2010. www.newsweek.com/what-does-mama-grizzly-really-mean-72001.

Millett, Kate. *CATERPILLARS: Journal Entries by 11 Women*. n.p.: Epona Press, 1977.

———. *Sexual Politics*. New York: Columbia University Press, 1970.

Mingus, Mia. "I Am Continuing the Work." In *The Wind Is Spirit: The Life, Love, and Legacy of Audre Lorde*, edited by Gloria Joseph, 253–55. New York: Villarosa Media, 2016.

Miranda, Deborah A. "Beth Brant: May Her Memory Be a Blessing." *BAD NDNS* (blog), September 11, 2015. https://badndns.blogspot.com/2015/09/may-her-memory-be-blessing.html.

———. "Extermination of the *Joyas*: Gendercide in Spanish California." *GLQ* 16 (2010): 253–84.

Mogul, Joey L., Andrea J. Ritchie, and Kay Whitlock. "Setting the Historical Stage: Colonial Legacies." In *Queer (In)justice: The Criminalization of LGBT People in the United States*, 1–19. Boston: Beacon Press, 2011.

Monahan, E. K., Y. Grewal-Kok, G. Cusick, and C. Anderson. *Economic and Concrete Supports: An Evidence-Based Service for Child Welfare Prevention*. Chicago: Chapin Hall at the University of Chicago, 2023.

Moniz, Tomas, and Ariel Gore. *Rad Families: A Celebration*. Oakland, CA: PM Press, 2016.

Montegary, Liz. *Familiar Perversions: The Racial, Sexual, and Economic Politics of LGBT Families*. New Brunswick, NJ: Rutgers University Press, 2018.

Moore, Lisa. *Sperm Counts: Overcome by Man's Most Precious Fluid*. New York: NYU Press, 2008.

Moore, Mignon. *Invisible Families: Gay Identities, Relationships and Motherhood among Black Women*. Berkeley: University of California Press, 2011.

Moraga, Cherríe. "Foreword: From Inside the First World." In *This Bridge Called My Back: Writings by Radical Women of Color*, 3rd ed., xv–xxxiii. Berkeley, CA: Third Woman Press, 2001.

————. *Waiting in the Wings: Portrait of a Queer Motherhood*. Ithaca, NY: Firebrand Books, 1997.

————. *Waiting in the Wings: Portrait of a Queer Motherhood*. 25th anniversary ed. Chicago: Haymarket Books, 2022.

Moraga, Cherríe, and Gloria Anzaldúa, eds. *This Bridge Called My Back: Writings by Radical Women of Color*. Watertown, MA: Persephone Press, 1981.

Moraga, Rafael Angel. "Afterword: 100 Nights." In *Waiting in the Wings: Portrait of a Queer Motherhood*, 25th anniversary ed., 121–24. Chicago: Haymarket Books, 2022.

Moran, Mary. "I Am Not Crazy." In "Surviving Psychiatric Assault and Creating Emotional Well-Being in Our Communities," edited by Elana Dykewomon, special issue, *Sinister Wisdom* 36 (1988/89): 15.

Moreau, Julie. "Lesbian Couple Sues Health and Human Services after Foster Care Application Rejected." NBC News, February 22, 2018. www.nbcnews.com/feature/nbc-out/lesbian-couple-sues-health-department-after-foster-care-application-rejected-n850371.

Moreau, Yves. "Crack Down on Genomic Surveillance." Nature.com, December 3, 2019. www.nature.com/articles/d41586-019-03687-x?sf225143202=1.

Moreira, Luciana. "Queer Motherhood: Challenging Heteronormative Rules beyond the Assimilationist/Radical Binary 1." *Journal of International Women's Studies* 19, no. 2 (2018): 14–28.

Morgan, Jennifer. *Laboring Women: Reproduction and Gender in New World Slavery*. Philadelphia: University of Pennsylvania Press, 2004.

Movement for Family Power. "Our Vision and Values." Accessed December 15, 2021. www.movementforfamilypower.org/indexa.

MSNBC. "Trump Lost, So Why Are Trump Ideas Watering Down Police Reform Bill in 2021?" Video, August 18, 2021, 00:05:16. www.msnbc.com/the-beat-with-ari/watch/trump-lost-so-why-are-trump-ideas-watering-down-police-reform-bill-in-2021-118996549509.

Muñoz, José Esteban. *Cruising Utopia: The Then and There of Queer Futurity*. New York: NYU Press, 2009.

Murphy, Michelle. *The Economization of Life*. Durham, NC: Duke University Press, 2017.

Musser, Amber Jamilla. "Re-membering Audre: Adding Lesbian Feminist Mother Poet to Black." In *No Tea, No Shade: New Writings in Black Queer Studies*, edited by E. Patrick Johnson, 346–61. Durham, NC: Duke University Press, 2016.

Mutcherson, Kimberly M. "Blood and Water in a Post-coital World." *Family Law Quarterly* 49, no. 1 (Spring 2015): 117–34.

———. *Reproductive Justice and Reproductive Technologies*. Oakland: University of California Press, forthcoming.

———. "Transformative Reproduction." *Journal of Gender, Race and Justice* 16, no. 1 (2013). https://ssrn.com/abstract=2313201.

Nagle, Rebecca. "The Supreme Court Case That Could Break Native American Sovereignty." *The Atlantic*, November 8, 2022. www.theatlantic.com/ideas/archive/2022/11/scotus-native-american-sovereignty-brackeen-v-haaland/672038/.

———. "Trojan Horse." Episode 6 of *This Land* podcast, September 20, 2021. Crooked Media. https://crooked.com/podcast/6-trojan-horse/.

National Association of Black Social Workers. "Position Statement on Trans-racial Adoption." September 1972. www.nabsw.org/page/PositionStatements.

Nelson, Alondra. *The Social Life of DNA: Race, Reparations, and Reconciliation after the Genome*. Boston: Beacon Press, 2016.

———. "The Social Life of DNA: Racial Reconciliation and Institutional Morality after the Genome." *British Journal of Sociology* 69, no. 3 (2018): 522–37.

Nelson, Maggie. *The Argonauts*. Minneapolis, MN: Greywolf, 2015.

Nessel, Dana. "Attorney General Nessel's Statement on Dumont v Gordon Settlement Agreement," YouTube video, 00:01:02, March 22, 2019. www.youtube.com/watch?v=-iJwG59drCs.

Nordqvist, Petra. "Feminist Heterosexual Imaginaries of Reproduction: Lesbian Conception in Feminist Studies of Reproductive Technologies." *Feminist Theory* 9, no. 3 (2008): 273–92.

Norman, Derek M. "A Glittering Goodbye to Hector Xtravaganza." *New York Times*, March 11, 2019. www.nytimes.com/2019/03/11/nyregion/hector-xtravaganza-memorial-death.html.

O'Brien, Michelle E. "To Abolish the Family: The Working-Class Family and Gender Liberation in Capitalist Development." *Endnotes* 5 (2020): 390–97.

Oliver, Kelly. "Marxism and Surrogacy." *Hypatia* 4, no. 3 (1989): 95–115.

Onyejiaka, Tiffany. "Why Black Patients Treated by Black Doctors Fare Better." *Ro* (blog), July 21, 2020. https://modernfertility.com/blog/racial-bias-disparities-black-womens-health/.

O'Reilly Andrea, ed. *Maternal Theory: Essential Readings*. Bradford, Ontario, Canada: Demeter Press, 2007.

Out History. "Gay Liberation in New York City." Accessed June 21, 2020. http://outhistory.org/exhibits/show/gay-liberation-in-new-york-cit/3rd-world/pg-1.

Owen, Gabrielle. *A Queer History of Adolescence: Developmental Pasts, Relational Futures*. Athens: University of Georgia Press, 2020.

Owens, Emily A. "Reproducing Racial Fictions: Critical Meditations on (a) Lesbian Pregnancy." *Signs: Journal of Women in Culture and Society* 44, no. 4 (2019): 859–82.

Oyewùmí, Oyèrónké. "Visualizing the Body: Western Theories and African Subjects." In *African Gender Studies, A Reader*, edited by Oyèrónké Oyewùmí, 3–21. New York: Palgrave, 2005.

Palestinian Feminist Collective. "The Palestinian Feminist Collective Condemns Reproductive Genocide in Gaza." May 27, 2024. https://palestinianfeministcollective.org/the-pfc-condemns-reproductive-genocide-in-gaza/.

Park, Shelley M. "Adoptive Maternal Bodies: A Queer Paradigm for Rethinking Mothering?" *Hypatia* 21, no. 1 (2006): 201–26.

———. *Mothering Queerly, Queering Motherhood: Resisting Monomaternalism in Adoptive, Lesbian, Blended, and Polygamous Families*. Albany: State University of New York Press, 2013.

Parker, Pat. Foreword to *Jonestown and Other Madness*. Ithaca, NY: Firebrand Books, 1985.

———. "Gay Parenting: Or Look Out, Anita." In *Politics of the Heart: A Lesbian Parenting Anthology*, edited by Sandra Pollack and Jeanne Vaughn, 94–99. Ithaca, NY: Firebrand Books, 1987.

———. *Jonestown and Other Madness*. Ithaca, NY: Firebrand Books, 1985.

———. "Legacy." In *Jonestown and Other Madness*, 67–75. Ithaca, NY: Firebrand Books, 1985.

———. "Revolution: It's Not Neat or Pretty or Quick." In *This Bridge Called My Back: Writings by Radical Women of Color*, 4th ed., edited by Cherríe Moraga and Gloria Anzaldúa, 242–71. New York: University of New York Press, 2015.

———. "Untitled Letter to Nancy K. Bereano." Schlesinger Archives, Harvard University, December 11, 1983.

———. "Untitled Letter to Whiteness." Schlesinger Archives, Harvard University, February 18, 1983.

Patton-Imani, Sandra. *Queering Family Trees: Race, Reproductive Justice, and Lesbian Motherhood*. New York: New York University Press, 2020.

Payne, Jenny Gunnarsson. "Grammars of Kinship: Biological Motherhood and Assisted Reproduction in the Age of Epigenetics." *Signs: Journal of Women in Culture and Society* 41, no. 3 (2016): 483–506. https://doi.org/10.1086/684233.

Petryna, Adriana. *When Experiments Travel: Clinical Trials and the Global Search for Human Subjects*. Princeton, NJ: Princeton University Press, 2009.

Pfeffer, Carla A. *Queering Families: The Postmodern Partnerships of Cisgender Women and Transgender Men*. Sexuality, Identity, and Society Series. New York: Oxford University Press, 2017.

Piepzna-Samarasinha, Leah Lakshmi. *Care Work: Dreaming Disability Justice*. Vancouver, BC: Arsenal Pulp Press, 2018.

———. *The Future Is Disabled: Prophecies, Love Notes and Mourning Songs*. Vancouver, BC: Arsenal Pulp Press, 2022.

Pierce, Joseph. "Trace, Blood, and Native Identity." *Critical Ethnic Studies* 3, no. 2 (Fall 2017): 57–76.

Plaster, Joseph. *Kids on the Street: Queer Kinship and Religion in San Francisco's Tenderloin*. Durham, NC: Duke University Press, 2023.

Pollack, Sandra, and Jeanne Vaughn, eds. *Politics of the Heart: A Lesbian Parenting Anthology*. Ithaca, NY: Firebrand Books, 1987.

Pratt, Minnie Bruce. *Crime against Nature*. Ithaca, NY: A Midsummer Night's Press, 2013.

———. "Justice, Come Down." In *The Dirt She Ate: New and Selected Poems*. Pittsburgh, PA: University of Pittsburgh Press, 2003.

———. "Shame." In *Crime against Nature*. New York: A Midsummer Night's Press, 1990.

Priest, Myisha. "Salvation Is the Issue." *Meridians* 8, no. 2 (2008): 116–22.

Puar, Jasbir. *Terrorist Assemblages: Homonationalism in Queer Times*. Durham, NC: Duke University Press, 2007.

Puig de la Bellacasa, María. *Matters of Care: Speculative Ethics in More Than Human Worlds*. Minneapolis: University of Minnesota Press, 2017.

Raina, Amy W. "Siblings vs. Diblings." *queermainemama* (blog), August 1, 2019. https://queermainemama.wordpress.com/2019/08/01/siblings-vs-diblings/.

Rajan, Kaushik Sunder. *Biocapital: The Constitution of Postgenomic Life*. Durham, NC: Duke University Press, 2006.

Rajani Bhatia, Lisa Campo-Engelstein. "The Biomedicalization of Social Egg Freezing." *Science, Technology, and Human Values* 43, no. 5 (2018): 864–87.

Reardon, Jenny. "Race without Salvation." In *Revisiting Race in a Genomic Age*, edited by Barbara Koenig, Sandra Soo-Jin, and Sarah S. Richardson, 304–19. New Brunswick, NJ: Rutgers University Press, 2008.

Rich, Adrienne. "Compulsory Heterosexuality and Lesbian Existence." *Signs* 5, no. 4 (1980): 631–60.

———. "Husband-Right and Father-Right" [1977]. In *On Lies, Secrets, and Silence: Selected Prose, 1966–1978*, 215–22. New York: W. W. Norton, 1995.

———. Introduction to *Legal Kidnapping: What Happens to a Family When the Father Kidnaps Two Children*, by Anna Demeter, xi-xxi. Boston: Beacon Press, 1977.

Rich, Camille Gear. "Contracting Our Way to Inequality: Race, Reproductive Freedom, and the Quest for the Perfect Child," *Minnesota Law Review* 104, no. 5 (May 2020): 2375–2470.

Richardson, Sarah. "Maternal Bodies in the Postgenomic Order: Gender and the Explanatory Landscape of Epigenetics." In *Postgenomics: Perspectives on Biology after the Genome*, edited by S. Richardson and H. Stevens, 210–29. Durham, NC: Duke University Press. 2015.

Ritchie, Andrea. *Practicing New Worlds: Abolition and Emergent Strategies*. Chico, CA: AK Press, 2023.

Ritchie, Christina. "Not Sick: Liberal, Trans, and Crip Feminist Critiques of Medicalization." *Journal of Bioethical Inquiry* 29 (2019): 1–13.

Rivers, Daniel. "Families." In *The Routledge History of Queer America*, edited by Don Romesburg, 276–87. New York: Routledge, 2018.

———. "'In the Best Interests of the Child': Lesbian and Gay Parenting Custody Cases, 1967–1985." *Journal of Social History* 43, no. 4 (Summer 2010): 917–43.

———. *Radical Relations: Lesbian Mothers, Gay Fathers, and Their Children in the United States since World War II.* Chapel Hill: University of North Carolina Press, 2013.

———. "Rally in Support of Jeanne Jullion." In *Radical Relations: Lesbian Mothers, Gay Fathers, and Their Children in the United States since World War II*, 86. Chapel Hill: University of North Carolina Press, 2013.

Ro. "Modern Fertility." Accessed July 17, 2023, https://ro.co/modern-fertility/?ro_ch=cpc&ro_p=google&ro_c=14494630967&ro_g=131133256946&ro_con=101&ro_a=649786582010&ro_t=kwd-1803625546008&ro_n=g&ro_d=c&gad=1&gclid=CjwKCAjwg-GjBhBnEiwAMUvNW6H5X-ZDZyYWBCRmrv5JS6vgliJWf8eGLXI-lqViJ5e4FgcFwEOHcRoC3B4QAvD_BwE.

Roberts, Dorothy. "Abolishing Policing Also Means Abolishing Family Regulation." *The Imprint*, June 16, 2020. https://imprintnews.org/child-welfare-2/abolishing-policing-also-means-abolishing-family-regulation/44480.

———. "I Have Studied Child Protective Services for Decades. It Needs to Be Abolished." *Mother Jones*, April 5, 2022. www.motherjones.com/criminal-justice/2022/04/abolish-child-protective-services-torn-apart-dorothy-roberts-book-excerpt/.

———. *Killing the Black Body: Race, Reproduction, and the Meaning of Liberty.* Toronto: Random House, 1998.

———. "Race, Gender, and Genetic Technologies: A New Reproductive Dystopia?" *Signs* 34, no. 4 (2009: 783–804.

———. *Shattered Bonds: The Color of Child Welfare.* New York: Civitas Books, 2002.

———. *Torn Apart: How the Child Welfare System Destroys Black Families—and How Abolition Can Build a Safer World.* New York: Basic Books, 2023.

Roberts, Dorothy, and Lisa Sangoi. "Black Families Matter: How the Child Welfare System Punishes Poor Families of Color." *The Appeal*, March 26, 2018, https://theappeal.org/black-families-matter-how-the-child-welfare-system-punishes-poor-families-of-color-33ad20e2882e/.

Rodríguez, Juana María. *Sexual Futures, Queer Gestures, and Other Latina Longings*. New York: New York University Press, 2014.

Roemer, Neoshia. "The Indian Child Welfare Act as Reproductive Justice." *Boston University Law Review* 103, no. 55 (2023): 55–116. www.bu.edu/bulawreview/files/2023/04/ROEMER.pdf.

Romesburg, Don. "Where She Comes From: Locating Queer Transracial Adoption." *QED: A Journal in GLBTQ Worldmaking* 1, no. 3 (2014): 1–29.

Rosario, Diana, Karen Hurtado, Karina Hurtado-Ocampo, and Brittney Washington. *All Aboard the Freedom Express*. Coloring book. Macorina Films, 2021. https://creativewildfire.org/wp-content/uploads/2022/01/all_aboard_the_freedom_express-small.pdf.

Rosenberg, Susan. *An American Radical: A Political Prisoner in My Own Country*. New York: Citadel Press, 2011.

Ross, Loretta, and Rickie Solinger. *Reproductive Justice: An Introduction*. Oakland: University of California Press, 2017.

Roy, Arundhati. "The Pandemic Is a Portal." Rethinking Schools, 2020. https://rethinkingschools.org/articles/the-pandemic-is-a-portal/.

Rubin, Gayle. "Thinking Sex: Notes for a Radical Theory of the Politics of Sexuality." In *Culture, Society and Sexuality: A Reader*, edited by Richard Parker and Peter Aggleton, 143–78. London: Routledge, 2002.

Rudrappa, Sharmila. *Discounted Life: The Price of Global Surrogacy in India*. New York: New York University Press, 2015.

Russell, Camisha A. *The Assisted Reproduction of Race*. Bloomington: Indiana University Press, 2018.

Schreiber, Melody. "Why Is This Group of Doctors So Intent on Unmasking Kids?" *New Republic*, February 22, 2022. https://newrepublic.com/article/165413/mask-mandates-kids-back-to-normal.

Schulman, Sarah. *Let the Record Show: A Political History of ACT UP New York, 1987–1993*. New York: Farrar, Straus and Giroux, 2021.

Schurr, Carolin. "The Baby Business Booms: Economic Geographies of Assisted Reproduction." *Geography Compass* 12, no. 8 (2018): 123–95.

Severance. "About Severance." Accessed June 8, 2021. https://severancemag.com/about-severance/.

———. "Conceiving People: Q&A with Daniel Groll." *Severance Magazine.* Accessed July 5, 2023. https://severancemag.com/tag/books/.

———. "Donor Conception." Accessed July 4, 2024. https://severancemag.com/donor-conception/.

Sexton, Jared. "People-of-Color-Blindness: Notes on the Afterlife of Slavery." *Social Text* 28 (2010): 31–56.

Shange, Savannah. "Black on Purpose: Race, Inheritance and Queer Reproduction." *Feminist Wire*, October 10, 2014. https://thefeministwire.com/2014/10/black-purpose-race-inheritance-queer-reproduction/.

Shapiro, Dani. *Inheritance: A Memoir of Genealogy, Paternity, and Love.* New York: Knopf, 2019.

Shapiro, Ilya. "Stop Treating Adopted Kids Differently Based on Race." *Cato at Liberty* (blog), January 13, 2020.

Shapiro, Susan. "Cancer as a Feminist Issue." *Sojourner Magazine*, 15, no. 1 (1989): 18–19.

Shear, Michael, Katie Benner, and Michael Schmidt. "We Need to Take Away Children,' No Matter How Young, Justice Dept. Officials Said." *New York Times*, October 28, 2021. www.nytimes.com/2020/10/06/us/politics/family-separation-border-immigration-jeff-sessions-rod-rosenstein.html.

Sheldon, Rebekah. *The Child to Come: Life after the Human Catastrophe.* Minneapolis: University of Minnesota Press, 2016.

Shellnutt, Kate. "America's Largest Christian Adoption Agency Lets LGBT Couples Foster in 1 of 35 States." *Christianity Today*, April 25, 2019.www.christianitytoday.com/news/2019/april/bethany-christian-services-michigan-foster-lgbt-couples.html.

Smietana, Marcin, and Charis Thompson, eds. "Making Families: Transnational Surrogacy, Queer Kinship, and Reproductive Justice." Special issue, *Reproductive Biomedicine and Society Online* 7 (2018).

Smietana, Marcin, Charis Thompson, and France Winddance Twine. "Introduction: Making and Breaking Families—Reading Queer Reproductions, Stratified Reproduction and Reproductive Justice Together." In *Reproductive BioMedicine and Society Online* 7 (November 2018): 112–39. http://eprints.lse.ac.uk/90977/1/Smietana_Introduction-making-and-breaking.pdf.

Smith, Lindsay. *Subversive Genes: Making DNA and Human Rights in Argentina*. Forthcoming.

Social Science Research / University of Amsterdam. "Amade M'charek—Race and Genetics." YouTube video, 4:30, March 25, 2015. www.youtube.com/watch?v=COHQ7F6q_ew.

Solinger, Rickie. *Beggars and Choosers: How the Politics of Choice Shapes Adoption, Abortion, and Welfare in the United States*. New York: Macmillan, 2001.

Somerville, Siobhan. "Scientific Racism and the Emergence of the Homosexual Body." *Journal of the History of Sexuality* 5, no. 2 (1994): 243–66.

Soohoo, Cynthia. "After Dobbs, Are Rights for Zygotes, Embryos, and Fetuses Next?" *CUNY Law Review Blog*, November 10, 2022. https://papers.ssrn.com/sol3/papers.cfm?abstract_id=4273309.

———. "An Embryo Is Not a Person: Rejecting Prenatal Personhood for a More Complex View of Prenatal Life." *Constitutional Law Now* 81 (March 2, 2023): 81–115.

Sotiropoulos, Karen. "Open Adoption and the Politics of Transnational Feminist Human Rights." *Radical History Review* 2008, no. 101 (2008): 179–90.

Spade, Dean. "Keynote Address: Trans Law and Politics on a Neoliberal Landscape." *Temple Political and Civil Rights Law Review* 18, no. 2 (Spring 2009): 353–74.

———. *Mutual Aid: Building Solidarity through This Crisis (and the Next)*. London: Verso Books, 2020.

———. *Normal Life: Administrative Violence, Critical Trans Politics, and the Limits of Law*. Durham, NC: Duke University Press, 2015.

———. "Shit's Totally FUCKED! What Can We Do? A Mutual Aid Explainer." YouTube video, July 9, 2019. 7:54. www.youtube.com/watch?v=PopmGAvsggg.

————. "Trans Law and Politics on a Neoliberal Landscape." In *Normal Life: Administrative Violence, Critical Trans Politics, and the Limits of Law*, 21–37. Durham, NC: Duke University Press, 2015.

Spade, Dean, and Craig Willse. "Norms and Normalization." In *The Oxford Handbook of Feminist Theory*, edited by Lisa Disch and Mary Hawkesworth. Oxford: Oxford University Press, 2015. www.deanspade.net/wp-content/uploads/2020/08/Norms_and_NormalizationFinal.pdf.

Spira, Tamara Lea. "For June." *Feminist Wire*, March 16, 2016. https://thefeministwire.com/2016/03/for-june/.

————. "The Geopolitics of the Erotic: Audre Lorde's Mexico and the De-colonization of the Revolutionary Imagination." In *Audre Lorde's Transnational Legacies*, edited by Stella Bolaki and Sabine Broeck, 177–90. Amherst: University of Massachusetts Press, 2015.

————. "Intimate Internationalisms: 1970s 'Third World' Queer Feminist Solidarity with Chile." *Feminist Theory* 15, no. 2 (August 2014): 119–40. https://doi.org/10.1177/1464700114528768.

————. "Life before Conception: Gamete Personhood in the Wake of Dobbs." *Nursing Clio*, December 13, 2023. https://nursingclio.org/2023/12/13/life-before-conception-gamete-personhood-in-the-wake-of-dobbs/.

————. *Movements of Feeling: Feminist Radical Imaginations in Neoliberal Times*. Seattle: University of Washington Press, forthcoming.

————. "Race, Sexuality and Indigeneity in Patricio Guzmán's Nostalgia for the Light: Toward a New Ontology and Archive of Revolution." *E-Misférica* 8, no. 3 (2012). http://hemisphericinstitute.org/hemi/en/e-misferica-91/spira.

Spira, Tamara Lea, Dayjha McMillan, Madi Stapleton, and Verónica Vélez. "ACAB Means Abolishing the Cops in Our Heads, Hearts, and Homes: An Intergenerational Demand for Family Abolition." In *Abolition Feminisms*, vol. 2, *Feminist Ruptures against the Carceral State*, edited by Alisa Bierria, Brooke Lober, and Jakeya Caruthers, 13–42. Chicago: Haymarket Books, 2022.

Sreenivas, Mytheli. "Introduction." *Frontiers: A Journal of Women Studies* 34, no. 3 (2013): vii–xiv.

Stacey, Judith. "Gay Parenthood and the Decline of Paternity as We Knew It." *Sexualities* 9, no. 1 (2006): 27–55.

———. "Queer Reproductive Justice? Symposium Making Families Commentary." *Reproductive BioMedicine and Society Online* 7 (2018): 4–7.

Stanley, Eric. "The Affective Commons: Gay Shame, Queer Hate, and Other Collective Feelings." *GLQ* 24, no. 4 (2018): 489–508.

Steinberg, Deborah Lynn. "A Most Selective Practice: The Eugenic Logics of IVF." *Women's Studies International Forum* 20, no. 1 (1997): 33–48.

Stimson, Charles. "How Low Can Far Left Go? Attacks on Barrett for Adopting Haitian Orphans Hit Rock Bottom." Heritage Foundation, October 1, 2020. www.heritage.org/courts/commentary/how-low-can-far-left-go-attacks-barrett-adopting-haitian-orphans-hit-rock-bottom.

Stockton, Kathryn Bond. *The Queer Child, or Growing Sideways in the Twentieth Century.* Durham, NC: Duke University Press, 2009.

Stoeckle, Anabel. "Rethinking Reproductive Labor through Surrogates' Invisible Bodily Care Work." *Critical Sociology* 44, nos. 7–8 (2018): 1103–1116.

St. John, Paige. "DNA Genealogical Databases Are a Gold Mine for Police, but with Few Rules and Little Transparency." *Los Angeles Times*, November 24, 2019. www.latimes.com/california/story/2019-11-24/law-enforcement-dna-crime-cases-privacy.

Stoller, Nancy E. *Lessons from the Damned: Queers, Whores and Junkies Respond to AIDS.* New York: Routledge, 1998.

St. Vincent Catholic Charities. "Family Is Forever." Accessed December 15, 2021. https://stvcc.org/family-is-forever/.

———. "Forever Family Christmas." Accessed December 15, 2021. https://stvcc.org/forever-family-christmas.

———. "Refugee Services History." Accessed December 15, 2021. https://stvcc.org/services/refugee-services/refugee-services-history/.

———. "St. Vincent Catholic Charities." Accessed December 15, 2021. https://stvcc.org.

———. "Why We Resettle Refugees." Video, 00:01:25. Accessed December 15, 2021. https://stvcc.org/services/refugee-services/resettle-refugees/.

Sullivan, Mecca Jamilah. Introduction to *Sister Love: The Letters of Audre Lorde and Pat Parker, 1974–1979*, edited by Julie Enszer, 11–24. Dover, FL: Sinister Wisdom, 2018.

Summers, A. K. *Pregnant Butch: Nine Long Months Spent in Drag.* Berkeley, CA: Soft Skull Press, 2014.

Tadiar, Neferti X. M. "If Not Mere Metaphor … Sexual Economies Reconsidered." *S&F Online* 7, no. 3 (Summer 2009). https://sfonline.barnard.edu/sexecon/tadiar_05.htm.

———. "Life-Times of Disposability within Global Neoliberalism." *Social Text* 31, no. 2 (2013): 19–48.

———. *Things Fall Away: Philippine Historical Experience and the Makings of Globalization.* Durham, NC: Duke University Press, 2009.

TallBear, Kim. "Making Love and Relations beyond Settler Sex and Family." In *Making Kin Not Population: Reconceiving Generations*, edited by Adele E. Clarke and Donna Haraway, 145–64. Chicago: Prickly Paradigm Press, 2018.

———. *Native American DNA: Tribal Belonging and the False Promise of Genetic Science.* Minneapolis: University of Minnesota Press, 2013.

Taylor, Sonya Renee. *The Body Is Not an Apology: The Power of Radical Self-Love.* Oakland, CA: Berrett-Koehler, 2018.

Them Before Us. "Them Before Us." Accessed April 20, 2021. https://thembeforeus.com.

———. "Who We Are." About. Accessed April 17, 2021. https://thembeforeus.com.

Third World Gay Revolution. "Sixteen Point Platform and Program." *Pinko*, October 15, 2019. https://pinko.online/pinko-1/third-world-gay-revolution-archive.

———. "What We Want, What We Believe." In *Out of the Closets: Voices of Gay Liberation*, edited by Karla Jay and Allen Young. New York: Douglas Book Corporation, 1972.

Thompson, Charis. *Making Parents: The Ontological Choreography of Reproductive Technologies.* Cambridge, MA: MIT Press, 2005.

Thompson, Julie M. *Mommy Queerest: Contemporary Rhetorics of Lesbian Maternal Identity.* Amherst: University of Massachusetts Press, 2002.

Thuma, Emily. *All Our Trials: Prisons, Policing, and the Feminist Fight to End Violence.* Chicago: University of Illinois Press, 2019.

————. "Lessons in Self-Defense: Gender Violence, Racial Criminalization, and Anticarceral Feminism." *Women's Studies Quarterly* 43, nos. 3/4 (2015): 52–71.

Thunberg, Greta. "Transcript: Greta Thunberg's Speech at the U.N. Climate Action Summit." National Public Radio, September 23, 2019.www.npr.org/2019/09/23/763452863/transcript-greta-thunbergs-speech-at-the-u-n-climate-action-summit.

Truong, Timmy. "Same-Sex Couple Carries Same Baby, Calls Experience 'Priceless.'" ABC News, October 28, 2018. https://abcnews .go.com/US/sex-couple-carries-baby-calls-experience-priceless /story?id=58768828.

Tsang, Daniel. "Third World Gays and Lesbians Meet." In *Remaking Radicalism: A Grassroots Documentary Reader of the United States, 1973– 2001,* edited by Dan Berger and Emily K. Hobson, 44–46. Atlanta: University of Georgia Press, 2020.

3andMe. "About." Accessed April 17, 2021. www.23andme.com/.

Twine, France Winddance. *Outsourcing the Womb: Race, Class, and Gestational Surrogacy in a Global Market.* New York: Routledge, 2015.

United Nations. "Convention on the Rights of the Child." United Nations Human Rights, Office of the High Commissioner. November 20, 1989. www.ohchr.org/en/professionalinterest/pages/crc .aspx.

Valdez, Natali. "The Redistribution of Reproductive Responsibility: On the Epigenetics of 'Environment.'" *Medical Anthropology Quarterly* 32, no. 3 (2018): 425–42.

————. *Weighing the Future: Race, Science, and Pregnancy Trials in the Postgenomic Era.* Oakland: University of California Press, 2021.

Vasquez, Christopher. "NCLR Relieved by Narrow SCOTUS Ruling in Fulton Allowing Governments to Prohibit Anti-LGBTQ Discrimination." National Center for Lesbian Rights, press release, June17,2021.www.nclrights.org/about-us/press-release/nclr-relieved-by-narrow-scotus-ruling-in-fulton-allowing-governments-to-pro-hibit-anti-lgbtq-discrimination/.

Vechery, Afton. "The Business of Fertility and Why It Took So Long." Interview by *Fortune Magazine*, December 11, 2019. YouTube video. www.youtube.com/watch?v=5Z1I5CBzuvI.

Vélez, Verónica. "Madres en la Lucha: Forging Motherhood as a Political Movement across Borders." In *The Chicana M(other)work Anthology: Porque sin Madres No Hay Revolución*, edited by Cecilia Caballero, 171–91. Feminist Wire Books. Tucson: University of Arizona Press, 2019.

Vertommen, Sigrid. "Resistance Is Fertile: Sperm Smuggling and Birth Strikes for Reproductive Justice in Israel/Palestine." Paper presented at the "Remaking Reproduction" conference, University of Cambridge, June 27–29, 2018.

Vider, Stephen. *The Queerness of Home: Gender, Sexuality, and the Politics of Domesticity after World War II*. Chicago: University of Chicago Press, 2022.

Vora, Kalindi. "After the Housewife: Surrogacy, Labour and Human Reproduction." *Radical Philosophy* 2, no. 4 (Spring 2019): 42–46.

———. *Life Support: Biocapital and the New History of Outsourced Labor*. Minneapolis: University of Minnesota Press, 2015.

Waldby, Catherine. *The Oocyte Economy: The Changing Meaning of Human Eggs*. Durham, NC: Duke University Press, 2019.

Ward, Myah. "At Least 3,900 Children Separated from Families under Trump 'Zero Tolerance' Policy, Task Force Finds." *Politico*, June 8, 2021. www.politico.com/news/2021/06/08/trump-zero-tolerance-policy-child-separations-492099.

Weeks, Kathi. "Abolition of the Family: The Most Infamous Feminist Proposal." *Feminist Theory* 24, no. 3 (2021). https://doi.org/10.1177/14647001211015841.

Wei, Wei. "Queering the Rise of China: Gay Parenthood, Transnational ARTs, and Dislocated Reproductive Rights." *Feminist Studies* 47, no. 2 (2021): 312–40. https://doi.org/10.1353/fem.2021.0018.

Weigman, Robyn. "Sex and Negativity; Or What Queer Theory Has for You." *Cultural Critique* 95 (Winter 2017): 219–43.

Weinbaum, Alys Eve. *The Afterlife of Reproductive Slavery: Biocapitalism and Black Feminism's Philosophy of History.* Durham, NC: Duke University Press, 2019.

———. "The Afterlife of Slavery and the Problem of Reproductive Freedom." *Social Text* 31, no. 2 (2013): 49–68.

Weston, Kath. *Families We Choose: Lesbians, Gays, Kinship.* Rev. ed. Between Men—between Women. New York: Columbia University Press, 1997.

Wheaton, Oliver. "Revolutionary New Surgery Could Allow Trans Women to Carry Children." *Metro*, November 22, 2015. https://metro.co.uk/2015/11/22/revolutionary-new-surgery-could-allow-trans-women-to-carry-children-5519000/.

Willey, Angela. *Undoing Monogamy: The Politics of Science and the Possibilities of Biology.* Durham, NC: Duke University Press, 2016.

Williams, Mai'a. "Radical Mothering as a Pathway to Liberation." *Millennium: A Journal of International Studies* 47, no. 3 (2019): 497–512.

———. *This Is How We Survive: Revolutionary Mothering, War, and Exile in the 21st Century.* Oakland, CA: PM Press, 2019.

Wilson v. Williams, Volume # FD-2021-3681 (2023), District Court, Seventh Judicial District, State of Oklahoma, Letter Ruling. www.documentcloud.org/documents/23649403-1053622896-20230214-105340-1?responsive=1&title=1.

Wilson-Williams, Rebekah. "Time to Be Brave." Accessed July 17, 2023. *Metro Family.* www.metrofamilymagazine.com/time-to-be-brave/.

Winnow, Jackie. "Lesbians Evolving Health Care: Cancer and AIDS." *Feminist Review* 41 (Summer 1992): 68–76.

Wise, Justin. "American Academy of Pediatrics President: Trump Family Separation Policy Is 'Child Abuse.'" The Hill, June 18, 2018. https://thehill.com/latino/392790-american-academy-of-pediatrics-president-trumps-family-separation-policy-is-child.

Witt, Charlotte. "A Critique of the Bionormative Concept of Family." In *Family-Making: Contemporary Ethical Challenges*, edited by Francoise Baylis and Carolyn McLeod. Oxford: Oxford University Press, 2014.

Youmans, Greg. *Word Is Out: A Queer Film Classic.* Vancouver, BC: Arsenal Pulp Press, 2011.

Zimmer, Carl. "Seven Big Misconceptions about Heredity." *Skeptical Inquirer* 43, no. 3 (May/June 2019). https://skepticalinquirer.org/2019/05/seven-big-misconceptions-about-heredity/.

INDEX

Founded in 1893,
UNIVERSITY OF CALIFORNIA PRESS
publishes bold, progressive books and journals
on topics in the arts, humanities, social sciences,
and natural sciences—with a focus on social
justice issues—that inspire thought and action
among readers worldwide.

The UC PRESS FOUNDATION
raises funds to uphold the press's vital role
as an independent, nonprofit publisher, and
receives philanthropic support from a wide
range of individuals and institutions—and from
committed readers like you. To learn more, visit
ucpress.edu/supportus.

www.ingramcontent.com/pod-product-compliance
Lightning Source LLC
Chambersburg PA
CBHW020821270326
41928CB00006B/397